CROSSING THE WATER AND KEEPING THE FAITH

NORTH AMERICAN RELIGIONS

Series Editors: Tracy Fessenden (Religious Studies, Arizona State University), Laura Levitt (Religious Studies, Temple University), and David Harrington Watt (History, Temple University)

In recent years a cadre of industrious, imaginative, and theoretically sophisticated scholars of religion have focused their attention on North America. As a result the field is far more subtle, expansive, and interdisciplinary than it was just two decades ago. The North American Religions series builds on this transformative momentum. Books in the series move among the discourses of ethnography, cultural analysis, and historical study to shed new light on a wide range of religious experiences, practices, and institutions. They explore topics such as lived religion, popular religious movements, religion and social power, religion and cultural reproduction, and the relationship between secular and religious institutions and practices. The series focus primarily, but not exclusively, on religion in the United States in the twentieth and twenty-first centuries.

The Notorious Elizabeth Tuttle: Marriage, Murder, and Madness in the Family of Jonathan Edwards
Ava Chamberlain

Suffer the Little Children: Uses of the Past in Jewish and African American Children's Literature
Jodi Eichler-Levine

Crossing the Water and Keeping the Faith: Haitian Religion in Miami
Terry Rey and Alex Stepick

Crossing the Water and Keeping the Faith

Haitian Religion in Miami

Terry Rey and Alex Stepick

Foreword by Archbishop Thomas Wenski

NEW YORK UNIVERSITY PRESS

New York and London

NEW YORK UNIVERSITY PRESS
New York and London
www.nyupress.org

References to Internet Websites (URLs) were accurate at the time of writing.
Neither the author nor New York University Press is responsible for URLs that
may have expired or changed since the manuscript was prepared.

LIBRARY OF CONGRESS CATALOGING-IN-PUBLICATION DATA

Rey, Terry.
Crossing the water and keeping the faith : Haitian religion in Miami / Terry Rey and Alex
Stepick; foreword by Archbishop Thomas Wenski.
pages cm. — (North American religions)
Includes bibliographical references and index.
ISBN 978-0-8147-7708-4 (cl : alk. paper)
ISBN 978-0-8147-7709-1 (pbk. : alk. paper)
1. Miami (Fla.)—Religion. 2. Haitians—Florida—Miami—Religion. 3. Haitian
Americans—Florida—Miami—Religion. 4. Catholic Church—Florida—Miami.
5. Vodou—Florida—Miami. I. Title.
BL2527.F6R49 2013
200.89'96972940759381—dc23   2013007856

New York University Press books are printed on acid-free paper, and their binding materials
are chosen for strength and durability. We strive to use environmentally responsible
suppliers and materials to the greatest extent possible in publishing our books.

Manufactured in the United States of America
10 9 8 7 6 5 4 3 2 1

In loving memory of Msgr. Gérard Darbouze, Micha Gaillard, Fr. Gérard Jean-Juste, Magalie Marcelin, Archbishop Joseph Serge Miot, and Michel-Rolph Trouillot, who inspired us and so many others by illuminating the struggle and leading the way.

CONTENTS

Foreword   ix
   Archbishop Thomas Wenski

Acknowledgments   xiii

Introduction: Haitian Religion in Miami   1

1 The Haitian Catholic Church in Miami: When the Saints
   Go Sailing In   33

2 Immigrant Faith and Class Distinctions: Haitian Catholics
   beyond Little Haiti   59

3 Feting Haiti's Patron Saint in Little Haiti: The Feast of Our
   Lady of Perpetual Help   83

4 Vodou in the Magic City: Serving the Spirits across the Sea   113

5 Storefront and Transnational Protestantism in Little
   Haiti: Harvesting the Gospel in the Haitian Church of the
   Open Door   151

Conclusion: Beasts, Gods, and Transnational
Transubstantiation   189

Appendices   203

Notes   227

Bibliography   237

Index   253

About the Authors   266

I welcome this book on the religious faith of Miami's Haitian community, which features Little Haiti's Notre Dame d'Haiti Mission, where I served for eighteen years as a parish priest. The authors are not theologians but social scientists, but their research and their insights derived from that research helps illustrate how religious institutions, which are usually regarded as "conservative," can creatively and imaginatively respond to new challenges and create new opportunities for marginalized people.

In the 1960s, Operation Pedro Pan, during which the Roman Catholic Church helped some 14,000 unaccompanied minors from Cuba to resettle in the United States, the establishment of *La Ermita de la Caridad* (the shrine dedicated to Cuba's patron saint), and the integration of thousands of young Cuban children into its parochial school system were just some of the ways that the local Catholic Church rose to the challenges and opportunities posed by the influx of Cuban refugees to Miami. In the late 1970s, the arrival of Haitian "boat people"—most of whom identified themselves as Catholics—posed new challenges to the archdiocese, challenges met in large part successfully by the establishment of Notre Dame d'Haiti in 1981 on what was previously the campus of a Catholic high school for girls.

The Roman Catholic Church in America, which began as an immigrant institution, moved up into the middle class and out to the suburbs after World War II. As a result, it became invisible to many poor newly arriving immigrants. The challenge in Haitian Miami was thus to make the Church visible to the new immigrants and vice versa. A subtext to the whole issue of immigration is, of course, class. America has always pretended to be unconscious of class; America's ambiguity toward race is more openly acknowledged. Yet, the key to understanding race relations in America lies in the acknowledgment of the underlying class conflict that so often influences the interactions between racial and ethnic groups.

A pastoral approach that works well in middle-class America will not necessarily correspond to the needs of immigrants who have not yet "transferred" into the middle class. One size does not fit all. To give a hypothetical example, in, say, a suburban Michigan parish, the two or three Peruvian cardiologists who may live there might have no problem feeling at home with their American-born neighbors. Indeed, if asked, they might not even feel any pressing need for Spanish language liturgy. Yet, within the territorial limits of this same suburban parish there may be a migrant labor camp of Mexican farm workers. They would probably not feel at home in the parish, for many reasons. For one thing, perhaps they are not as bilingual as our hypothetical cardiologists. And, perhaps more importantly, class differences between middle-class denizens of suburbia and these possibly undocumented farm workers would mitigate against their successful integration into the life of that parish even if the parishioners bent over backwards to welcome them. Given factors beyond the control of people's best intentions, to count on that parish's being a vital force in the lives of those Mexican farm workers would be very Pollyannaish. In reality, they would most likely remain invisible to the wider Church and the Church itself would be invisible to those farm workers. They simply would not see the institution as "theirs." Without providing for ecclesial structures, like a "national" or ethnic parish, which would allow those farm workers a sense of ownership and would make them stakeholders in the Church, all our talk about the "preferential option for the poor" remains just that—talk.

My many years of experience as a pastor in South Florida's Haitian community taught me that. Notre Dame d'Haiti in Miami is a mission church designed on the national parish model, a model used by the Roman Catholic Church in the United States to integrate millions of immigrants during the late nineteenth and early twentieth centuries. Notre Dame has no English masses but five Sunday masses in Haitian Creole. The parish is entirely made up of Haitians, many of whom fled to South Florida in rickety boats. The newly arrived Haitians struggled to achieve legal status, and to learn English and marketable skills in the American workforce. In the 1980s anti-immigrant sentiment was more focused on these poor, black migrants from the hemisphere's second republic. Their petitions for political asylum were routinely dismissed and, unlike Cuban "refugees," the Haitians were regarded as merely "economic migrants."

There are many Haitian professionals who live in Miami—doctors, nurses, accountants, and the like—but they don't usually go to Notre Dame. If they go to church, they go to the parishes in the suburbs where they live. They integrate very well there because they are already the social and economic equals of the Americans who sit side by side with them in the pews. They perhaps don't need a Notre Dame, at least not to the extent that the three thousand or four thousand people that attend Notre Dame every week need it.

Notre Dame d'Haiti gives these Haitians a sense of belonging in a society that has often proved hostile to them: remember that in the 1980s "Haitian" was one of the four H's identifying "risk" for HIV-AIDS. Notre Dame d'Haiti gives Haitians a place that allows them to do for themselves. They are the ushers, choir members, youth group leaders, catechists, readers, and sodality leaders. For six days a week, they might be reminded that they are foreigners, and unwelcome ones at that. At least on Sunday (and of course, not only on Sunday) at Notre Dame, they feel at home.

Notre Dame has provided for these Haitians the "position of strength" that assures successful integration both into the Church and into the broader society. This could not be easily duplicated in the territorial parish. In territorial parishes, because of mass schedules and other activities for the "real" parishioners, the newcomers are assigned to a midafternoon and generally inconvenient time slot. And, of course, they are admonished, "be sure to be finished by four and pick up after yourself!" But, as a Cuban proverb puts it: "If you want a man to walk with you, make sure he has comfortable shoes." Evangelization, to be successful, must really take root within the culture to which the gospel is brought. So when evangelization is successful, it is enculturation. Enculturation allows the gospel message to be expressed in its integrity but within pastoral structures that are culturally sensitive and culturally appropriate—in other words, ones that are "comfortable shoes."

Culture is like the skin that envelops our bodies. The task of enculturation then is to have the good news of Christ penetrate and become one with a people's skin. To strip away a people's culture by forcing assimilation is to expose their society to shock, then to disease and death. Research among children of immigrants bears this out. Those most comfortable with their ethnic identity, those more at ease with their parents' language and culture, do better academically and socially in American society than those who, because of shame or pressure to conform, Americanize themselves too rapidly. The mean streets of too many American cities underscore the fact that rootless people tend to become also ruthless people.

The trauma that brought these people to the United States in the first place—civil unrest, oppression, grinding poverty—and the difficulties of adapting to American life, such as learning a language, immigration status, family separation, can conspire to weaken or injure the "skin" that is one's culture. These wounds present real dangers, and they require the opportunity to be healed. Without Notre Dame, these wounds would have gone undiagnosed and untreated by the Church's pastoral ministry because the wounded would have remained invisible.

The experience of Notre Dame d'Haiti Mission and Miami's Haitian community offers the social scientist a rich and interesting field to study. Notre Dame d'Haiti has served this community (even those who are non-Catholic) so well because it is both truly Catholic and truly Haitian. This volume showcases how the faiths of Miami's Haitians, Catholic or other, offer mechanisms of social cohesion to otherwise marginalized immigrants and help them negotiate a strange and often unwelcoming new home

Archbishop Thomas Wenski
Miami, July 2012

ACKNOWLEDGMENTS

This book was a long time in the making and its realization relied heavily on the generous support and insights of many people in many places. Our gratitude is thus as far reaching as it is sincere, though most of it is grounded in, and springs from, Miami and Haiti. Above all, we thank the many Haitian and Haitian American believers, family members, and friends who have so kindly shared with us the depths and contours of their fascinating religious lives, and the priests, priestesses, bishops, pastors, prophets, prophetesses, preachers, and herbalists who have guided them and us along the way. We could not have even conceived of this project without the open arms that received us into a wide array of Haitian religious congregations, Catholic, Protestant, and Vodouists, which are far too many to name here.

For their assistance with our research in Miami, we are especially grateful to Oungan Michelet Tibosse Alisma, Manbo Margaret Armand, Rev. Fritz Bazin, Fr. Patrick Charles, Rev. Jacques Clotaire, Rev. F. F. Duclair, Rev. François Duclair, Rev. Emmanuel Eugène, Rev. Jonas Georges, the late Monsignor Gérard Darbouze, Fr. Lesley Jean, Fr. Reginald Jean-Mary, Jose Antonio Lammoglia, Rev. Wilner Maxi, Manbo Danièle Mangones, Fr. Jean Pierre, Rev. Fandor Saint-Felix, Fr. Juan Sosa, Rev. Harold Vieux, Emile Villard, and Archbishop Thomas Wenski. In Haiti we were very fortunate to have been spoken to and been welcomed and guided by Br. Ameleon, Fr. Whistler Angrand, Fr. Emmanuel Charles, Fr. Gabriel Charles, Joel Jean-Baptiste, the late Fr. Gérard Jean-Juste, Ira Lowenthal, Yolette Mengual, the late Archbishop Joseph Serge Miot, Francesca Pascal, Archbishop Guire Poulard, Mira Toussaint, and by a number of leaders in the National Haitian Protestant Pastors Association.

Much of our research was funded by the Pew Charitable Trusts as part of their Gateway Cities Initiative, and we gratefully acknowledge this support and particularly that of our program officer at Pew, Kimon Sargeant. The Pew project also resulted in the book *Churches and Charity in the Immigrant City,* which we co-edited with the project's other principal investigator, Sarah Mahler. Also affiliated with that project were postdoctoral fellows Katrin Hansing, Christine Ho, and Yves Labissiere. Graduate research assistants were Terry Tsuji, Aidil Oscariz, Isabel del Pino Allen, Su Fink, Eileen Smith-Cavros, Noemi Baez, and Ann Reeder Goraczko.

We began this study of Haitian religion in Miami more than ten years ago while both of us were on the faculty at Florida International University. We enjoyed fruitful collaborations related to this book with a host of talented scholars there, especially Marvin Dunne, Deborah O'Neil, and Carol Dutton Stepick. Meanwhile, FIU's Immigration and Ethnicity Institute and the university's Center for Labor Research and Studies, where the institute is housed, provided the space for our Pew-funded research and many other resources that were essential to its success. We also owe a special word of thanks to several professional colleagues from other universities and institutes who are experts on Haitian religion, especially Dimitri Béchacq, Rachel Beauvoir-Dominique, Leslie Desmangles, Benjamin Hebblethwaite, Laënnec Hurbon, Bertin Louis, Elizabeth McAlister, Karen McCarthy Brown, Margarita Mooney, and Karen Richman, who have so graciously shared their work and ideas with us over the years; Leslie and Margarita, in fact, along with two other anonymous reviewers, read the entirety of an earlier draft of our manuscript and provided invaluable feedback that made this a much better book.

Many thanks also to Jason Martin for creating two of the book's maps, to Jerry Berndt for contributing his magnificent photographs to this project, to Gayle Schooley for patient and priceless technical and logistical assistance, and to Serge Rey for helping us think spatially about our work. More recently, we have benefited in many ways from our wonderful collaborators at New York University Press, especially Mary Sutherland, Despina Papazoglou Gimbel, Constance Grady, and Jennifer Hammer, our most able editor, and we gratefully acknowledge their support, along with that of the editors of the series in which this book resides, Tracy Fessenden, Laura Levitt, and David Harrington Watt. *Antouka mèsi anpil pou tout bèl soutyen ki te pèmèt liv sa realize!*

Haitian Religion in Miami

Spiritually, poetically, and politically it is altogether fitting that the heart of Haitian life in Miami beats precisely at the intersection of streets named for the great Haitian poet Félix Morisseau-Leroy and the great African American civil rights leader Martin Luther King Jr. Félix Morisseau-Leroy was the first major writer to compose plays and poetry in Haitian Creole, the language of the Haitian masses, a language whose official recognition by the Haitian government—a status previously reserved for the French of the Haitian elite—was in large part the result of the bard's advocacy and international acclaim. Like so many of his compatriots, "Moriso," as he is affectionately known to Haitians, had to flee Haiti in 1953 because of political oppression and take refuge abroad, first in France and then in several African countries before settling in Miami in 1981. There, in the "Magic City," he would pass the last seventeen years of his life, just as Miami's Haitian diaspora was beginning to swell, a community in which he "was hailed as the forerunner of many of their efforts; as one of them said on his death: 'He realised that for people to understand the problems, they need to be taught in their own language, not a language they don't understand. Otherwise, they're being mystified, they're being shown a lack of respect'" (Caistor 1998). Martin Luther King's profound commitment to the gospel and to social change toward securing civil rights for African Americans, meanwhile, exemplifies the faith and resilience of another African-descended people, Haitians, who have come to America in search of life, of a better life, for themselves, their loved ones, and for Haiti.

On any given Sunday, multitudes from the Haitian diaspora congregate at the intersection of these two streets at the intersection of King and Morisseau-Leroy in Little Haiti. Most of them gather at Notre Dame d'Haiti Catholic Church, while others shuffle to their

Protestant storefront churches, toting Bibles; others purchase herbs or have a spiritualist reading done by a Vodou priestess in a temple, and others pick up cornmeal, red beans, and ground Haitian coffee in the Caribbean Market. Just across the street from the market, Notre Dame d'Haiti, the primary Haitian Catholic Church in Miami, literally overflows with prayerful, beseeching believers, many clutching rosaries or photographs of loved ones who remain across the water, in Haiti. Not only are the pews full but people are standing in the back and in the doorways of the sanctuary and outside on the patio and in the parking lot. Speakers hung on an exterior wall project the liturgical prayers and lively hymns to those who didn't make it in time to find a spot inside the church, a squat building that was originally designed as a high school cafeteria. The parking lot is also overflowing with cars; every marked spot is taken, forcing dozens to park their vehicles haphazardly on the grass or in more orderly fashion outside the churchyard curbside along two of the neighborhood's busiest commercial corridors. Nearer to the building a few women oversee small temporary food stands and a few others sell novena manuals and icons of Jesus and the Virgin Mary, while a group of adolescents take to the basketball court for a pickup game of hoops; beyond them several people pray the rosary before the grotto of Our Lady of Lourdes. All of these activities ensure that, even between each Sunday's five masses, Notre Dame and the vicinity teem with Haitian life.

But, the main draw is the mass. Men and women, the elderly and the youth, families and singles, all crowd inside the church. Eventually they are swaying to music driven by Vodou drums that infuse the congregation with African rhythms, joyfully singing hymns of praise in French and Haitian Creole. The homily is bilingual, primarily in Creole, but also in English for the second-generation youth who prefer it. Although Notre Dame continues to attracts more Haitians than any other Roman Catholic Church in South Florida, and though it remains the spiritual home and springboard to new lives for thousands of Haitian immigrants in Miami, there are many more Haitians now living elsewhere in the Roman Catholic Archdiocese of Miami, which currently offers Creole and French masses at no fewer than fourteen other churches.

Because Saint-Domingue, later the Republic of Haiti, was born out of the French colonial project that enslaved hundreds of thousands of Africans and Creoles, historically Haiti has been a predominately Roman Catholic—and Vodouist—country, although Protestantism also has a long history in the Caribbean nation and has grown considerably influential over the last three generations. All of these historical and contemporary religious and demographic realities are increasingly transnational as evinced by the scores of Haitian Protestant churches in Miami. Little Haiti, a 50-x-12 block swath of inner-city Miami that despite the spread of Haitians and Haitians Americans throughout South Florida, remains the densest concentration of Haitians outside of Haiti. It is home to over one hundred Haitian Protestant churches, most of them located along the neighborhood's chief commercial corridors, though some are tucked away less visibly on side streets in private homes, which are transformed into sanctuaries for worship services on Sundays. A few of them we have managed to find only because the inspired sermons preached by their pastors or the lively hymns sung by their choirs are amplified by loudspeakers and echo down the streets, beckoning the wayward and the seeker alike.

Though fewer by far, there are scattered among Little Haiti's churches about a dozen *botanicas*, religious goods stores that cater to practitioners of African-derived religions, in this case Vodou, the religion of a slight but declining majority among Haiti's national population and one of the three sides to what Drexel Woodson (1993: 157) refers to as a "religious triangle of forces" that pervades Haitian society and culture. To be sure, Vodou is alive and well in Miami, as testified not just by the city's Haitian botanicas but by the home-based and ambulatory practices of the estimated two hundred *oungan* and *manbo* (priests and priestesses) who currently lead that faith in South Florida, and by a few operative temples.[1] And, even among those Haitian Christians in Miami who reject Vodou as satanic, belief in its reality is no less forceful in the diaspora than in Haiti. Indeed, comments made to us by several Little Haiti residents that while doing our fieldwork, we should be careful to avoid the Sabel Palm Court housing complex for fear of encountering *loup garou* or *zonbi* (werewolves and zombies of Vodouist lore) in that densely populated part of the neighborhood. We have been left to wonder whether residents of the neighboring Jewish nursing home are aware of such nemeses!

All of these churches, botanicas, practices, and beliefs powerfully reflect how central religion is to most Haitians and Haitian Americans in Miami. Survey data indicates that the majority of Haitian immigrants in Miami attend religious services more than once a week, making them one of the most (if not *the* most) religiously active immigrant groups in the United States (Stepick 1998).[2] In her extensive fieldwork among transnational religious communities comprised of Haitians in Palm Beach County, Florida, and Leogane, Haiti, Karen Richman (2005a; 2007) similarly concludes that for most Haitian immigrants in South Florida, the church itself is central to life, perhaps even more so than it had been in the homeland. Less scientifically, we have taken numerous visitors of a wide array of ethnic and economic backgrounds to Sunday church services and/or botanicas in Little Haiti, and almost all of them have remarked to us how devout and "spiritual" they find Haitians in Miami to be. We taught at Florida International University, a public university in southwest Miami, which probably has more Haitian and Haitian American students than any other university in the United States. There we often found that asking Haitian students, especially those who were shy or withdrawn, about their churches invariably inspired fairly open conversation—the ultimate ice-breaker, as it were.

This book is a historical and ethnographic study of Haitian religion in Miami, based on many years of formal fieldwork in the city as well as in Haiti, and extensive archival research. While intending generally to contribute to our understanding of "new immigrant" religion in the United States—an interdisciplinary academic field that has received much attention over the past twenty-five years—more particularly our study aims to advance our understanding of Haitian religion, with especial contributions in mind for two subcategories of the study: (1) Haitian immigrant religion in the United States, and (2) Haitian religion approached holistically, that is, in consideration of the three major forms of Haitian religion taken together, namely Catholicism, Protestantism, and Vodou. Toward developing our thinking and research design of Haitian religion in the United States, we have benefited handsomely from several excellent studies on the topic, namely single-authored books by Karen McCarthy Brown (1991), Elizabeth McAlister (2006), Karen Richman (2005b), and Margarita Mooney (2011). The first three of these books focus primarily on Haitian Vodou and are based in large part on fieldwork in Haiti, although Richman's also contains important discussions of Protestantism, while Mooney's study focuses on immigrant Haitian Catholics in three diasporic locations, including Miami, the chief site of our own research. Like all four of these scholars, our methodological approach has been primarily ethnographic, based on extensive participant observation and many interviews.

In our conceptual orientation, we follow the leads of Paul Brodwin (1996) and André Corten (2001) in seeking to view Haitian religion as a whole, despite a sometimes violent history of strife between Catholicism, Protestantism, and Vodou. Brodwin and Corten, too, both approached their subjects ethnographically, and their studies are focused entirely on religion in Haiti. Thus, *Crossing the Water and Keeping the Faith* is in part patterned on these two subcategories of the study of Haitian religion, even though it moves beyond the first in approaching Haitian immigrant religion holistically, and beyond the second by doing so while focusing on Haitian religion in Miami. Consequentially, making any sense of Haitian religion in Miami required us to make numerous trips to Haiti over the years, the religious lives of Haitian immigrants being so profoundly transnational. And, at the end of it all, we make two central novel arguments: (1) that underlying and transcending religious difference in Haiti and the Haitian diaspora there can be identified a unifying *Haitian religious collusio*, and (2) that Haitian religion in the diaspora is largely explicable in terms of the generation of and quest for "salvation goods" in the form of luck (*chans*), magic (*maji*), protection, health, prosperity, and, especially, *worthiness*.

A Word on Haitian Religious Demographics

A tired cliché has it that "Haitians are 90 percent Catholic, 10 percent Protestant, and 100 percent Vodouist." In its wild statistical inaccuracy, this popular myth greatly oversimplifies the transnational Haitian religious field. In reality, the best statistical data on religion in Haiti clearly demonstrates that the community of Protestants throughout the country, who generally condemn Vodou as diabolical, has blossomed in the last three decades to constitute roughly one-third of the entire national Haitian population (Hurbon 2001: 126). In light of the putatively traditional reluctance of Haitians to reveal their Vodouist affiliation to social scientists and journalists, these figures are as sound as one can have on the percentage of Vodouists in Haiti by way of subtraction: If

Protestants generally do not practice Vodou (practice here defined as routinely performing devotions to spirits and/or ancestors and *not* as merely the occasional consultation with an *oungan* or *manbo*), then at a maximum, Vodouists today constitute three-fourths of the Haitian population, though probably considerably less than this because there are more *katolik fran* (lit. "frank Catholics"—Haitian Catholics who do not also practice Vodou) than is generally acknowledged in scholarly or journalistic literature. Judging by the proliferation of Haitian Protestant storefront churches in cities like Boston, Chicago, Miami, Montreal, Newark, New York, Philadelphia, and Washington, the figure is certainly even higher in the Haitian diaspora.[3]

This proliferation of Protestant storefront churches in the Haitian diaspora is hardly surprising in light of the statistical data available on religion in Haiti. From 1982 to 1997, for instance, the number of Protestants in the Haitian capital city of Port-au-Prince, home to roughly one-fourth of country's total population, had doubled to nearly 40 percent of the city's total population (Houtart and Rémy 1997: 34); rural statistics from around the same time indicate that the Protestant population in Haiti was then between 27 percent and 33 percent (Woodson and Baro 1996: 54; 1997: 38). With no indications of any subsequent decline in Protestant affiliation either in Port-au-Prince or the countryside, one could reasonably estimate that today Haiti is already more than one-third Protestant and, as François Houtart and Anselm Rémy (1997: 35) conclude in one of the two largest demographic studies of religion conducted in the country, that "Haiti is on pace to becoming a country of a Protestant majority." Furthermore, as Drexel Woodson and Mamadou Baro (1996: 54) assert in the other study, because throughout Haiti "the mixture of *sèvis lwa* [Vodou] with Protestantism is rare," and because many Haitian Protestants consider Vodou to be satanic and the source of Haiti's many trials and tribulations, including the tragic 2010 earthquake, it is likely that more than one in three people in Haiti today (and certainly more in the Haitian diaspora), does not practice Vodou. If we add to this population the number of *katolik fran* in Haiti, it would appear that today Vodouists in Haiti constitute a slight but seemingly declining majority of the population, far from "100 percent," certainly.

That said, most people in Haiti still practice Vodou; many others nominally and/or situationally enter the religion, usually for guidance, healing, or protective magic. Nonetheless, just about everyone's understanding of the universe and her place and purpose therein is influenced in some way by the religion, which is a cornerstone of the Haitian religious collusio. Pierre Bourdieu (2000: 145) coined the term "collusio" to mean "an immediate agreement in ways of judging and acting which does not presuppose either the communication of consciousness, still less a contractual decision, [which] is the basis of practical understanding, the paradigm of which might be the one established between members of the same team, or, despite the antagonism, all the players engaged in the game." And, even among Haitian Evangelicals or Pentecostals who demonize Vodou, there is little or no doubt that Vodou is real—that it effectively accesses and negotiates a supernatural reality that is objectively existent. Thus like any nationally popular religion, Vodou's ethos spreads well beyond the confines of the personal and communal spiritual lives of its actual practitioners. This is very much the case in Haiti, and to a noticeably lesser extent, it remains the case in Haitian Miami. Comparatively speaking, Vodou functions for most Haitians, whatever their religious persuasion, somewhat like Calvinism does in the United States for Americans of an even wider range of religious or secular commitments: although not all Americans are Calvinists, the Protestant work ethic, inspired in large part by Calvinist theology, broadly influences how Americans of all ethnic and religious backgrounds understand life.[4] So, just as many American Christians can believe that money is the root of all evil while being nevertheless materialistically self-indulgent in good conscience, so do some Haitian Pentecostals use their Bibles as amulets much like their Vodouist ancestors would have used a gourd filled with water or a packet of leaves.[5] We know, for instance, of some illiterate *botpipel* who attribute their successful crossing of the water to Miami to pocket-sized copies of the New Testament that they carried with them at sea. Of course, such forms of *maji* do not always work, as reflected in one journalist's description of the tragic scene of the drowning of thirty-three Haitian migrants just off shore from Hillsboro Beach in 1981: "Lying near the body of one expectant mother was a waterlogged burlap sack containing a small cellophane bag of hair curlers and a small, blue soft-bound New Testament" (Gersuk 1981).

Conceptualizing a Haitian Religious Collusio

Not all Haitians are religiously devout; in fact, we personally know a few Haitians who are atheists or agnostics, and one of us recalls hearing the owner of a travel agency in Port-au-Prince reject his employees' request for a day off on a major Catholic feast day by dismissing the widely popular national Catholic tradition as "a bunch of superstition" (*yon pakèt siperstisyon*). Yet, for most Haitians in Miami, as in Haiti, religion is a central guiding force in life. Furthermore, over the course of many years of research and living in Miami and in Haiti, we have come to believe that even though the forms of worship in which Haitians and Haitian Americans engage are diverse and sometimes theologically and socially at odds with one another, there is a generally shared substratum of features that runs beneath this diversity and animosity.

In conversation with our own field experience, a careful review of the literature on religion in Haiti and the Haitian diaspora would seem to confirm this sense that there is indeed, across religious difference, something like a Haitian religious collusio. It would not be unfair to think of collusio as a kind of collective habitus, or at least as the predictable and relative uniformity of habitus of all members of a given delineated collectivity or social status group, be it family, class, race, or ethnicity. By habitus, which is perhaps Bourdieu's (1977: 95) most signature theoretical notion, is meant the "matrix of perception" through which one makes sense of the world and the seat or generator of one's dispositions, inclinations, and tastes.

Because it unites people even across denominational difference and "antagonisms" and permits people on opposing "teams" to play on the same playing "field," collusio is a much better concept to use in speaking about Haitian religion holistically than the related notion of habitus, which is more individualized, though as thoroughly socially constructed, in Bourdieu's theory of practice. More specifically, Bourdieu (1971: 319) conceives of the religious habitus as "the principal generator of all thoughts, perceptions and actions consistent with the norms of a religious representation of the natural and supernatural worlds." To speak of a generalized Haitian religious habitus would gloss over very real and important differences between a Haitian Catholic habitus, a Haitian Protestant habitus, and a Haitian Vodouist habitus, the notion of habitus being fundamentally about perception and inclination. For example, a Haitian Catholic habitus will *incline* a Haitian Catholic to reach for the holy water and cross herself upon entering a Catholic church, but a Protestant habitus would not. The habitus of a Haitian Protestant who comes across a Vodou ceremony would not *incline* him to *perceive* of what is happening as holy and would likely *incline* him instead either to leave or to denounce what he *perceives*. A Vodouist habitus, furthermore, *inclines* one to *perceive* of both a Vodou temple and a Catholic church as sacred spaces, whereas a Protestant habitus would not. A Vodouist habitus would likely not *incline* a Vodouist to enter a Protestant church, but if he did so, he would not *perceive* of a great deal of religious capital, there being neither icons of saints nor much other religious paraphernalia there. These are real differences that a claim for a unifying Haitian religious habitus would unsoundly mask, distort, or deny; however, what is still shared is a Haitian religious collusio, a collusio in which Catholic, Protestant, and Vodouist religious habitus all operate. "As such, habitus is the basis of an *implicit collusion* among all the agents who are the products of similar conditions and conditionings, and also a practical experience of the transcendence of the group" (Bourdieu 2000: 145, emphasis in original). Put otherwise by Catherine Robinson (2002: 9), "habitus and a commonality of experience are important in the production of *collusio*, a collusion of subjects which in turn assures the shared investment, and maintenance of, the habitus." Furthermore, for Bourdieu (1992b: 110), "everything is social" and socially constructed, and so characteristics of the members of any given collectivity can generally be explained in terms of the socially (and culturally, politically, religiously, and economically) environmental factors that shape them. Members and participants in any given collectivity thereby coherently belong and participate by virtue of collusio, or the shared "feel for the game" that their common socializations have inculcated into their habitus (Bourdieu 1992a: 66). Whether that habitus be Haitian Catholic, Haitian Protestant, or Haitian Vodouist, it operates according to the generalized contours of the Haitian religious collusio, "the collective and tacitly affirmed understanding of 'the done thing'" in Haitian religion conceived of holistically (Rey 2007: 154).

The Haitian religious collusio consists in large part of a "a practical sense" (Bourdieu 1980) that life in this world is inhabited by invisible, supernatural forces that are to be served and which can be called upon and operationalized toward healing ills, mitigating plight, enhancing luck, and achieving goals. In one of the only two other major ethnographic studies of Haitian religion to engage at once Catholicism, Protestantism, and Vodou, Brodwin (1996: 1) reaches a similar conclusion that central to such a collusio lies a disposition to turn to religion for healing, one that inclines Haitians in general "to ally themselves with a morally upright source of healing power—connect to one or another spiritual being—and ardently denounce the competing religious options." In the other study, Corten (2001: 30) aims to understand Haitian religion holistically and to identify long-standing and/or emergent unifying threads across Haitian religious diversity. He, like Brodwin, concludes that in being confronted with ever deepening levels of poverty and despair, Catholicism, Protestantism, and Vodou in Haiti all operate "around 'a persecutory conception of evil': occult forces persecute us, and one must protect oneself."[6]

In this conceptual scheme, the meaning or purpose of religion is thus inflected by one's social position. For those who are privileged, religion serves to legitimate their status—a sense that they are *worthy* of their privileged social positions. For those who are not so materially fortunate, religion functions to provide a sense of dignity that may be otherwise absent—a sense that they are *worthy* in spite of it all; as such, Weber (1963: 106) states that religion provides members of "dis-privileged classes" with "a worthiness that has not fallen their lot, they and the world being what it is."[7] Religious habitus thus *inclines* people to embrace symbolic systems that pronounce for them their worthiness, systems that are predicated upon the existence of supernatural forces, and thus orient their lives in accordance with them. When laypersons embrace the symbolic systems of a given religious institution, say, the Catholic Church, as legitimate, they do so, according to Bourdieu's theory of the "religious field," because that institution has secured in them the recognition (or the "misrecognition") that it possesses "religious capital." Fundamentally a form of power to consecrate and thereby produce salvation goods for one's consumption, this religious capital in turn ensures adherence to the Church instead of the "heresiarch."[8] In such recognition lies the key to a given religious institution's gaining the upper hand in the competition over souls that structures any given religious field (Rey 2004; 2007).

Immigrant Religion, Symbolic Capital, and Salvation Goods

For immigrants, religious congregations clearly can be a source of social support, solace, and identity formation, as numerous studies have demonstrated (e.g., Abdullah 2010; Kurien 1998; Min 2005). These forms of support can be conceived of different kinds of "symbolic capital," for example, as resources that can be transformed or "transubstantiated" into material capital (Bourdieu 1983; Coleman 1988; Portes 1998). Many immigrants benefit from social relations forged in American churches by landing jobs, finding affordable babysitting, or accessing professional medical care at free health fairs. Immigrant congregations are thus commonly the sites of the formation of social capital that is utilized in the adaptation to the host society (Ebaugh and Chafetz 2000b; Richman 2005a).[9] Korean immigrants, for example, develop and reinforce social ties through their churches that they self-consciously use for business purposes (Chai 2000; Hurh and Kim 1990; Kim and Kim 2001; Kwon, Ebaugh, and Hagan 1997; Min 2000; Suh 2001; Yoo 1998). And, in fortifying relations in these ways in diasporic contexts, religious congregations often provide immigrants with an arena for the maintenance of their homeland cultural identity, wherein they also accrue these and other forms of symbolic capital.

Whether or not they employ these theoretical concepts explicitly, most studies of immigrant religious life in fact focus primarily on symbolic capital. The literature broadly demonstrates religion's role in reinforcing and perpetuating migrants' ties to the homeland culture as a mechanism for both easing the psychological distress occasioned by immigration and providing a community of co-ethnics who can assist each other in adjusting to life while retaining ties to those they left behind (e.g., Chou 1991; Legge 1997; Min 2005). Jay Dolan (1992: 153) finds that certain nineteenth-century letters of first-generation Italian immigrants in New York reflected an "understanding of the afterlife as a place of reunion" that mirrored immigrants' separation from their loved ones in the homeland. Religion has thus served to tie immigrants to each other socially and to the homeland symbolically (see also, e.g., DeMarinis and Grzymala-Moszczynska 1995; Tweed 1997), just as it has helped provide a meaningful sociocultural identity, thereby reinforcing immigrant ethnic and national home country identities (e.g., Al-Ahmary 2000; Tiryakian 1991).

During the "old immigration" (i.e., at the end of the nineteenth and beginning of the twentieth centuries), the American Catholic Church self-consciously created ethnic parishes that made it easier for immigrants to continue practicing their faith (e.g., Juliani 2007; Orsi 1988; Tomasi 1975). Such is no longer formally the practice in Catholic archdioceses and dioceses in the United States, but in reality many churches in America remain effectively ethnic parishes. As Ann Chih Lin and Amaney Jamal (2001) indicate, for contemporary immigrants religion indeed continues to forge cultural identity and social purpose (see also Bankston 1997). Congregations that immigrants attend often are (or soon become) perceived locally as serving a particular ethnic group, often in languages that exclude native-born Americans.[10] Mainly for social and cultural reasons, though often also for less obvious theological ones, such congregations naturally draw people of similar ethnic composition to those already seated in the pews. In all, immigrants and religion are almost invariably closely linked in contemporary America (as has generally been the case throughout American history), and this is especially true in the case of Haitians in Miami.

The study of Haitian religion in immigrant contexts can shed useful light on the function of religion for other groups among "the new immigrants" in the United States. Haitian immigrants in Miami are not unique in attending church more frequently than native-born Americans. Carl Bankston and Min Zhou (2000) observe that Vietnamese Catholics in New Orleans attend with similar frequency, as do Korean immigrants, mostly as Presbyterians (Kim and Kim 2001) in that case. Reasons offered to explain such high church attendance among Korean religious practice in the United States might help us understand Haitian immigrant religion. Nationwide surveys of Presbyterians reveal that 70 percent of first-generation Koreans in Los Angeles are members of Korean ethnic churches in the United States, in part because such denominational affiliation not only generates social capital for adherents but also aids in the assimilation process in a majority Christian host society (Hurh and Kim 1984; see also Min 1992; Kim and Kim 2001). The scholarly literature further demonstrates that many Koreans adopt Christianity upon migrating to the United States, and that the maintenance of national cultural identity is a driving force in the preponderance of Korean religion in America (Min 2005: 99). These religious trends among Korean immigrants, in our view, also help explain why Haitian immigrants in Miami are so religious and why a smaller percentage practice Vodou in South Florida than in Haiti. Richman (2003; 2005a; 2005b) notes a trend among Haitian immigrants in West Palm Beach of abandoning Vodouist devotions in part to gain better control over remittances that they send to Haiti. Likewise in Miami, we have heard some recent Haitian immigrants witness in churches that they are committing themselves to Christ as part of the new life that they hope to make in America for themselves and their families. This sometimes is stated when newcomers at Protestant church services are asked to stand, introduce themselves, and say what brings them there on this particular Sunday (or Saturday, in the case of Seventh Day Adventists). At one worship service in 2005 at the Philadelphia Church of God, a Haitian storefront located on NE 54th Street in Little Haiti, for instance, one young man stood and explained: "I am here because I am looking for a church where I can rest my weary head. I don't speak English and had a very hard time coming to Miami. I am tired of the lwa and that old stuff [*vye bagay sa yo*]; I came here looking for life and I want a new life in Jesus."

In this book, we reify such general findings in the scholarly literature on religion and the new immigrants by carefully describing and theorizing the religious lives of Haitian immigrants in Miami, while highlighting an additional factor that is perhaps somewhat unique to them among immigrant communities in general: Among Haitian Catholics, Protestants, and Vodouists alike, Haiti is conceived of as being a place of profound religious importance, whether as a nation chosen by God to act out some divine plan (McAlister 2012), as a site of choice for Marian apparitions (Rey 1999; 2002), or as the residing place of Vodou spirits and the dead, who are both deeply tied to the land (Lowenthal 1988; Richman 2007). This conceptualization among Haitian immigrants serves to deepen the religious aspect of their transnational lives. Some salvation goods, in fact, can be acquired only in Haiti, while others still are of greater value if acquired in the homeland than in the diaspora. There seems to be, from the perspective of Haitian immigrants in Miami, more religious capital in Haiti than in the United States, which is one reason why church attendance increases considerably when a priest or pastor from the homeland is in Miami to preach or celebrate mass.

Bourdieu (1991: 22, emphasis in original) perceives of religious capital as "power durably to modify the representations and practices of laypersons by inculcating in them a *religious habitus*. This religious capital is the generative basis of all thoughts, perceptions, and actions conforming to the norms of a religious representation of the natural and supernatural world." Put otherwise, religious capital is the power possessed by religious institutions and their ordained representatives to produce "salvation goods" and effectively market them to the laity in the "religious field." Derived from Weber, by the term "salvation goods" (*Heilsguten/biens de salut*), Bourdieu means especially sacraments and any officially recognized membership in an ecclesial community, which is regarded as requisite to salvation (Stöltz 2008). The concept proves especially useful for understanding the transnational Haitian religious field when one considers the etymology of the word "salvation." The first thought that the word usually brings to mind is that of heaven, of being redeemed from sin and delivered to an eternal life of glory with God. Indeed, Catholic sacraments are important salvation goods in this sense of the word, though etymologically "salvation" connotes health, vitality, wholeness, and well-being, along with holiness. As Leonard Swidler (1992: 16) explains:

> The term comes from the Latin *salus*, "health," whence a number of English and Romance cognates are derived, all fundamentally referring to health: salutary, salubrious, salute, salutation. The Germanic counterpart is *Heil*, "salvation," and as an adjective *heilig*, "holy," whence the English cognates health, hale, heal, whole, holy. To be "holy" means to be (w)hole. "Salvation" ultimately means attaining, preserving or restoring a healthy, holy, whole human life—however understood.

To drive home the relevance of these etymological observations for the study of Haitian religion, we allude to conclusions reached by Brodwin (1996) and Brown (1989) respectively that *healing* is an ultimate concern in Haitian religion (in Brown's case the reference is to Vodou alone). More generally speaking, in African and African-derived contexts, religion is likewise fundamentally about helping people live *whole* lives through infusing those lives with a force that derives ultimately from God on high, a *holy* force accessed chiefly through communal ritual, a force that is called *uzima* in Swahili, *nguya* in Lingala, *ashe* in Yoruba, and *nam* in Haitian Creole (Murphy 1993; Tempels 1959; Washington 1972).

In employing the concept of salvation goods, we intend for these etymological considerations to be kept in mind. It should also be noted that the notion of religious capital as understood in the Weber-Bourdieu lineage differs markedly from the ways in which leading proponents of microeconomic theory of use the term, viewing religious capital as the personal religious know-how of the laity (e.g., Stark and Finke 2002; Iannaccone 1992). Whereas Bourdieu conceives of the "religious field" as a sociocultural arena dominated by institutions that horde religious capital, meaning that the religious field is shaped from the top down, American economists and sociologists of religion, like Laurence Iannaccone and Rodney Stark, generally portray "religious markets" as being shaped largely by consumer demand, markets in which local churches compete with one another over "consumers" and in which both the church leaders ("CEOs") and the consumers act rationally in the religious market "so as to maximize their net benefit" (Iannaccone, 1992: 124). This differs significantly from Bourdieu's position that religion is ultimately gerrymandered to benefit ruling classes in capitalist societies. Generally speaking, microeconomic theory of religion, "a powerful theoretical paradigm for understanding why certain faith-based organizations thrive while others stagnate and fail" (Chesnut 2003: 7), is a straightforward extension of rational choice theory, which has affected all social science disciplines, most obviously economics (popularized in the recent *Freakonomics* book and subsequent columns and blogs [Levitt and Dubner 2009]). In plainer words, it argues that peoples' behaviors are rational in that they calculatingly choose what best fits their needs among a range of available alternatives.

In applying rational choice theory to religion generally and to Haitian diasporic religion particularly, we find it to be of some limited utility, notwithstanding certain compelling criticisms that some scholars have made of this approach (e.g., Bruce 2002, 1999; Chaves 1995; Sharot 2002). In particular, there is a wide range of religious congregations and worship styles in Miami from which Haitians immigrants may choose, and there are surely reasons why some are more attractive to them than others. Some individual Haitian immigrants do actively choose a church because it may have a more engaging, emotional style of worship, although such choices are dictated at least as much by "practical sense" and inclined as much by habitus and collusio as by rational calculation (see chap. 5).

Among Haitian immigrants in Miami, the tremendous popularity of Notre Dame d'Haiti Catholic Church can be soundly explained less in terms of the choices of those who worship there than in the powerful resonance between its leadership's ecclesiology and political vision, and the religious habitus of Catholic Haitian immigrants settling in Little Haiti (see chap, 2). Notre Dame's founding priest, Msgr. Thomas Wenski, who is now the archbishop of Miami, combined extensive pastoral and social service work with engaged preaching that addressed political issues in Haiti while shepherding Notre Dame. At the same time, Notre Dame d'Haiti and some of Miami's Haitian Protestant churches are so large that they incorporate a number of different worship styles and programs, and offer prayer services in different languages (Haitian Creole, English, and, to a lesser extent, French). They offer both social services and worship, and they orchestrate traditional worship and charismatic services at different times—something for everyone, as it were.

Because of this complex diversity across and within congregations, it is difficult to apply rational choice theory of religion toward developing a holistic understanding of Haitian religion in Miami. Should it focus on congregations or particular activities within congregations? Should we examine what individuals do most commonly or the look at the entire range of what they do, even if that varies considerably? Should one give priority to congregational worship or to "lived religion" (Orsi 2003)? We argue and document in the following chapters that there is some ecclesiological and sociological resonance between given congregations and the religious tastes of people in their pews or *peristil* (temples); while hardly surprising, this resonance is not always demonstrably "rational" because believers are themselves often unclear about their "choices" of a given congregation over all others. We demonstrate, for example, that individuals often attend a particular congregation for emotional "reasons." To some, this might amount to an oxymoron that invalidates rational choice theory. For others, it might simply confirm a weaker version of rational choice theory in demonstrating that there is indeed a demonstrable link between motivations and religious practice.

Moreover, many people cannot articulate their reasons for attending a particular church, or they may only do so inconsistently and incompletely. Some simply state that it's because a friend recommended it, only to later reveal that they also received advice on how to find a job, attend free language classes or health fairs, that there are occasionally visiting pastors from their home region, or that they heard rumors that a certain pastor might have magical prayers to help secure a green card, and a nearly endless number of other so-called rationalizations.

Furthermore, microeconomic theories of religion do not address what produces the market in the first place, or what forces create and maintain the choices available, and limit or even eliminate other choices. We find that some religious institutions have considerable resources that promote them and make them "obvious" choices. For example, the Roman Catholic Church had a strong, visible presence in Miami before any Haitian boat people showed up on Florida shores, and when they began arriving in large numbers in the late 1970s and early 1980s, they had practically nowhere else to turn—they had little or no choice. Some observers and advocates criticized the Church for responding slowly and inadequately to the influx of largely Catholic Haitians, but when it did respond, it created what became the largest, most influential religious institution in the Haitian diaspora, Notre Dame d'Haiti. Some emergent Haitian Protestant churches also drew upon resources from larger church bodies in the United States through denominational affiliation, like Grace United Methodist Church, but other religious institutions have been entirely on their own, as were virtually all Vodouist congregations. This means that the place of some institutions in the religious market is much less visible and that their lack of comparative "success," as measured by size, may be more reflective of deficient material resources than of any lack of religious capital that they possess or any devaluation of the salvation goods that they have to offer.

For everything else that it might be from their own theological perspectives, for most Haitian immigrants, from a sociological perspective, religion can said to provide symbolic capital as a substitute for material capital and a springboard to obtaining material capital, and also to furnish the assurance of worthiness in a world that denies them a material sense of worthiness—a key salvation good in immigrant religion, especially for Haitians in Miami. That most Haitians suffer material deprivation is widely documented (e.g., Fass 1988; Francisque 1986; Maternowska 2006). Most Haitians, whether in Haiti or in the diaspora, inhabit and negotiate unequal and often oppressive socio-economic worlds in which their labors are exploited or in which they turn to uncertain market enterprises in the "informal sector" (Lundhal 1992; Manigat 1997; Trouillot 1990). The present study does not cover such social conditions in Haiti, but it does consider the racial discrimination and prejudice that Haitians have been forced to confront and endeavor to overcome in South Florida, which they have largely done with admirable success. These realities should be kept in mind when considering the rather impressive statistic that nearly 90 percent of Haitian immigrants in Miami attend church at least monthly (Stepick and Portes 1986: 346). The data thus demonstrates that religion is a critical, central component of the lives of many, indeed most, Haitian immigrants in the United States, and our findings in Miami only corroborate this. We thus hypothesize that, in general, the deeper the discrimination that any given immigrant group experiences upon arrival in the United States, the greater value that salvation goods in the form of worthiness will have. This is not to propose yet another iteration of tired deprivation theories of religion; wealthy Haitians are also generally very religious people, and, although our hypothesis is based on a premise that material deprivation plays an important role in Haitian religion, it does not follow that religious practice among Haitian immigrants in Miami amounts to any form of escapism, fatalism, or "alienation," as Marxist theory would suggest (see chap. 1). Instead, their religious practice indeed yields demonstrable material benefits.

Haitians in South Florida

Today there are roughly half a million Haitians and Haitian Americans living in Florida, more than in any other state in the country. Many of them arrived as refugees and started their new lives in Little Haiti, where almost invariably they received material assistance from local churches' social programs and spiritual fulfillment in the form of sacraments administered by a Catholic priest, healing hands laid upon them by a Protestant pastor, or divination performed by a Vodou priestess: these are salvation goods. South Florida's Haitian community is the largest in the United States and the largest beyond the island of Hispaniola, where roughly 10 million people live in Haiti and another million Haitians live across the border in the Dominican Republic. But it is only relatively recently that Haitians made South Florida such a key part of their diaspora, and they did so against tremendous odds, in one of the most negative contexts of reception that America has ever created for immigrants.

Like most Caribbean islanders, Haitians have a long history of migration out of their homeland. Until the late 1950s there were almost no Haitians in the United States. However, there were a few important exceptions in the forms of the occasional migrations of groups or individuals who made their marks on earlier American history. For example, Jean Baptiste Point Du Sable (1750–1818), born in Saint Marc, Saint-Domingue, migrated as a young man to the largely unsettled Northwest, establishing a trading post on the banks of the Chicago River where it feeds into Lake Michigan. This station was thriving enough by 1776 to earn Du Sable the title of "Founder of Chicago." The pioneering naturalist John James Audubon (1785–1851) was also born in Saint-Domingue, as Jean-Jacques Audubon, on his father's sugar plantation in Les Cayes, and he immigrated to Philadelphia, via France, in 1803. Audubon found a thriving francophone community in Philadelphia, one with deep ties to Saint-Domingue. Meanwhile, during the Haitian Revolution, which raged intermittently between 1791 and 1804 and transformed Saint-Domingue into the Republic of Haiti, several thousand French colonists fled the conflict, many of them bringing some of their African and Creole slaves with them, and they settled in New Orleans and Philadelphia. In New Orleans, some of these Dominguean refugees contributed to the development of the American version of Vodou ("Voodoo"), for which the Big Easy is famous. Yet, these migrations were far more French than African-descended experiences and as such they did not produce an enduring Haitian community in the States.

Not until the 1960s did substantial Haitian communities begin to appear in American cities, primarily New York but also Boston and Chicago. Given that during the last quarter of the twentieth century the American government so actively deterred Haitians from arriving in South Florida, it is painfully ironic that the first major migration of Haitians to the States was abetted by the American Embassy in

Haiti during the early 1960s. François "Papa Doc" Duvalier assumed the Haitian presidency in 1957 and soon initiated a thoroughly vicious campaign of oppression against potential and perceived political enemies, driving many into exile. In response, the Kennedy administration instructed the U.S. embassy in Haiti to ease entry requirements for Haitians seeking visas, a process parallel to what was already in place in Cuba and in the neighboring Dominican Republic. Most of these early migrants from Haiti were professionals and members of their country's mulatto elite; they were soon followed by members of the nation's newly emergent black middle class. Changes in U.S. immigration law in 1965 allowed immigrants to sponsor relatives, and gradually the flow of émigrés from Haiti became more socioeconomically diverse, with seven thousand Haitians gaining permanent residency and twenty thousand more securing temporary visas each year by the end of the decade (Stepick 1998: 4).

At that time, Miami and all of Florida was deeply embroiled in the civil rights struggle, with segregation just beginning to be legally dismantled and with anti-black racism still widespread. The city was very much a part of the Deep South, with "'whites only signs'" being then "as prevalent in Miami as they were in other southern cities" (Dunne 1997: 171). Many among the early Haitian migrants were mulatto elites who had enjoyed considerable privilege in Haiti, like Morisseau-Leroy, though once settled in the United States they would be simply classified as "black" according to the informal "one-drop rule" that once dominated perceptions of race and racialized social structures. The first flows of Haitians, being fully aware of inherent racism there, thus bypassed Florida and the rest of the South; they headed to cities where they were more likely to be welcome, or at least less likely to provoke a negative reaction. New York was a first choice of black Caribbean migrants in general, some of them contributing to the Harlem Renaissance of the 1920s and 1930s (Kasinitz 1992). In 1932, for example, Langston Hughes, one of the giants of that cultural movement, visited Haiti for several months and met the great Haitian writer Jacques Roumain, whose classic novel *Gouverneurs de la rosée* Hughes translated into English as *Masters of the Dew* (Roumain 1947).

In the wake of the dismantling of legalized segregation in the Deep South, a few Haitians from elsewhere in the United States moved to

Florida, and especially Miami, as the climate there was more similar to their homeland's and it was much closer to Haiti than Boston, Chicago, or New York, making return trips to the native land and a transnational existence logistically easier. Yet, it was not until small boats of refugees began arriving directly from Haiti that Haitians became visible as a distinct immigrant community in South Florida. The first Haitian boat people claiming persecution in Haiti arrived in September 1963. All twenty-three on board were denied asylum and deported, however, signaling a rising swell of incipient rejection to come (Little and Newhouse al-Sahli, 2004).[11]

Seafaring Haitian refugees, called *botpipel* in Haitian Creole (a phonetic appropriation of the English term "boat people"), were relatively few until the late 1970s. When they did begin to arrive more frequently by the end of that decade, the United States created an extremely negative context of reception, with the federal government instituting a consistent, resolute policy to keep Haitians out of South Florida. From the 1980s through the end of the twentieth century, Haitians had the highest rejection rate of political asylum petitions among all arriving national groups. Beginning in 1981, the U.S. Coast Guard began patrolling Haitian waters to intercept boats of potential refugees from Haiti, and although authorities were tasked with interviewing Haitians and reviewing their petitions for political asylum, virtually all interdicted migrants were repatriated to Haiti. As for Haitians who have managed to evade the Coast Guard and make it to Florida shores only to later be arrested, the United States routinely jails them in immigration detention centers. And this remains the case today. Contrariwise, refugees from Cuba who arrive on U.S. shores are paroled into American society and given legal papers, a contrast that we profile briefly in chapter 4.

Periodically, policies against Haitian *botpipel* have been relaxed, either under order of the federal courts or by temporary relief from the federal administration. For example, in 1980, the United States welcomed more than 125,000 Cuban migrants. Under political pressure from civil and human rights groups about disparate, racialized treatment between Cubans and Haitians, President Carter decreed that Cubans and Haitians would be treated equally. But the order applied only to those who arrived before a specific date, October 10, 1980. For quite some time, no Cuban *balseros* (rafters) arrived after that date, but

Haitian *botpipel* did, and they again confronted prejudice and formidable obstacles to settling in the United States. Reportedly, an influential South Florida congressman bellowed behind closed doors at the head of what was then called the Immigration and Naturalization Service (INS, now known as ICE, Immigration and Customs Enforcement), "We don't want any more god damn black refugees in South Florida!" (Stepick 1998: 101).

Such American racism toward Haitians has a long history, which reaches to the peaks of national political power. William Jennings Bryan, President Woodrow Wilson's secretary of state, was shocked to learn that there were actually francophone literati in Haiti, quipping in disbelief: "Imagine! Niggers speaking French!!!" One of Wilson's military leaders of the first U.S. occupation of Haiti (1915–34), Colonel Littleton Waller was acquainted with some French-speaking Haitians and was a bit more philosophical: "These people are niggers in spite of the thin varnish of education and refinement. Down in their hearts they are just the same happy, idle, irresponsible people we know of" (in Maxwell 2004). Meanwhile, Franklin Delano Roosevelt visited Haiti in 1917 and was told by an American companion that Haiti's minister of culture "would have brought $1,500 at auction in New Orleans in 1860 for stud purposes," a comment that Roosevelt recounted ruefully to one of his own cabinet members when he returned to Haiti seventeen years later (Chomsky 1993: 201).

In due course, "diseased" was foregrounded among such pernicious stereotypes about Haitians, who had long been perceived of in American collective consciousness as being poor, superstitious, backwards, illiterate, and inferior.[12] All of these stereotypes proved to be untrue of course, but the most damaging was the one that asserted Haitians were responsible for bringing AIDS into the United States. With AIDS science then in its infancy, in 1983 the Centers for Disease Control (CDC) marked Haitians as one of the special at-risk groups for carrying the communicable disease (along with homosexuals, heroin addicts, and hemophiliacs—the infamous "Four H Club"), while researchers from MIT suggested in a medical journal that the practice of "voodoo" in Haiti was in part responsible for the disease's spread there (Farmer 1992). The CDC subsequently disavowed this list, but as so often happens, many people remembered the original news rather than the

correction, and the damage was done. In Haiti, a once-thriving tour-
ist industry collapsed altogether, while Haitians in the United States
found themselves facing new forms of racism tied to blame for allegedly bringing the dreaded disease to the country and for being themselves likely infected. Haitians were often shunned, frequently denied
work, evicted, and even picketed. In high schools, the label "Haitian"
became an epithet, driving many Haitian youths to deny their heritage
and become "cover-ups," with Pierres becoming Peters, Jeans becoming
Johnnies, and Maries becoming Marys (Stepick 1998: 1).

Yet, the early waves of Haitian refugees in South Florida did receive
some support, both locally and nationally, chiefly from civil rights organizations and churches. First to publicly advocate on behalf of Haitians
were a few local African American churches. Although African Americans were generally uninterested in assisting the refugees, as Marvin
Dunne (1997: 323) explains, "[a] small coalition of blacks led by the
Reverend James Jenkins of Liberty City's Friendship Missionary Baptist
Church and a small group of black ministers called the Black Baptist
Alliance helped to provide food, shelter, and clothing to the newcomers." The Reverend Ray Fauntroy, the African American leader of the
Miami chapter of the Southern Christian Leadership Council, which
had been founded by Martin Luther King Jr. in Atlanta in 1957, also
"became an early and visible advocate for Haitian refugees." Meanwhile,
in 1975 the National Council of Churches (NCC) established the Christian Community Service Agency "to act as a conduit of church funds to
assist Haitian refugees." The agency would later be renamed the Haitian
Refugee Center (HRC). A Haitian-born Catholic priest, Rev. Gerard
Jean-Juste, became its executive director from the time he arrived in
Miami from Boston in 1977 until 1990, when he left Miami for Haiti
to take up a ministerial post in the national government of the newly
elected president Jean Bertrand Aristide, a like-minded Catholic priest
who was committed to the teachings of liberation theology.

Jean-Juste had originally left Haiti as a young man and attended
seminary in Puerto Rico. In 1971, an exiled Haitian bishop in New York
ordained him—the first Haitian Roman Catholic priest in the United
States. After his ordination, the priest taught English to Haitians in
Boston. When he moved to Miami, he criticized the local Catholic
hierarchy for its failure to advocate on behalf of Haitian refugees, an

action that resulted in his being barred from saying mass in the then-Diocese of Miami, despite a dire need of Creole-speaking Catholic priests in South Florida.[13] Throughout his time in Miami, *"Pè Njeri"* (Father Jerry), as he was lovingly called by *botpipel*, relished his role as a constant reminder to the local establishment's conscience concerning Haitians, and he was the most frequently quoted Haitian spokesmen, a charismatic leader with a keen knack for manipulating the press. His vocal opposition to the status quo eventually irked the NCC, however, such that they withdrew their funding for the HRC. The Ford Foundation stepped into the breach for the ensuing fifteen years, and the priest continued to rail against his church for failing to support immigrants.

In retrospect, Pè Njeri's criticism is somewhat ironic in the sense that the Cuban refugee influx can be said to have created the Catholic Church in Miami. Although that is not literally true, before the arrival of Cuban refugees in Miami in the early 1960s, the Church was relatively small. The Roman Catholic Diocese, for example, was then headquartered in Palm Beach—not in Miami. Miami residents were far more likely to be Baptists (a legacy of being a southern state) or Jewish (a result of Miami's tourism and retirement communities). But with the arrival of Cuban refugees who were fleeing a predominantly Catholic country, the Roman Catholic Church became South Florida's first resettlement agency to be funded by the U.S. government. Whereas by Latin American standards Cubans had generally not been fervently devout in their homeland, the Catholic Church became a critical institution for them in Miami. As such, in the 1970s Haitians were not the primary social concern of local Catholic Church's outreach ministry to immigrants. The local Catholic bishop, Msgr. Edward McCarthy, actively opposed the creation of an ethnic parish for Haitians even though he generously supported one that already existed for Cubans.[14]

Throughout the 1980s and 1990s, the HRC was the epicenter of political activity in Little Haiti, located on one of the neighborhood's main commercial corridors, NE 54th Street. *"Senkant Kat"* (fifty-four, in Haitian Creole) became so synonymous with the HRC that many newly arriving immigrants who had no personal contacts in the city would simply seek out a Haitian cab driver (of whom there are many in Miami) and ask to be brought to *Senkant Kat*. When the dictator Jean-Claude Duvalier was driven out of Haiti in 1986, Haitians celebrated on *Senkant Kat* in front of the HRC. When the military assumed control through repeated coups, demonstrations filled the same street each time. When Aristide campaigned for the Haitian presidency by visiting Miami in 1989, the HRC organized rallies to support him. After a coup deposed Aristide in 1991, the center organized massive marches in support of democracy. Whenever the national or local media wanted a quote concerning either Haitian refugees or politics in Haiti, they first went to the HRC.

While Jean-Juste's and the HRC's political activities were highly visible, the less-heralded legal services rendered by the center were more critical to the formation of Miami's Haitian community. Much of their work involved supporting Haitian immigrants in asylum hearings through collaborations primarily with non-Haitian lawyers and Haitian legal aides. The center's most significant efforts took the form of class-action lawsuits on behalf of Haitians' asylum claims. These legal victories frustrated the U.S. government efforts to repress the flow of Haitians to South Florida. For example, concerning the work for HRC by a white female lawyer named Cheryl Little, one immigration official complained that "I think she should get married, get a husband, have some children, cook for him, let him support her, and help him contribute to society" (in Schmich 1991).

During the 1980s the U.S. Catholic Church, and particularly its Diocese of Miami, emerged as a forceful supporter of Haitian immigrants, offering legal services to individual Haitian immigrants and criticizing U.S. policies that discriminated against Haitians. Most of their efforts were channeled through Notre Dame d'Haiti Catholic Church and the adjoined Pierre Toussaint Haitian Catholic Center. Without the legal victories of the HRC and the criticism from the Catholic Church and others, it is likely that the U.S. government would have succeeded in its efforts and that a critical nucleus of Miami's Haitian community never would have formed. In short, mainstream churches, namely the Roman Catholic Church and member institutions of the NCC, successfully militated against governmental efforts to keep Haitians out of, or down and out in, Miami.

As the government and advocates for *botpipel* squabbled over policies pertaining to the rights of Haitians to remain in the United States, a visible Haitian community gradually took shape in Miami, with those who managed to stave off deportation being supplemented by secondary migrants from New York and elsewhere in the States, by new migrants coming directly from Haiti (often with relatives already settled in Miami), and by the emergence of a second generation. The densest and most visible Haitian concentration arose in what came to be known as Little Haiti, a neighborhood formerly called Lemon City, which lies within the formal municipal boundaries of City of Miami. Consisting today of a roughly 50 x 12-block inner-city zone, Little Haiti is located just north of downtown Miami, squeezed between a small, upscale, predominately white community next to Biscayne Bay on the east, the ethnically mixed and middle-class neighborhood of Miami Shores on the north, and Miami's densest concentration of African Americans, in Liberty City, one of Miami's poorest neighborhoods, on the west.

The Little Haiti storefronts leap out at you. Bright blues, reds, and oranges seem to vibrate to the pulsing Haitian music blaring from sidewalk speakers. The multilingual signs advertise distinctively Haitian products—rapid money-transfer to any village in Haiti, the latest Haitian music, custom-tailored French-styled fashions, and culinary delights such as *lanbi nan sos* (conch in Creole sauce) and *griot* (fried pork chunks). Murals of Haitian revolutionary heroes and Catholic saints adorn grocery stores and restaurants, and Haitian flags flutter here and there. Pedestrians abound. Places of worship pervade the neighborhood, primarily Protestant storefronts but also a few Catholic and mainstream Protestant churches and several Vodou temples in or behind botanicas or in private homes. On NE 2nd Avenue, the Caribbean Marketplace gives one a distinct feeling of actually being in a small incarnation of Port-au-Prince's famous Iron Market.

The side streets and back alleys present a different panorama. In between a few immaculate, spruced-up houses are a majority of neglected, deteriorating dwellings. The homes are typical American Sunbelt housing from the 1940s and 1950s, mostly small, single-family, one-story bungalows on tiny lots. Many once-grassy lawns have turned to dirt, some with cars parked on them; few are in the driveways. Most blocks have a trash pile in front of at least one house. It is not too uncommon to see bullet casings, crack phials, and discarded condoms on sidewalks or curbside.

The streets of Little Haiti thus reflect some of the diversity of economic conditions for Haitians in South Florida. Many Haitians are highly entrepreneurial and some have been quite successful in their business enterprises. But Little Haiti is a community primarily of the recently arrived and those who have not been able to move up and out of the ghetto. Haitians who live in Little Haiti are less likely than their compatriots residing elsewhere in Miami to have achieved economic prosperity. Many struggle to survive, bouncing between regular jobs in the formal sector, unemployment, and small-scale self-employment in the underground economy or the informal sector. The largest five occupational groups employing Miami-Dade Haitians are office support, building maintenance, food preparation, sales, and transportation. These are among the lowest paying occupations in the region. In fact, the five lowest-paying occupations (food preparation, farming, building maintenance, personal care, and healthcare support) employ 31 percent of Haitian workers but only 15 percent of all Miami-Dade workers.

In Miami-Dade County, the Haitian median household income is about $20,000, $16,000 less than the county's median household income and $29,000 less than the average income of the county's white residents. A similar disparity holds true for poverty rates. In Miami-Dade County the overall poverty rate is 18 percent, but the poverty rate for Haitians living in Miami is 37.5 percent, more than double. These figures mask the emerging diversity of Haitians and Haitian Americans in South Florida, however, particularly those Haitians immigrants who have been economically successful, some bringing much of their wealth from the homeland. The entrepreneurs and professionals who have stores or offices in Little Haiti tend to be those who have moved to other neighborhoods. Haitians and Haitian Americans in South Florida who reside outside of Little Haiti generally have more education, higher incomes, and larger homes, and they send their children to "better" schools and generally need not fear crime close to home. As more Haitians began settling in what became Little Haiti, some started moving northward to higher-income neighborhoods in communities such as Miami Springs, North Miami, and North Miami Beach, in Miami-Dade County, and Pembroke Pines, Miramar, and Wilton Manors in Broward County, which is immediately north of Miami-Dade. To the south, in Kendall and Perrine, meanwhile, a sizable middle and upper class segment of Haitian Miami has emerged, while today Palm Beach County is also home to a large Haitian community, as is the city of Orlando, much farther north, in Orange County.

By 2000, the metropolitan area that encompasses Miami-Dade County, Broward County, and Palm Beach County had become home to more than one-third of all Haitians and Haitian Americans in the United States, while the New York/New Jersey metropolitan area had just under 30 percent, with all other areas with visible Haitians populations (like Boston, Chicago, and Philadelphia) each having around 5 percent, if that. Among recent Haitian immigrants, more than 70 percent enter the United States based on family relationships, while just over one-fifth arrive as refugees or asylum seekers. Moreover, more than half of Haitian-born permanent residents are eligible to become U.S. citizens, and Haitians are more likely than other immigrants to become citizens (Terrazas 2010). More Haitians than other new immigrant groups also have had some college education, and fewer Haitians than other immigrants had no high school diploma. Furthermore, Haitian immigrants today are less likely to live in poverty than other new immigrant groups. Considering the great challenges that Haitians have faced in their journeys to America, these facts are quite impressive.

Although Haitians have spread out from Little Haiti over the years, and one can find residential concentrations and Haitian businesses scattered throughout South Florida, Little Haiti remains the heart of the Haitian community. Not only is it the best place to find specifically Haitian goods and the most delicious Haitian food this side of Port-au-Prince, but it also has the densest concentration of Haitian churches in Miami. It is still the case today that, although Notre Dame remains by far Miami's largest Haitian church, some of the most thriving Haitian religious congregations in South Florida are found outside of Little Haiti and even outside of the City of Miami, with Haitian Catholic ministries now flourishing from Homestead in the south to West Palm Beach in the north, with Protestant storefronts scattered throughout Miami-Dade, Broward, and Palm Beach Counties, and with one of the Haitian diaspora's most impressive Vodou temples located in the northern reaches of North Miami, several miles from Little Haiti. Our focus in this book is on Haitian religion in Miami-Dade County, with considerable material included from our field work in Haiti, necessitated because Haitian religion in Miami is so deeply transnational, such that making sense of the religious lives of Haitian immigrants requires visiting Haiti and observing religion there.

How the Book Is Organized

Crossing the Water and Keeping the Faith consists of this introduction, five chapters, and a conclusion, followed by a three appendices. Chapter 1 focuses on Notre Dame d'Haiti Catholic Church in Little Haiti, which is arguably the most significant cultural institution in the Haitian diaspora, and includes coverage of relevant periods of Haitian political history in order to illustrate some of the "push" forces that led to the creation of the Haitian diaspora. Although chapter 1 focuses on the Catholic side of the Haitian religious triangle of forces in Miami, it also serves as historical background for the entire book. Chapter 2 moves beyond Notre Dame and Little Haiti to consider some of the increasingly diverse, both economically and spiritually, forms that Haitian Catholic lives are taking in Miami. Meanwhile, Chapter 3 remains on the Catholic side of the triangle, returning to Little Haiti and focusing entirely on a single week of exuberant religious celebrations at Notre Dame d'Haiti Catholic Church, which center upon the Feast of Our Lady of Perpetual Help, Haiti's patron saint.

Moving to the Vodouist side of the triangle, chapter 4 describes challenges that practitioners of Haiti's most popular religion face in carrying on their homeland faith traditions in South Florida and the ways in which they have adapted those traditions in the diaspora. The botanica, for instance, is Vodou's most public face in Miami, even though such stores are virtually nonexistent in Haiti, where we know of only one such business enterprise in Port-au-Prince. Because Vodou is so strongly tied to the land in Haiti, in some ways it is even more transnational than Haitian Catholicism and Haitian Protestantism, and several examples of the contours of Haitian Vodouist transnationalism are profiled in this chapter. We also discuss various ways in which the religion has found its way into Miami courtrooms, an increasingly common phenomenon.

If, as demographic statistics suggest (Woodson and Baro 1996; 1997; Houtart and Rémy 1997), Haiti's national population is today roughly one-third Protestant, a community that has been steadily growing since World War II, we believe that the figure is even higher in the Haitian diaspora, where it may already be the case that there are as many Haitian Protestants as Catholics, and very many more Protestants than

Vodouists. Already by 1985, 40 percent of Haitian immigrants in Miami were Protestant (Stepick and Portes 1986), likely much higher than it was in Haiti at that time. Even the casual observer who tours Little Haiti cannot but be deeply impressed by how many Haitian storefront churches—nearly one hundred—are packed into the neighborhood. We have attended worship services in many of them and interviewed dozens of Haitian Protestant pastors and laypersons. We limit our focus to just two churches in an effort to illustrate more generally the place of the storefront church in Haitian life in Miami (see chap. 5).

Over the course of this book, the reader will meet several Haitian immigrant believers and a number of their most influential religious leaders. It has long been our impression that the anthropology and the sociology of religion are at their best when biography and ethnography are frequently woven into the narrative, and we have chosen to do such weaving throughout this study. We hope that our theorizing does not cloud the more important story of the place of religion in the lives of Haitian immigrants from their own perspective. If at times we sound as if we are making faith statements instead of scholarly observations, it is because we wish to reflect what is perhaps the most fundamental truth about Haitian religion in general—that it is rooted in the unshakeable faith of those who practice it, a faith that God and other spiritual beings exist and intervene in the lives of human beings, that miracles happen, and that life's ultimate meaning is religious. In other words, we are consciously following Wayne Proudfoot's (1985: 195–96) directive that in the study of religion "An emotion, practice or experience must be described in terms that can plausibly be attributed to the subject . . . terms that would be familiar to, incorporating beliefs that would be acknowledged by, the subject." That is, we have aimed to *describe* Haitian religion in terms that would discursively resonate with Haitian believers themselves, though when we turn to theory and analysis, turning our efforts to *explanation*, as with our application of Bourdieuian or Weberian theory, this "need not be couched in terms familiar or acceptable to the subject."

Our conclusion briefly offers some parting observations and summations of material covered in this book, driving home one of the most powerful points that one can make about Haitian immigrants in general and about their religion in particular: that what they have achieved for themselves and for their loved ones in Haiti is nothing short of remarkable, especially in light of the extraordinary challenges that they have faced in a society that never wanted them in the first place (Stepick 1992). And, to a person, were you to ask Haitians in Miami how this has been achieved, the response would be "by the grace of God." This answer might of course be worded in various ways depending upon individuals' specific faith commitments, but it is nonetheless integral to the Haitian religious collusio. This achievement, furthermore, is in part responsible for the resurgence of Haitian pride that we have approvingly witnessed in recent years in Miami, where just twenty years ago it was painfully elusive, and for a decrease in the denial of Haitian identity that once plagued the first generation of *botpipel* and their children as they sought new lives in and around Little Haiti. This is really quite an astounding and admirable testimony to the human spirit, but one that should not be so surprising coming from a people whose ancestors pulled off world history's only successful national slave revolt. That, too, they generally attribute to God, saints, and spirits.

1

The Haitian Catholic Church in Miami

When the Saints Go Sailing In

A colorful mural adorns the northern interior wall of Miami's Notre Dame d'Haiti Catholic Church (see fig. 1.1). It depicts bright skies over the shimmering blue waters and the high green mountains of the Caribbean nation of Haiti. Soaring through the skies is an Air d'Haïti passenger jet, while plying the waters is an overcrowded wooden sailboat. They are both departing and they are both watched over maternally by Our Lady of Perpetual Help. For those aboard the plane with intentions to emigrate, voyagers who could afford an airline ticket and possessed the required valid passport and visa to board, the immigration and settlement experience in Miami differs vastly from those with no other choice than to squeeze onto a sailboat in a desperate and dangerous attempt to make it to *lot bo dlo*, to the other side of the water, as the Haitian diaspora is called in Haitian Creole. For those on the boat who actually make it to Miami, chances are that they eventually would find themselves in the pews of Notre Dame and in the hallways and erstwhile classrooms of its adjacent Pierre Toussaint Haitian Catholic Center, accessing any number of the social services offered there. An able leadership greets them with the generous support of the Roman Catholic Archdiocese of Miami. Together, the church leadership and the Haitian immigrant congregants have made this the epicenter of Little Haiti, an impoverished inner-city neighborhood that has been called both the "Ellis Island" and the "living room" for Haitians in Miami.

Notre Dame d'Haiti is very much the heart and soul of Little Haiti, the densest concentration of Haitian immigrants in Miami, if not the entire world, and one of the poorest neighborhoods in one of the poorest cities in America. And, although the jet airliner is depicted in the mural, this church began as a congregation of those who came on the boat, of thousands of Haitian refugees, of *botpipel,* who first began arriving in the late 1970s, followed by a large wave of some ten thousand coming in 1980 alone. They and their boat are also depicted in a stained-glass window behind the altar, right next to another stained-glass window of the Venerable Pierre Toussaint.[1] There is no memorial window of the plane, though, and so it is clear that this is a church of the *botpipel* and of the poor, however many wealthier Haitians may have gravitated here over the years. Haitian class distinctions, as everything else in Haitian culture and society, extend transnationally into Miami. The Polish American monsignor Thomas Wenski, one of the founders of Notre Dame and the spiritual father of Haitian Miami, understood this from the very beginning of his ministry: "I figured out pretty quickly that the doctors and lawyers didn't need me—their Haitianess was a sort of social tea kind of thing, like at Christ the King," a reference to an upper middle-class parish elsewhere in the Archdiocese of Miami that has a weekly French/Creole language Mass. And, one of the ways in which Wenski expressed his solidarity with the Haitian poor and endeared himself to his inner city flock was "by not learning French."[2]

For those touching down on the Air d'Haïti flight at Miami International Airport (some of them the French-speaking doctors and lawyers who didn't need Wenski), chances are that they already owned fine houses somewhere else in Miami-Dade County than Little Haiti, or that they were welcomed into the living rooms of relatives to embark upon settlement experiences that did not require any assistance from the Toussaint Center on the grounds of Notre Dame d'Haiti. Many from this flight and thousands of others like them have never even stepped foot in Little Haiti. Most of them are devout Catholics who, like the Catholic *botpipel,* bring their faith with them when crossing the water. But, the ones from the plane find themselves worshipping, usually as minorities, in Catholic churches other than Notre Dame, in other Miami neighborhoods, where masses are celebrated regularly in French or Haitian Creole. They are members of an increasingly upwardly

Figure 1.1. Mural inside of Notre Dame d'Haiti Catholic Church in Little Haiti, Miami, depicting Our Lady of Perpetual Help, Haiti's patron saint, watching over departing boat people and air passengers leaving Haiti for Miami. Photo by Jerry Berndt.

mobile and economically, culturally, and generationally diversifying Miami's Haitian community that today counts roughly a quarter of a million people. And, just as they have diversified economically, culturally, and generationally, so too have Haitian and Haitian American Catholics in Miami diversified religiously

This chapter is a historical and ethnographic portrayal of Notre Dame d'Haiti Catholic Church, the leading cultural and religious institution in Haitian Miami and one of the most significant "ethnic parishes" in American Catholic history. Time and time again, Haitian immigrants have flocked to Notre Dame for solidarity and prayer, whether in the midst of tumult in Haiti or in the struggle to survive in a "host" society that never wanted them. More regularly, Notre Dame has also effectively served as the spiritual home for tens of thousands of Haitian Catholic immigrants over the years, and the Toussaint Center has served thousands more Haitians and Haitian Americans of whatever religious or secular persuasion with its myriad of social assistance programs.

Prayers and Tears in the Living Room

"When I learned about the earthquake," explains Fr. Reginald Jean-Mary, "I opened the church so that people could come and pray" (WLRN 2010). What else was there to do in the immediate aftermath of the devastating earthquake in Haiti on January 12, 2010? For thirty years Haitian immigrants had come to "the living room," as Fr. Jean-Mary likes to call his church, to pray: regularly for Mass but also whenever news of some major event in Haiti reaches Miami: of coups-d'état; of violence at the polls; of AIDS and cholera epidemics; or of migrants lost at sea. On October 27, 1983, for instance, when Msgr. Wenski led 140 Haitian immigrants in mournful procession beneath the towering oak trees in the churchyard behind Notre Dame. The processors and their priest prayerfully joined hands in a circle and planted a large wooden cross in the ground to commemorate the thirty-three seafaring Haitian migrants who drowned when their sailboat, *La Nativité*, capsized within sight of the lights of the South Florida coast at night two years earlier, their bodies washing up on Hillsboro Beach by the following morning. "This wasn't only for those who died aboard *La Nativité*," noted Wenski. "It's for the hundreds whose bodies were never found [in other unsuccessful attempts to reach the United States]" (in Vaughan 1983b).

Just over twenty years later, in 2004, Haiti celebrated its bicentennial, marking the republic's independence from French colonial rule, a feat achieved through world history's only successful national slave revolt. Lampposts throughout Little Haiti were adorned with banners of red and blue, the colors of the Haitian flag. Thousands of Haitians walked beneath them on New Year's Day to Notre Dame d'Haiti for an effusive and worshipful outdoor Mass and jubilee, which, even by Notre Dame's standards, was an extraordinary occasion, perhaps the most celebratory in the church's history. January 1 is also the feast day of the Solemnity of Mary, Mother of God, which certainly added spiritual meaning to the gathering, as most Haitian Catholics attribute the independence and the care of their homeland nation to the Blessed Mother, but especially to Our Lady of Perpetual Help (Rey 1999; 2002). To Haitian Catholics, Notre Dame d'Haiti, Our Lady of Haiti, *is* Our Lady of Perpetual Help. The sociologist Margarita Mooney (2009: 4) was in attendance among the estimated four thousand people at Notre Dame that festive sunny day, and she helpfully reflects some of the celebration's broader import:

> The celebration at Notre Dame on January 1, 2004, marked not only two hundred years of Haitian independence but also a significant amount of progress in the Haitian community in Miami. In the 1970s, Catholic leaders in Miami celebrated Mass for thousands of Haitian asylum seekers being detained in Krome Detention Center and opened their doors to thousands of boat people who showed up at the church doorstep seeking help. Today, some twenty-five years later, Haitians in Miami have overcome tremendous prejudice in their journey from being . . . "the refugees nobody wanted" to becoming proud Haitian Americans with their own community organizations, elected political leaders, religious institutions, and distinct cultural identity.

That New Years Day gathering at Notre Dame d'Haiti was a celebration not only of Haitian independence and the Virgin Mary but of the rich stores of worthiness, justice, and dignity that Haitians in Miami have gained over the years from and through this church, through the material and spiritual support of Notre Dame d'Haiti and the Toussaint Center.

The joy of January 1, 2004, would last only two months: on February 29—this was a leap year and the first day of Lent—Haitians in Miami awoke to learn that a rebellion in their beloved homeland had driven the democratically elected president Jean-Bertrand Aristide from power, and that he was being whisked off to exile, for the second time in recent history. Once again, upon receiving news of upheaval or disaster in Haiti, hundreds of Miami Haitians dropped whatever they were doing that morning and flocked to Notre Dame. They came, as they always have, to pray for Haiti and to try to gain some sense of meaning amid yet another tragedy back home. In a moving expression of solidarity with Haitian Catholics, a group of Cubans and Cuban Americans made pilgrimage from the Shrine of the Virgin of Charity of El Cobre to Notre Dame, led by the spiritual father of the Cuban exile community, Bishop Augustín Roman. Journalists also came, knowing that if Haiti is anywhere in Miami, it is here. Conspiracy theories were quick to hit the city's Creole airwaves and circulate via *teledjòl* (word-of-mouth).

The one with the greatest currency had it that Presidents George W. Bush and Jacques Chirac had initiated a Franco-American coup d'état in Port-au-Prince to please the Haitian economic elite and foreign investors, Aristide's most vociferous opponents. By 8:00 a.m., the pews of Notre Dame were filled with sobbing people overcome with an all-too-familiar sense of disbelief in the seemingly inevitable. During Fr. Jean-Mary's stirring impromptu sermon, a woman in a rear pew cried out *"Aba George Bush! Aba George Bush!"* (Down with George Bush! Down with George Bush!). Jean-Mary seized the opportunity to place emphasis on the dire need for Haitian unity, which is one of the most common exhortations that we have heard preached in Haitian churches over the years: "Madame! Madame! That is not it! That is not what we need right now at all! It is not the time for blame and division, but for unity, prayer, and healing!" For Haitian Catholics in Miami, there is no better place to turn for these things than Notre Dame d'Haiti, where their faith and spirituality have transformed a drab high school cafeteria into one of the most moving religious sanctuaries in the American Catholic Church.

Thus, for most Haitian Catholics in South Florida, when tragedy strikes the homeland you go to Notre Dame and you pray and you weep and you console and you come together with family and strangers alike, uniting in a repeating drama of faith and longing and for a time when Haiti has peace and food and shelter and health care and education and jobs for all. But January 12, 2010, was unlike any other tragedy-induced gathering at Notre Dame, something much worse than any coup d'état imaginable. The earthquake created devastating violence in Haiti, crushing its capital city and killing a quarter of a million people in a few terrifying minutes. Jean-Mary got word of the quake and, like so many of us, tried immediately to call Haiti for news. "I was able to talk to a priest in Haiti. The only word I heard was 'catastrophe' and then it cut off" (in Romero and Lacy 2010). Then he opened the church for people to pray: "They were crying, they were leaning on each other . . . some would throw themselves on the ground to find strength" (WLRN 2010). The living room was once again swept with tears and prayers, this time more cascadingly than ever in Notre Dame's thirty years. But the people who had crossed the water kept the faith, as they always have, through it all and despite it all.

Founding the Haitian Catholic Church in Little Haiti

Haitian refugees began arriving in South Florida in significant numbers in the early 1970s; by the end of that decade they numbered around
fifty thousand, most of them initially settling in Miami just seven hundred miles from Haiti, and most of them were Catholics. The Haitian
community's rapid growth and pressing needs prompted Archbishop
Edward McCarthy to establish the Pierre Toussaint Haitian Catholic
Center in 1978 at the Cathedral of St. Mary in Lemon City, a neighborhood that would soon become known as Little Haiti. That year he also
appointed a recently ordained native Floridian named Thomas Wenski
to serve at Corpus Christi Catholic Church, a few miles to the south,
where Masses had been said in French and eventually in Creole for the
migrants since 1973. As the son of Polish immigrants, Wenski was especially sensitive to the concerns of South Florida's newly arriving Haitians: "I've always considered myself an ethnic. As a kid, I was always
the Pollack. I wore my Polishness as a badge of honor. That sense of
ethnicity always helped me when I learned Spanish to identify with the
Cuban community and also when I learned Creole to identify with the
Haitian community" (in Shaffer 1989).

Soon thereafter, Archbishop Coleman Carroll's plea to the Catholic
Church of Haiti to send a priest to help serve Miami's swelling Haitian
population was granted, and Fr. Gérard Darbouze, a native of Les Cayes
who had been a priest of the Haitian Diocese of Jérémie, left Haiti in
1980 to join Wenski to minister to Haitian refugees in South Florida.
By then, Wenski had been named director of the archdiocesan Haitian apostolate and pastor of Notre Dame d'Haiti Catholic Church,
which was still without a home independent of the cathedral. In 1980
Darbouze and Wenski said Mass in Haitian Creole at the cathedral in
Miami, and other Creole services less frequently at Corpus Christi and
at Catholic churches in Pompano Beach, Belle Glade, and Fort Lauderdale, as well as at the Krome Detention Center.

To Wenski, 1981 was a year of "divine providential timing" for the Haitian Catholic Mission in Miami. May 1981 witnessed the last graduating
class of girls from Notre Dame Academy at the corner of NE 62nd Street
and NE 2nd Avenue. Then the school merged with Archbishop Curley
High School because of dwindling enrollments, and the archdiocese

decided to cede the premises to the Haitian Catholic Mission. The cafeteria was transformed into the church, while the two stories of classrooms housed the rectory and the multitude of social service programs offered by the Haitian Catholic Center: ESL classes, job placement counseling, health screenings, legal assistance, and the like. Almost immediately, the center drew throngs of beneficiaries. Because more than ten thousand Haitian refugees had arrived in South Florida in 1980, Wenski understandably perceived the hand of providence in the transfer of the school grounds to the Haitian apostolate. By August, masses were being said in Creole for the mission's approximately one hundred members, even though Notre Dame's official consecration, by Archbishop McCarthy, did not take place until November 15. By 1982, Notre Dame had absorbed Corpus Christi's weekly Creole Mass and the Cathedral of St. Mary's daily morning Creole Mass. They offered in the new "quasi-parish" two Creole masses per day, the first at 9:00 a.m. and the second at 5:30 p.m., with Wenski as pastor, a role that he assumed enthusiastically and thoughtfully: "Immigrants integrate into American society best from positions of strength, which is precisely what the ethnic church fosters. . . . Establishing an ethnic parish was key to giving Haitians a sense of identity, and a sense of belonging. . . . The whole idea was to make the Church visible to Haitians and to make Haitians visible to the Church."[3]

Politics, Protest, and Prayer in Little Haiti

A Haitian American proverb has it that "When Haiti sneezes, Miami catches a cold." Because it was so closely attuned to, and created by, the social and political upheaval that rocked Haiti in the 1980s and 1990s, Notre Dame d'Haiti cannot be understood without focusing on the remarkable events that brought to an end thirty years of brutal dynastic dictatorship in Haiti under the Duvaliers and the ensuing (and shorter-lived) Namphy and Cédras regimes.[4] As it had throughout Latin America, liberation theology took root in Haiti in the 1970s, creating a new breed of Catholic priests in the country who envisioned the church as the prophetic "Bride of Christ" who should exercise a "preferential option for the poor." For what seemed like the first time in Haitian history, Catholic leaders began to forthrightly confront and denounce the causes of poverty and injustice that had always plagued Haitian society, the very forces that drove thousands of Haitians to sea and to seek asylum in Miami. Many of the first generation of congregants at Notre Dame brought this new conception of the church—of *Tilegliz* (Little Church)—with them to Miami, where their expectations of a socially and politically engaged church resonated harmoniously with Wenski's own ecclesiology, hence its actualization at Notre Dame d'Haiti.

Momentous sanction for the Tilegliz came with the visit of Pope John Paul II to Port-au-Prince on March 9, 1983. Much to the chagrin of Jean-Claude "Baby Doc" Duvalier, John Paul's speech before thousands of enthusiastic Haitians at Port-au-Prince's international airport amounted to a powerful exhortation for an end to political oppression and social injustice, punctuated with the resounding insistence that *"Il faut que quelque chose change ici"* (Something must change here). Haitians in the diaspora closely followed the pontiff's historic visit. In Miami, the Notre Dame community was especially overjoyed to hear their pope denounce the abuses of the Duvalier regime and acknowledge that in Haiti there was "a deep need for justice, a better distribution of goods, more equitable organization of society and more participation" (Juan Pablo II 1986: 192).

Wenski was in Haiti for the occasion. Before returning to Miami, a few days after the pope's visit, he managed to interview Gérard Duclerville, a Catholic lay activist who had been imprisoned and tortured by agents of the Duvalier regime. His recording of the Duclerville interview was played on Haitian radio in Miami, and one hundred copies were made and sold at Notre Dame. The flip side of the cassette tape was John Paul II's homily at the Port-au-Prince airport. Wenski later published the interview with photos in *Lavwa Katolik*, Florida's only Creole newspaper, which he founded and edited. In response, the Haitian government lodged a formal complaint to the Archdiocese of Miami, recognizing that although Notre Dame d'Haiti was located abroad, it was clearly integral to the popular struggle against political repression in the Haitian homeland (McCarthy 1983a).[5] It also served to establish a harmonious rhythm between Wenski's charisma and his flock's liberation ecclesiology: "That's probably when I proved to the Haitians here that I'd paid my dues . . . I was saying mass in Creole every week. Whenever something happened in Haiti, we said mass for the victims. I think that gave us credibility in the community" (in Viglucci 1995).

Emboldened by their pontiff, courageous and progressive clergy of the Haitian Catholic Church, like Hugo Triest, Antoine Adrien, Jean-Bertrand Aristide, Jean-Marie Vincent, Gilles Danroc, Max Dominique, and Bishop Willy Romélus (all of whom at one point in time have visited and/or said Mass at Notre Dame in Miami), took a leadership role in the events of 1985/86 that precipitated the political demise of Jean-Claude Duvalier. Haitian Catholic protest against the Duvalier regime had taken on transnational form, especially at Notre Dame in Miami, where Wenski's sermons often criticized the regime's human rights abuses. At a special Wednesday morning Mass and prayer vigil sponsored by the six bishops of the Haitian Catholic Church on February 9, 1983, the priest employed a Haitian proverb to express his view of the deteriorating political situation in Haiti: "If the bull knew its force, it would not let the little boy tie a rope around its neck . . . and it seems the bull is recognizing its force" (in Balmaseda 1983). The bull was symbolic of the rising popular Catholic Church in Haiti, while the boy symbolized the brutal but teetering dictator. A local Duvalierist radio station, WGLY (widely believed to be financed by the Haitian government), accused Wenski of inciting violence, broadcasting couched threats on the life of the pastor whom they nicknamed "*Pè Kiki*"—"Father Kiki" (Vaughan 1983c). Notre Dame's own radio broadcast, "*Chita Tande*" (Sit, Listen), responded simply and indirectly by keeping Miami Haitians abreast of political developments in Haiti.

Meanwhile, in the summer of 1985 the Duvalier regime deported three Belgian priests for criticizing its government: Hugo Triest, Ivan Pollefeyt, and Jean Hostens. One week after their deportation from Haiti, Pollefeyt and Hostens came to Little Haiti to say mass at Notre Dame, on August 4, 1985. In preparation for their visit, Wenski called for a day of fasting and led a candlelight procession as a gesture of support to the church in Haiti: "It is a gesture of solidarity with the church in Haiti, and a way of giving moral support to the priests to show them that the Haitian people, if not the government, are with them" (in McCarthy 1985b). In October, Wenski hand-delivered a message of thanks to Pope John Paul II for his inspiration and support for the Haitian people's struggle against oppression. The message was signed by a group of Haitian Catholic priests in Miami, Wenski, and many of his flock. It was also read repeatedly over Miami's Creole-language radio (McCarthy 1985c).

On the eve of Duvalier's ouster, hundreds of Haitian immigrants gathered daily in celebration before Notre Dame d'Haiti, chanting "Duvalier is Gone. Praise the Lord!!!" At times their joyful anticipation of the regime's fall was dramatic: on January 30, when around one thousand people took to the streets to stage a mock funeral procession, "stuffing a straw man with newspapers and parading through the streets, playing bongo drums and singing a Haitian funeral dirge" (Bohning 1986). On February 7, 1986, their prayers were answered when Duvalier was whisked out of Haiti by the U.S. government and off to exile in France. Two days later, on the first Sunday after Duvalier's departure from Haiti, an extraordinary Mass was celebrated at Notre Dame d'Haiti. Archbishop Edward McCarthy recalled that he "woke up early Friday and heard a lot of happy horns tooting. Haiti is free—hallelujah." McCarthy said Mass for more than three hours before two thousand ecstatic Haitians in the Notre Dame churchyard, proclaiming in English on behalf of the archdiocese that "we will be with you in your joy and your anxiety. We love you and admire your pilgrimage to freedom." In an outpouring of religious and political faith, the chants of thousands of Haitians of "*Libete!*" "*Libete!*" (Freedom! Freedom!) echoed from Notre Dame and throughout Little Haiti (Cottman 1986).

Significantly, Msgr. Willy Romélus, bishop of the Haitian Diocese of Jérémie and among Haiti's six bishops the most outspoken (and often sole) opponent to the Duvalier regime, visited Miami a few weeks after the government was finally toppled. Romélus celebrated Mass to more than two thousand people over several days, both at Notre Dame and at Corpus Christi, where the local Catholic ministry to Haitians was born a little more than ten years earlier (McCarthy 1986). The next year, Pope John Paul II made Miami the first destination on his second visit to the United States as pontiff. On September 10, the pope was greeted by President Ronald Reagan, kissed a Haitian girl named Nancy Bourjolly on the head, and then was driven to Little Haiti. Several thousand people were waiting there to greet him at the Cathedral of St. Mary, many of them Haitian immigrants living within walking distance, like Myrlende Mathurin, who lauded the pontiff as being "the pope of little people like us, you can see he cares" (in Suro 1987). In what was surely one of the most powerful moments in the history of Haitian Catholicism in Miami, in addressing the faithful "Pope John Paul spoke in

Creole about the problems Haitians have suffered in their homeland. He prayed for them" (May 1987: 10).

With the Duvalier dictatorship toppled, a new Haitian Constitution was ratified in 1987 and hopes abounded for a renaissance of justice and human rights. Haitians on both sides of the Straits of Florida were cautiously optimistic when elections were called for November of that year; they found it difficult to place any trust in the Haitian Army, which remained in control of the country under General Henri Namphy. In the days leading up to the elections, Haitians in Miami were praying "practically around the clock" for the peace at the polls in the homeland. "For this thing to come off," noted a realistic Wenski, "it will need a miracle" (in Gaither 1987).[6] Instead of a miracle, however, there was another tragedy, and the Notre Dame faithful were once more transformed into grieving protestors after soldiers and paramilitary agents opened fire on voters in Port-au-Prince, killing at least thirty-four and causing cancellation of the elections. Six days later, some six thousand Haitians gathered in Little Haiti around Notre Dame to embark on a march of protest against the Namphy regime (Evans 1987). Nothing had changed: whatever joyous smoke still wafted in the transnational Haitian air following Jean-Claude Duvalier's ouster the year before, whatever exuberant hope remained for a new era of justice and human rights in Haiti, was cleared away on that "Bloody Sunday," November 29, 1987. Regrettably, a series of constitutionally illegitimate governments proceeded to exercise state power in Haiti, the nation's rigid class structure remained intact, and the poverty of the masses somehow worsened, leading some observers to speak of "Duvalierism without Duvalier" (Fernandez 1991).

Led by Aristide, Tilegliz nonetheless continued the struggle for justice in the same uncompromising spirit embodied by the pope's 1983 speech in Port-au-Prince. The Haitian Catholic bishops, meanwhile, were widely believed to have been instructed by the Vatican to tone down their church's political activism. Excepting Bishop Romélus, they endeavored to silence Aristide, eventually having him banished from the Salesian Order and to a rural parish far from the politically explosive shantytowns of the capital. Now bereft of the support of the church hierarchy and because of his outspokenness against political oppression and social injustice, Aristide became the target of a number of orchestrated attacks. Among these acts of violence, the brazen September 11, 1988, attack during Mass on Aristide's own slum parish, St. Jean Bosco, ranks as "one of the most lurid crimes ever perpetrated against the church in Latin America" (Farmer 1994: 145). Thirteen parishioners were killed.[7] Shaken but defiant, Aristide continued to be the leading inspiration for popular protest in Haiti.

The faithful at Notre Dame in Little Haiti, along with their pastor, Fr. Wenski, were tremendously inspired by Aristide. The *Miami Herald* columnist Andres Viglucci (1995) explains:

> In 1983, Wenski came across the writings of a young seminarian named Jean-Bertrand Aristide in a Creole church monthly, biblical commentaries that had a lot of applications to Haiti. Wenski reprinted the articles in a Creole newspaper that he published at the time. For many Haitians in Miami, it was their initial exposure to the priest who was to become the first democratically elected president of the country.

Aristide's enormous popularity culminated with his election to the Haitian presidency in late 1990, which sparked triumphant celebrations in Little Haiti and throughout the Haitian diaspora. On February 7, 1991, the day of Aristide's inauguration, Notre Dame d'Haiti was packed with jubilant worshippers for a Mass to celebrate the occasion. Following the service, a young acolyte named Dorcely Jean hoisted an eighty-pound, nine-foot wooden cross upon his shoulders and led a procession of several hundred people from the church and down NE 2nd Avenue to NE 54th Street and location of the Haitian Refugee Center, where the crowd had swelled into a sea of red and blue. Jean's words summed up the collective hope of the Haitian faithful: "I'm so happy. The cross is very heavy, but I don't feel it because we have a new life. That's why I carry the cross. To thank God" (in San Martin 1991). Support to the new president by Little Haiti's Catholic community went beyond the symbolic and moral. In early April 1991, Notre Dame held a fund-raiser for the Aristide government (Herald Staff 1991).

However, Dorcely Jean's joy, along with that of millions of other disenfranchised Haitians in the homeland and the diaspora, soon turned to sadness and outrage, and whatever funds that Notre Dame had raised for the first Aristide government went to an ill-fated cause. It was of little surprise to anyone familiar with Haitian history when Aristide was overthrown in a coup d'état just nine months after he began his first term as president, orchestrated by General Raoul Cédras with the backing of important elements of the Haitian economic elite on September 19, 1991. Because they took Aristide's vision of a new social order to be little more than an incendiary promotion of class warfare (for one thing, the "little priest" had the audacity to double the minimum wage to about 75 cents a day!), those who coordinated and bankrolled the coup saw fit to banish the priest-*cum*-president from Haiti.

Within days of the coup a new wave of *botpipel* began to flee Haiti, as the Cédras regime committed some of the most vicious brutality in the nation's history, this time against Aristide supporters. By early December 1991, the U.S. Coast Guard had detained more than six thousand Haitian migrants and transported them for detention at the naval base in Guantanamo Bay, Cuba; the following year the Coast Guard rounded up more than thirty-seven thousand, which remains the all-time high for a single year (U.S. Coast Guard n.d). As part of an appeal by the U.S. Catholic Bishops Conference, a special offering collected $1,000 at Notre Dame. Wenski used the money to purchase more than two hundred Creole hymnals to bring to Guantanamo, where he made a pastoral visit, celebrating Mass in all six refugee camps, teaching military chaplains the Creole Eucharistic liturgy, and recruiting assistants for them from among *botpipel* (David 1991). He then returned to Little Haiti with more than six hundred handwritten notes from the refugees to family in Miami. Some of the notes supplied phone numbers of relatives for Wenski to contact. Others he read at Mass and on Creole radio. One of them said, "Tell mommy not to cry. I am still alive" (in Markowitz 1991).

Thousands of others in Haiti were not so fortunate and died at the hands of the Cédras junta, and tens of thousands more were persecuted (Commission Justice et Paix du Diocèse de Gonaïves 1995; Marotte and Razafimbahiny 1997; Rey 1999, 2006). Among those who did manage to flee were certain Tilegliz leaders like Fr. Gilles Danroc, who was driven from his parish in Haiti's Artibonite Valley by the Haitian military. With such exiled priests residing at Notre Dame for weeks while awaiting word that it was safe to return to Haiti, the Little Haiti church became something of a command center for Tilegliz in the diaspora. A *Miami Herald* reporter wrote:

Danroc and a handful of others have been able to stay involved in their struggle by running an underground communications network, of sorts, out of a church office in Little Haiti. . . . They use the office's fax machine, phones, and computer to exchange dispatches on conditions in Haiti with activists back home and religious and human rights organizations throughout Europe and North America. (Maass 1992)

Over the next three years of junta rule in Haiti, Notre Dame remained engaged in the struggle spiritually, politically, and socially. Not only did the church hold frequent Masses for victims of the junta, but many donated money to aid them. In August 1992, for example, more than fifteen hundred people responded to Notre Dame's call to donate funds toward meeting the victims' pressing medical needs and daily subsistence. On one day alone more than $30,000 was raised at the church (*Miami Herald* Staff 1992). Wenski, meanwhile, regularly used both the radio and the pulpit to denounce the illegitimate junta in Haiti.[8] The summer of 1994 was especially grueling, as the Clinton administration heightened its efforts to topple the Cédras junta, which responded by ramping up its oppression, driving a massive exodus of over twenty-five thousand refugees to sea (Rey 2006; U.S. Coast Guard, n.d.). In a gruesome parting shot, the junta assassinated the longtime Tilegliz leader Father Jean-Marie Vincent in a Port-au-Prince churchyard on August 29, 1994, just weeks before the United States and the United Nations finally occupied Haiti militarily, forcing Cédras and other members of the Haitian Army's high command into exile and restoring Aristide to power. At Notre Dame, a memorial Mass was said that September for Vincent and the thousands of others who were murdered in Haiti from September 1991 to September 1994 (Casmir 1994).

Passing the Torch but Not the Flame: Notre Dame in the Post-Wenski Years

In a moving ceremony before twelve thousand people at the Miami Arena on September 2, 1997, Msgr. Thomas Wenski was invested as the auxiliary bishop of Miami (Witt 1997). The new bishop's move from Notre Dame to the archdiocesan offices, where among other things he was director of Catholic Charities, and his move out of the ghetto rectory to a house on Biscayne Bay, left Msgr. Gerard Darbouze to pastor Notre Dame d'Haiti, a position that he officially assumed at the beginning of 1999. Notre Dame's status was also then formally changed from mission to parish. At the age of sixty-nine, Darbouze was about to celebrate his twentieth year of service to Miami's Haitian Catholic apostolate. He made it clear that he had no intentions of carrying on Wenski's indefatigable commitment to social and political activism: "My concern is not to have an impact outside my parish, but model Haitian unity here. . . . I'm not a politician. I'm not an activist. I'm a minister. That's it" (in Witt 1998).

Having served as a priest in the Haitian Archdiocese of Jérémie for twenty-five years prior to arriving in Miami, Darbouze's approach to ministry could be described as that of a scrupulous "old school" Haitian Catholic priest, one trained before liberation theology transformed Haitian Catholicism in the 1970s and '80s. Prior to those years, the Catholic seminary in Haiti had trained priests primarily for pastoral service and education. The ultraconservative Haitian archbishop of Port-au-Prince François Wolff Ligondé, who had close ties to the Duvaliers, would not tolerate liberationist tendencies among his clergy. He had raised no objection, for instance, when Papa Doc Duvalier deported the Jesuits from Haiti in 1962 upon suspecting the order of inciting popular discontent with his dictatorship, while in 1980 he officiated over his son Baby Doc's $3 million wedding to Michèle Bennett (Rohter 1994). Darbouze viewed pastoral service as the church's true mission, and so he was often irked by Wenski's high-profile political and social activism. In 1983, when the Haitian government complained to the Archdiocese of Miami because of Wenski's publicizing his interview with Gérard Duclerville on radio and in the press, Darbouze also lodged a complaint about Wenski to Archbishop McCarthy. Ten years later, in 1993, with the junta having then been in power for more than a year and then showing no signs of relenting, Miami's Creole radio programs consistently expressed outrage at the political and human rights nightmare that Haiti had once again become. At that point, in objection to the political activism of Wenski and other Catholic clerics in Haiti and the Haitian diaspora, Darbouze commented to one reporter, on the eve of inaugurating his own pastoral broadcast, "They [Haitians in Miami] are sick of that. They expect to get something better from priests, and they will" (in Maass 1993).

When Darbouze took over at the helm at Notre Dame, one of the first things he did was to raise funds to erect a black iron fence around the church yard. By 1999, the church was able to pay Rich Iron Company $70,000 for the project (Mardy 1999). Because Little Haiti is a densely populated urban neighborhood with little public park space, the churchyard is the largest, greenest vista in the area. Typical inner-city problems such as drug abuse, prostitution, and homelessness had become increasingly acute in Little Haiti as its poverty worsened and its population increased in the 1990s, and the churchyard regularly drew them into its midst. Wenski's response to the problem was not to build a fence but to pressure the city and county governments to foot the bills for the clean up: "It's not like we're generating the trash; this is a social problem that we have nothing to do with" (in Casimir 1996). By the mid 1990s, the problem had gotten so bad in the ten-acre churchyard, home to some of the city's most majestic oaks, that every year before its carnival the church was paying upwards of $3,000 to have the all of the mattresses, clothing, boxes, and other trash removed.

The fence might have been taken a sign that Notre Dame would change considerably under its first Haitian pastor, Msgr. Darbouze, who, again, explicitly gave primacy to pastoral over social concerns. For one thing, the long-standing monthly all-night vigils were cancelled out of security concerns. For another, Catholic Charities, which Wenski had been overseeing for the Archdiocese of Miami, took over the direction of the various social programs offered at the Toussaint Center. But this reorientation of parish goals cannot be understood merely in terms of Darbouze's ecclesiology and leadership style, anymore than Notre Dame's political posture can be understood by consideration of Wenski's "ethical charisma" alone (Weber 1963: 55). The social and political success of Notre Dame d'Haiti Catholic Church resulted from a confluence of Wenski's leadership and the deep influence of liberation theology on his Haitian flock, which had become accustomed in Haiti to a Church engaged in the struggle for justice and human rights. By the time Darbouze became Notre Dame's head pastor in 1999, the Tilegliz movement in Haiti was all but dead. And, because Notre Dame is not merely a parish in the Archdiocese of Miami but a leading Catholic institution in the transnational Haitian religious field, the death of liberation theology in Haiti portended its demise at Notre Dame.

Another noteworthy distinction between the Wenski and Darbouze is identifiable in the respective ways that each negotiated the question of Vodou while pastoring Notre Dame. Though the religion is not nearly as widespread in the Haitian diaspora as in Haiti, there are Vodouists among Haitians in Miami whose religious practice includes attendance at Mass and other services at Notre Dame. But during the Wenski years, denunciation of Vodou from the pulpit was far less common than what one routinely hears in Catholic churches in Haiti. Despite his rather strict, conservative interpretation of Catholic canon law, Msgr. Wenski cultivated a rather "hands off" approach to the question of Vodou, in part because of his awareness of his own outsiderhood, however Haitianized he might have become over the years: "People don't appreciate being told they're s——. They have to realize things on their own. Also, I have to remember that I'm not Haitian. They might not accept certain things from a white guy. . . . A guest can't go and rearrange the furniture. I've felt that advice serves me very well" (in Viglucci 1995).[9] As an insider, Darbouze, during his roughly twenty years of ministry to Haitian Miami, was at home railing against Vodou, something that most Haitian Catholic priests have always done, underscoring a priestly role that had been emphasized in his seminary training.[10] In the weeks leading up to Halloween, for instance, Darbouze was known to discourage trick-or-treating because it hearkens to Vodou's Feast of Gede (the spirit of the dead). This is Vodou's most important communal ceremony, as it seizes the occasion of the Catholic All Saints and All Souls Days to commemorate the distant and tragically anonymous ancestors of Africa (Rey 2009).

Although ecclesiological deviation in leadership from Wenski to Darbouze might have indeed resulted in a fence, less Vodou, and a less politically oriented Notre Dame, the church's social engagement endured even as its pastors changed and priorities shifted. Perhaps more important is that Notre Dame parishioners would insist this activism to be the work of God and the result of formidable and constant prayer. Mooney (2009: 103) captures this central reality at Notre Dame beautifully:

> Notre Dame illustrates one way in which social action and intense prayer experiences can complement rather than compete with each other. If in some cases prayer detracts from social action or vice versa,

we might find that the reason lies more in the leadership style of the pastors and lay leaders rather than in a contradiction between prayer and action. Although clergy and lay leaders at Notre Dame admitted that some people may use prayer as a refuge from having to confront problems in their lives, prayer gave the majority of people greater courage to face their problems as individuals and as a group. The people I interviewed did not think it irrational to call on supernatural grace to bring about change in this world; in their minds, prayer precedes rather than supplants action.

Prayer, as much as social and political engagement, is what has secured Notre Dame's place as the *poto mitan* (center post) of Little Haiti, and the church's institutional momentum is so strong that the changes made by Darbouze during his tenure as pastor from 1997 until his retirement in 2004 have had little lasting effect, as much as he remains a beloved figure in the memory of local Haitian Catholics.[11] Furthermore, the contrast between Darbouze's his ecclesiology and Wenski's is perhaps a bit exaggerated, for Wenski also always gave primacy to the pastoral over the social: "my thinking was that you build a community starting with the Eucharist" (Mooney 2009: 60). Moreover, clerical leadership at Notre Dame has never been a "one man show," however enormous Wenski's influence and legacy have been. Many of the dozens of Haitian priests who have served periods of residency at the parish do not share Darbouze's condescending attitude toward Vodou or his distaste for political activism. Notre Dame's present pastor, the Haitian-born and U.S.-trained Fr. Reginald Jean-Mary writes that "Vodunists in South Florida express their belief in the Supreme Deity or *Bondye* or *Granmet*. It is a *viable* means by which Voodoo devotees establish contact with the Sacred and the Divine as well as with one another" (Jean-Mary 2000, emphasis added). Instead of occupying himself with any efforts to combat Vodou, *"Pè Reji"* (Fr. Reggie), as the faithful affectionately call him, is especially concerned with the mounting inner-city problems threatening Little Haiti's youth, and he has become renowned for both his activism and his passionate sermons in this regard: "It is my dream to develop the social consciousness and the morality of the youth . . . to help the youth become more human so they can be better Christians."[12]

A New Shepherd, a New Church, and
the Tragic Earthquake of 2010

Upon Darbouze's retirement in 2004, Pè Reji was appointed as pastor of Notre Dame d'Haiti. In the interim years between then and the tragic earthquake of 2010 in Haiti, Pè Reji mobilized a number of church improvement projects, making Notre Dame aesthetically quite different than the way it looked when we began our fieldwork for this book in the late 1990s. For example, the choir has now moved to the opposite side of the church, alongside of the *botpipel* stained-glass window. The tabernacle is now where it should be, behind the altar to the right. No longer are there wooden pews but cushioned maroon chairs that interlock to form pewlike seating; all have individual kneelers that fold up. The entire interior has been likewise redone, with a newly tiled floor, freshly painted walls, the mural not just touched up but redone (the plane is now American Airlines and no longer Air d'Haïti, a long defunct Haitian airline). The drop ceiling is gone, and now there are chandeliers. The entry from the sanctuary into the restrooms has been eliminated; one must now walk out of the sanctuary toward the backyard and around the back wall of the church to get to the restrooms, which have also been refurbished, the cockroaches no longer in residence. On a linguistic level, English factors more heavily at masses at Notre Dame than ever before; there are bilingual Creole/English services now twice each Sunday. Behind the church and school are several notable changes, too. There is a new playground, just behind the exterior makeshift diner where one can get a good, cheap Haitian meal. A bit deeper into the churchyard is a new, white statue of the Holy Family, with a small landscaped waterfall at its base. To the west, against the fence, is a maroon, life-sized statue of the risen Christ with outstretched, welcoming arms. The grotto, which dates from 2004 and houses a statue of Our Lady of Lourdes, now features a landscaped waterfall and an elaborate garden (see fig. 1.2). It is all beautiful, tranquil, and evocative of prayer and meditation, and one can usually find a few people sitting contemplatively or saying the rosary on ornate concrete benches before the Virgin. Others stand directly before the statue, usually women, arms outspread, audibly imploring the Virgin in most familiar terms, just as is common in Catholic churches throughout Haiti.

Figure 1.2. A woman prays before the grotto housing an icon of Our Lady of Lourdes in the churchyard of Notre Dame d'Haiti Catholic Church, Little Haiti, Miami, reflecting the deep Marian piety that characterizes Haitian and Haitian American Catholicism. Photo by Jerry Berndt.

The biggest change at Notre Dame is still to come. Msgr. Wenski, who was installed as archbishop of Miami in 2010 after having served for six years as coadjutor bishop of the Diocese of Orlando, said Mass at Notre Dame in late June 2011 to celebrate the church's thirtieth anniversary. He announced that a new church edifice would be built for Notre Dame at the cost of $3.2 million, then he lead the faithful outside to bless the ground where construction was soon to begin. By then, a six-year fund-raising effort at Notre Dame had garnered over $2 million and the church secured a loan from the archdiocese for the balance. Once completed, the new church will have a seating capacity of fifteen hundred worshippers (Green 2011a). The plan hit a snag, however, when the City of Miami denied Notre Dame a permit to remove eleven oak trees to make space for the construction and an expanded parking lot. Members of a local neighborhood association and environmentalists protested the plan to kill the trees, seven of which "are considered live specimen oak trees, meaning the trees are more than twenty-four inches in diameter." It remains to be seen whether the building's design, which is already complete, will be altered, but in the meantime the church has appealed the rejection (Candido 2011). When asked about the issue, Pè Reji alluded to the growth of the congregation as necessitating a larger church building: "People have a right to contest it, the environment belongs to everyone. We care about the environment. But people in the church are sitting under the sun, the rain because we don't have a place to put them. This is an injustice. We are trying to build a sacred temple here. That is all" (in Green 2011).

The two most impressive and important things about Notre Dame have not changed, though, and would never be expected to change, namely the worshipful depths and uniquely Haitian rhythms of its spiritual life and its generous material support for Haitian immigrants. Mass at Notre Dame is a thoroughly joyous, prayerful, and artful experience, with conga drums accompanying the beautiful voices of the choir, drawing all of the faithful to join in singing hymns of praise in Haitian Creole and sometimes in French (see fig. 1.3). People stand and

Figure 1.3. Masses at Notre Dame d'Haiti in Little Haiti are jubilant affairs, featuring lively hymns of praise that are often driven by traditional African drumming rhythms. Here, women in one corner of the sanctuary join in the jubilation. Photo by Jerry Berndt.

sway to the music, arms outstretched toward heaven, many of them with rosaries dangling from their hands. There is standing room only for Sunday Mass, with speakers mounted outside for those not arriving early enough to find a seat. Hundreds and sometimes thousands more come to Notre Dame for special occasions, such as the Feast of Our Lady of Perpetual Help, a week-long celebration that is the highlight of each year for Haitian Catholics.

As for social services, upwards of one thousand people a day come to the Toussaint Center for everything from ESL classes and legal assistance with immigration proceedings to job placement counseling and help with their monthly bills.[13] Several church groups are central to the assistance efforts at Notre Dame, like the St. Vincent de Paul Society and the Legion of Mary (Mooney 2009: 85). All of these efforts, of course, were momentously rocked and challenged by the tragedy of the 2010 earthquake, a tragedy in Haiti that drew thousands to the church to seek news of relatives in Haiti, to weep, to pray, to unite for consolation and strength, and to perhaps ask God the painful question, *Why Haiti?*

After presiding over a memorial Mass for the dead the day after earthquake, Pè Reji spearheaded the fund-raising for the relief effort at Notre Dame, setting up a collection center and organizing medical missions to Haiti. By July 2010, the church had amassed enough materials to fill twenty-seven shipping containers, and Chicago donated two ambulances, which Notre Dame arranged to ship to Port-au-Prince (LeMaire 2010). The young priest had by then made countless trips to Haiti, partnering with Catholic parishes in and around Port-au-Prince to orchestrate service delivery to thousands left homeless, maimed, bereft, and bereaved by the massive *goudougoudou*, as the quake is called in Haitian Creole, onomatopoeia for the terrifying sound the earth made in Haitian just before five o'clock on the afternoon of January 12, 2010.

Numerous churches in the Archdiocese of Miami raised funds and mobilized relief efforts in the days, weeks, months, and now years after the earthquake—including Fr. Jean Pierre's effort to raise $750,000 at St. James in North Miami to construct and staff a new health clinic in Port-au-Prince. Notre Dame, to no one's surprise, became the focus of the Catholic aid initiative. This was made resoundingly clear when between September 22 and 26, 2010, all of Haiti's Catholic bishops, along with the papal nuncio to Haiti, visited Notre Dame to launch an orchestrated

international effort to rebuild some of the churches and other buildings belonging to the Catholic Church in Haiti that were crushed in the
quake, including the majestic Cathedral of Our Lady of the Assumption
in Port-au-Prince, the nation's largest church, and St. Rose de Lima in
Leogane, the nation's oldest. Called PROCHE (Partnership for Reconstruction of the Church in Haiti; the word *proche* also means "near" in
French, in Haitian Creole it's *pwoch*), this structural effort is essentially
"a steering committee chaired by the president of the Haitian Bishops'
Conference and composed of representatives of the Holy See, the Haitian bishops, religious orders working in Haiti and donor dioceses and
agencies" (Rodriguez-Soto 2010). The September gathering to launch
PROCHE was extraordinary not only in bringing to Notre Dame the
papal nuncio, all of Haiti's bishops, and Catholic bishops from eleven
other nations, but in being host to a plenary session of the Haitian bishops and receiving a message to the Haitian church from Pope Benedict
XVI. Perhaps the most resounding words of the papal missive to the
Haitian faithful, an immigrant Catholic flock still struggling to come to
terms with the earthquake were these: "Entrusting you to the maternal
intercession of Our Lady of Perpetual Help, patron saint of Haiti, the
Pope sends to you all his Apostolic Blessing, as well as to all of those
who collaborate with you in your efforts."[14]

Two weeks later, the ninth annual "Jericho Revival" at Notre Dame
was transformed from a metaphoric spiritual gathering "about tearing
down the walls in our hearts and renewing our faith" into a memorial
that drew several thousands to commemorate those who were crushed
by real walls that collapsed in the earthquake. "After ten months, you
can tell people are feeling dispirited," explained Pè Reji. "Jericho is about
boosting their sense of hope" (in Miller 2010). Jericho 2010 also linked
the Notre Dame faithful to the Haiti Memorial Database, a project
launched by the *Miami Herald* to record names of dead earthquake victims, so many of whom went nameless to mass graves outside of Port-
au-Prince, and to give "survivors a place to register love ones' names,
photos, and memories" (Tracy 2010a). Wenski's message to the faithful
during Mass at the 2010 Jericho Revival: "Keep praying, without weary-
ing" (in Tracy 2010b). A few months later, Wenski returned to Little
Haiti to further memorialize the victims with a Mass marking the one-
year anniversary of the earthquake. This took place at the Cathedral of

St. Mary, whose bells tolled at 4:53 p.m., the exact moment when the earth began to quake in Haiti the year before. The Mass was followed by an ecumenical candlelight prayer vigil at Notre Dame, which lasted until midnight (Tracy 2011).

A Brief but Temporary Conclusion

Events such as the plenary session of the Haitian Catholic Bishop's Conference and the Jericho Revival are reminders to all of the Notre Dame faithful that helping Haiti through its gravest catastrophe since slavery is as much a spiritual as a material effort. Pè Reji echoes the reminder regularly: "We just have to pray, we just have to be active, and just have to be committed, to be accountable, and to really do things from our hearts" (WLRN 2010). Those words sum up succinctly what Notre Dame d'Haiti Catholic Church is really all about. There is no end in sight, meanwhile, to the needy Haitian immigrants whom Notre Dame and the Toussaint Center will serve in carrying on an exemplary legacy of Christian charity and service. Sadly, political turmoil and abject poverty in Haiti continue to drive its people to the sea in hopes of finding a better life in Miami. And tragically, those who die trying to escape—like the forty-five *botpipel* off the coast of Cuba in December of 2011 (BBC 2011)—will continue to have masses said for them at Notre Dame, just like the thousands who died in the earthquake. Those who do make it to South Florida, meanwhile, will be received with open arms and will be faithfully assisted in making the transition to life in Little Haiti, in America. And in the face of all of these incredible challenges, Notre Dame is, above all, an indelibly joyful, spiritual, and inspirational sanctuary of Catholic faith, faith kept among those who have crossed the water.

2

Immigrant Faith and Class Distinctions

Haitian Catholics beyond Little Haiti

Overview

Many Haitians in recent years have experienced migration to and settlement in Miami in quite different ways than the throngs of *botpipel* who
came in the late 1970s and early 1980s and in ensuing intermittent waves
spurned by political upheaval and poverty in the homeland. There is a
growing number of Haitians in South Florida who have either moved up
and out of the poverty of Little Haiti or who migrated with the means to
settle in the United States without the trademark daunting struggles of
Haitian refugees. Some of them are lighter-skinned members of the Haitian bourgeoisie, wealthy immigrants who own second homes in Miami
and have little or nothing to do with Little Haiti, in part because of long-
standing class antagonisms in Haitian society and culture, and these,
too, are transnational. And, they generally do religion differently, though
in ways that nonetheless reflect their participation in the same Haitian
religious collusio, which transcends religious difference and socio-economic class divisions. Many still believe deeply in unseen supernatural forces to whom they turn in the quest for healing, luck (*chans*), and
magic (*maji*), and for protection against "persecutory" forms of evil
(Brodwin 1996; Corten 2001). Thus, to give a fuller and truer picture of
Haitian Catholicism in Miami and to further demonstrate the transcendent reach of the Haitian religious collusio, we look beyond Little Haiti
to offer a glimpse into the lives and religious practice of Haitian Catholics in middle- and upper-class Miami neighborhoods like West Kendall
and Perrine. In particular, we discuss their participation in sacramental

rites at a Traditionalist Catholic shrine in Little Havana, the Shrine of St. Philomena, at Our Lady of Lourdes Catholic Church in Kendall, and at Christ the King Catholic Church in Perrine, as well as their participation in the Catholic Charismatic Renewal, a Pentecostal movement that has radically transformed the Catholic Church in Haiti, which, like virtually everything else discussed in this book, is transnational.

Crossing Class Lines and Keeping the Catholic Faith

Reflective of a long trend in American immigration history, over time many members of the Haitian community of South Florida have embarked on upwardly mobile socioeconomic trajectories, with some moving out of Little Haiti and into "better" neighborhoods like North Miami Beach or Miramar. Other Haitian migrants have arrived with enough economic and social capital to rent apartments or purchase homes in middle- and upper-middle-class neighborhoods like Kendall and Per- rine. For those Haitian Catholics who moved out of Little Haiti but did not go too far, some have remained parishioners at Notre Dame, making com- mutes for masses and other occasions there, while others have discov- ered different churches where masses are said in French and/or Haitian Creole. Among them is St. James Catholic Church, in North Miami, just a few miles north of Notre Dame, pastored by Fr. Jean Pierre who in 1988 was the first Haitian to be ordained a Roman Catholic priest in Miami. Farther north still is St. Bartholomew Catholic Church, in the middle- class neighborhood of Miramar, in southern Broward County. About half of St. Bartholomew's seventeen hundred parishioners are Haitian or Haitian American, helping to make this church the home of a robust and vibrant Haitian ministry.[1] This ministry is served by a full-time Haitian parochial vicar, Fr. Jean Jadotte, and two Haitian deacons, and includes a French/Creole mass each Sunday afternoon at 3:00, a Haitian charismatic prayer group, Amour, Sagesse et Paix (Love, Wisdom, and Peace), which meets each Friday evening at 7:30, a monthly mass in French/Creole as part of the Adoration of the Blessed Sacrament, a Haitian choir, and an outreach ministry, which sometimes travels to Haiti. St. Bartholomew's website offers a link in French with information about the parish and directs the reader to the Pierre Toussaint Haitian Catholic Center in Little Haiti and the Haitian Catholic Center in Fort Lauderdale for "resources"

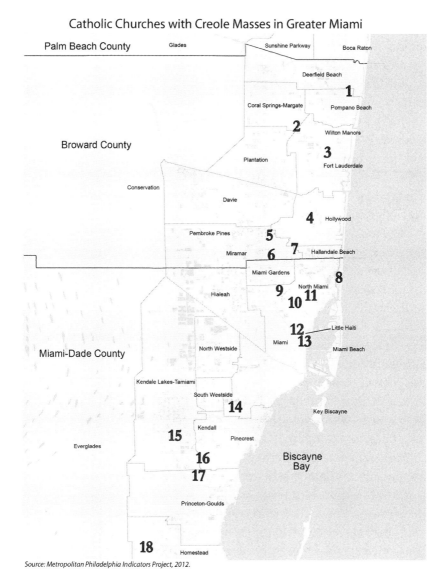

Catholic Churches with Creole Masses in Greater Miami

Palm Beach County   Glades

Sunshine Parkway

Boca Raton

Deerfield Beach

1

Coral Springs-Margate   Pompano Beach

2

Wilton Manors

3

Broward County

Plantation

Fort Lauderdale

Conservation

Davie

4   Hollywood

Pembroke Pines   **5**

Miramar   **6**   **7**   Hallandale Beach

Miami Gardens

8

North Miami

9

10 **11**

Hialeah

12   Little Haiti

Miami   **13**

North Westside

Miami-Dade County

Miami Beach

Kendale Lakes-Tamiami

South Westside

14

Key Biscayne

Kendall

15

Pinecrest

Everglades

16

Biscayne
Bay

17

Princeton-Goulds

18   Homestead

Source: Metropolitan Philadelphia Indicators Project, 2012.

Figure 2.1. By 2012, eighteen churches in the Archdiocese of Miami had established Haitian Creole and or French masses or some other form of bilingual or trilingual ministerial
services to the Haitian community, reflective of the spread of Haitians in South Florida
beyond Little Haiti. See appendix 1 for corresponding church names and addresses.

(stbartholomew.com). The church's weekly bulletin appears in English, Spanish, and French, with a notice about the schedule for confessions and masses in Haitian Creole. One version of the bulletin from early December 2011 advertised two day "Haitian Advent" retreat and a Haitian community Christmas celebration, featuring dinner, dancing, and live music.

In all, there are at least fourteen churches in the Archdiocese of Miami that celebrate at least one mass in Haitian Creole and two others that have a weekly French language mass, presumably to serve middle- and upper-class Haitian parishioners (miamiarch.org; see also appendix 1). Two additional churches, while not yet offering Creole or French masses, have Haitian or Haitian Americans priests in residence who hear confessions and officiate over baptisms, weddings, and funerals in Haitian Creole or French. Some churches list the Creole masses as "French/Creole" or "Creole/French," surely in part because the hymns at Haitian services are sung as often in French as in Creole and because the biblical readings are also frequently in French.

The 2009 closure of the Divine Mercy Haitian Mission in Fort Lauderdale notwithstanding (Rodriguez-Soto 2009), the fact that Creole and French language masses are said at so many churches in the Archdiocese of Miami is powerful testimony to the growth of South Florida's Haitian community and to the endurance of Haitian Catholic faith in the diaspora. Moreover, Haitian Catholic life in Miami extends far beyond the walls of those Catholic churches where ministries to Haitians have been formally established. Because of devotions to particular Catholic saints that they brought with them from Haiti, many Haitian immigrants in Miami practice their faith at multiple places, for instance at the Shrine of Our Lady of Charity of El Cobre (Tweed 1997: 59–60), the Shrine of St. Philomena, St. Ann Mission, and at occasional gatherings, small and large, in prayer groups and charismatic revivals either in churches, in private homes, or even in arenas. In addition, Haitian class distinctions are indeed reflected in where Haitians and Haitian Americans in South Florida worship.

The Shrine of St. Philomena

Despite our earlier study of religion in Miami (Stepick, Rey, and Mahler 2009), one in which two-thirds of Miami-Dade County were mapped to identify nearly one thousand churches, we had never heard of the Shrine of St. Philomena in the city's Little Havana neighborhood until we received an invitation *from Haiti* to attend the baptism of the newborn daughter of two Haitian friends. Given that the shrine is Catholic, missing it in our study was even more surprising because the Archdiocese of Miami keeps a comprehensive registry of its churches and shrines, readily available for all to see on its website. The shrine is not listed there, however, because the archdiocese does not formally recognize it, in spite of its pastor's ardent petitions for recognition, and despite the shrine's housing a first-class relic of St. Philomena, a particle of bone, which arrived from Rome in 1991 accompanied by an official Vatican letter confirming its authenticity.

The baptism took place one Saturday morning in 2001, and it was late getting started because the godparents were not on time, having gotten lost on the way. There were roughly fifty people in attendance, the vast majority of them Haitians or Haitian Americans who resided in South Florida, mostly in Miami, and a few relatives from New York and from Port-au-Prince. Presiding over the ritual was Fr. Timothy Hopkins, a British priest who became the shrine's second administrator in 1989. Because the shrine is part of the Traditionalist Catholic movement that conducts sacramental rites in accordance with church teachings prior to the Second Vatican Council (1962–66), the baptism was conducted mostly in Latin. Vatican II had made many significant changes to Catholic rituals, such as moving the altar closer to the laity and having much of the liturgy recited in vernacular languages rather than in Latin. Despite the support of a Catholic cardinal for the shrine's petition for incorporation into the Archdiocese of Miami, the archbishop "was not so gracious" as to favor the petition and tried to run Fr. Timothy "out of his territory" (shrineofsaintphilomena.com). The issue remains under consideration at the Vatican, though Fr. Timothy cites canon law in assuring the faithful that their religious obligations as Catholics can be legitimately met at the shrine. The Haitians we have met at the shrine, meanwhile, seem unconcerned with the issue; for them, it is quite simply a "very mystical" Catholic church and the diasporic homeland of a saint that is very popular in Haiti (O'Neil and Rey 2012).

The baptism was a serious but jovial affair in the small, rectangular, ornate shrine. Everyone present was very well dressed and conducted themselves with somber reverence throughout the ceremony. With few exceptions, the women and girls all had their heads covered with veils, as had been the tradition in Catholic sacramental services prior to Vatican II. The ritual lasted for about forty-five minutes, and then Fr. Timothy invited everyone to gather in the sacristy for a sumptuous Haitian meal. On offer were foods typical of what one would find at such a gathering in Haiti, namely patties of shredded chicken or ground beef (*pate poule ak pate vyann*), a shredded ham salad (*chiktay*), white rice and red beans (*diri kole ak pwa*), white rice with black mushrooms (*diri djon djon*), roasted goat (*kabrit boukane*), fried pork chunks (*griot*), fried plantains (*banan peze*), cold Presidente beer (*Preval glase*), and Haitian soda (*Cola Couronne*). Expenses for the entire festive gathering were covered in advance by a handsome donation to the shrine made by the parents and godparents of the newly baptized child, who was taken back home to Haiti the following Monday morning.

Present at the baptism was Mirlène Jeanty, a thirty-five-year-old Haitian immigrant who enjoys a life of privilege and bounty rather than enduring one of struggle and want.[2] She is also very active in the Charismatic Renewal and is a parishioner at Our Lady of Lourdes in the southwest Miami-Dade neighborhood of West Kendall. For Jeanty, an aunt of the baptized infant who migrated from Haiti during the UN embargo on the country in 1993, the baptism was her first time visiting the Shrine of St. Philomena, a place that she recalls immediately feeling to be *"très mystique"* (very mystical): "There is just this power there, something I feel with all of my senses, and then the Latin connects me to the great saints of the past ages in my church's history. I feel their presence there, in addition to Saint Philomena and the Virgin Mary and Jesus." Having been recently diagnosed with breast cancer, Jeanty also believed that the shrine could hold the power to heal her. So, at the feast of Haitian cuisine following the baptism, she approached Fr. Timothy to request that he say a healing Mass for her at the shrine in the near future. The priest granted her request, and the Mass for Jeanty's intention was organized a few weeks later.

The mass for Jeanty was attended by many of the same Haitian immigrants who had attended the baptism a few weeks earlier, even though none of the relatives who had returned home to Haiti was able to attend. The service at the shrine was conducted almost entirely in Latin and shrouded in the billowing clouds of incense smoke that wafted throughout the small sanctuary. The ceremony was somber yet hopeful, mysterious yet focused.

After the Mass was over and cheerful goodbyes said, on the drive back to Kendall an aunt described for Jeanty how she had seen Fr. Timothy conduct masses in private homes, and that they should invite him to her own home for such a service. She did. Again, the priest agreed, and one evening a few weeks later a second healing mass was arranged. Jeanty's extended family spent days preparing for the event, and though there was some disagreement as to whether the dining-room table that was to serve as the altar should face the front door or the rear sliding glass doors, no one either preparing the event or in attendance expressed the slightest concern that the Archdiocese of Miami might not condone the gathering, or that their own parish priests, whether at Our Lady of Lourdes or at Christ the King, might have something objectionable to say about their relationship to the shrine or about the sacraments that they sought from its priest. Other Catholics associated with the shrine had allegedly been "subject to un-Christian persecution from the Archdiocese of Miami. It was all rather like being Catholics in Elizabethan England" (shrineofsaintphilomena.com). Jeanty's own two children, who were both born in Haiti, were at that time enrolled in CCD (Confraternity of Christian Doctrine) classes at Our Lady of Lourdes in preparation for their First Communion, and in Jeanty's view the church politics at play over the shrine were of no ultimate concern:

> Saint Philomena is much bigger than any archbishop or doctrine, and she calls Father Timothy to serve her children, us—that is who we are. It is sad that the archdiocese doesn't recognize the shrine, but that is really kind of petty because what is more important is that God does and that his little saint is truly there at the Shrine. The archbishop should go and experience that for himself, and then things would be different.

Our Lady of Lourdes Catholic Church

By all appearances, Our Lady of Lourdes Roman Catholic Church, located in West Kendall, is a different kind of Catholic sanctuary from the Shine of St. Philomena or Notre Dame d'Haiti. Its congregation is comprised of middle- and upper-class immigrant Catholics from throughout Latin America and the Caribbean. Furthermore, it is located in a more recently developed part of Miami comprised mainly of large single-family homes and comfortable town houses with private yards, and carefully zoned shopping malls with franchises of virtually every major chain restaurant and retail outlet in America. It is thus somewhat misleading to speak of West Kendall as an "urban" neighborhood at all; it is far more evocative of a suburb than the narrow streets and small, crowded, and closely nested residences of Little Havana or Little Haiti. In fact, these two areas are both parts of the municipality of the City of Miami, whereas West Kendall and its sprawling adjacent neighborhoods, which now reach to the Everglades to the west and the citrus plantations and nurseries to the south, enjoy the moniker "Miami" only by virtue of the South Florida postal zoning system and to a 1997 referendum that changed the name of the county in which they happen to be located from "Dade" to "Miami-Dade." Why? Because, as the politically ambitious Dade County mayor Alex Penelas explained, "There is a magic to the name Miami. . . . Quite frankly, no one knows what Dade County is. By adding Miami to our county's name, we will be able to better identify and market our community throughout the world" (Yanez 1997).

For 161 years , Miami-Dade County had been simply "Dade County," with "Miami" an identifier reserved for the municipality of the City of Miami, Miami Beach, North Miami, North Miami Beach, and South Beach, and perhaps for decidedly less "urban" neighborhoods like Miami Gardens, Miami Lakes, Miami Shores, Miami Springs, South Miami, and South Miami Heights. Like much of what is today referred to commonly as "Miami," West Kendall is not part of any city at all, and many immigrants with the means to do so choose to purchase homes here, rather than in the *real* City of Miami, and send their children to the neighborhood's higher quality schools and to enjoy the peace of mind of its relatively low crime rate.[3] These are chief reasons why Mirlène Jeanty settled in West Kendall, where several of her relatives lived, and why she and her family became members of the parish of Our Lady of Lourdes.

Visually, there is nothing about West Kendall that evokes Haiti. There are no murals of Catholic saints or heroes of the Haitian Revolution, no Haitian flags, no Haitian restaurants, no Haitian bookstores, bakeries, music shops or cultural centers, and no Haitian storefront churches (there are actually no storefront churches at all in West Kendall, as far as we can tell). Haitians here are clearly a minority among a large and thriving White Hispanic majority. Among Blacks in this part of Miami-Dade, Haitians are also outnumbered by Jamaicans. We have found only one botanica in West Kendall, not too far from Our Lady of Lourdes, though closer to the new Lexus dealership, and it is Cuban. Home ownership in West Kendall is roughly double what it is in the City of Miami. The houses and town houses of West Kendall tend to be spacious, surrounded by well-manicured lawns, and often located in developments or "housing communities" with quaint names like "Palmetto Breeze," "The Crossings," "Country Walk," and "Devonaire." In 2000, the median household income in Kendall was $61,300 (city-data.com), compared to that of Little Haiti, which was then less than $20,000 (City of Miami 2011). Kendall is also home to one of Florida's best hospitals, the main campus of Miami-Dade College, and the Miami Metro Zoo. Furthermore, to our knowledge there are no street gangs in Kendall, and we have never seen anyone selling crack cocaine or sex there, forms of commerce that we have sometimes noticed in Little Haiti over the years.

About the only things that West Kendall does have in common with Little Haiti are palm trees, a flat topography, a subtropical climate, and Haitian Catholics. The Haitian Catholics in this neighborhood in southwest Miami-Dade County are generally members of the Haitian elite and/or the Haitian American middle or upper class. Traveling via American Airlines with valid passports, visas, and money to pay attorneys to work on their residency papers, their immigration and settlement experiences in South Florida have been radically different from those of the Haitian refugees who flocked to South Florida in the late 1970s and early 1980s, and in intermittent ensuing waves since then, and who endured imprisonment, poverty, and socio-political marginalization in the United States. It is tempting to suggest that the immigration experience of wealthier Haitians has not been as "theologizing" as that of their less fortunate compatriots, leading one to suspect that religious practice among middle- and upper-class Haitians might be not as regular as theirs (Smith 1978). To our knowledge, no survey research has been done on the religious lives of wealthier Haitians in Miami, but we are convinced that socioeconomic status has little, if any, determining influence on whether or not Haitian migrants practice religion. The

Haitian religious collusio can thus be said to hold for wealthy Haitians, generally speaking, thus transcending socioeconomic class difference as well as religious difference. Although we have no data to illustrate this definitively, we believe that upper-class Haitians, whether in Haiti or the diaspora, are less likely to be Protestants or Vodouists than Catholics. As such, in addition to establishing Creole-language masses in parishes in Little Haiti and North Miami, the Archdiocese of Miami eventually found it necessary to offer Creole- or French-language masses in much wealthier neighborhoods like Perrine and West Kendall.

Haitian immigrants themselves are keenly aware of the differences between Kendall and Little Haiti. Consider, for instance, the comments made by a Haitian cab driver, a Little Haiti resident, while driving one of us from Miami International Airport to Kendall one afternoon in 2004: "As for me, I want nothing to do with Kendall, because it's full of a bunch of bourgeois people. It's totally Duvalierville" (*"Mwen mem, mwen pa vle ayen pou we ak Kendall. Se chaje ak yon paket boujwa. Se Duvalyevil net!"*). "Duvalierville" is a not uncommon moniker in Haitian Miami for Kendall, Little Haiti's distant wealthy cousin roughly twenty-five miles to the southwest. When asked to reflect upon the differences between the two neighborhoods, meanwhile, an upper-middle-class, middle-aged Haitian immigrant and her American-born teenage son had the following to offer: "Haitians in Little Haiti are really very different than Haitians in Kendall, and many Haitians in Kendall have never even been to Little Haiti; they think it's like Cité Soleil or something," a reference to Port-au-Prince's sprawling seaside slum. Her son added, "In Little Haiti the Haitians live more like they are still in Haiti, and some of them don't even speak English, but us in Kendall, we live more like Americans."[4]

Our Lady of Lourdes Catholic Church was founded in 1985 and celebrated its first Mass in a gymnasium at Boystown, near the location of the present large church edifice at 11291 SW 142nd Avenue, in West Kendall, just a few miles from the Everglades to the west, a unique natural environment, which is increasing menaced by Miami-Dade's westward sprawl. Archbishop Edward McCarthy dedicated the church at its present location on the Feast of Our Lady of Lourdes in 1990, but the new church was seriously damaged two years later by Hurricane Andrew. The congregation persevered, rebuilt its church, and continued to grow, opening the Our Lady of Lourdes Parish School in 1997, whose first eighth-grade class graduated in 2002. In May 1997, a successful fund-raising campaign enabled the construction of a large "Mediterranean-style church, with the capacity to seat 1,200 people. . . . What a positive impact this spiritual and structural Church has had on our community." Today Our Lady of Lourdes counts more than six thousand members in its registry, "a vibrant community poised and ready to minister to many, creating a spiritual foundation for a multi-cultural community in West Kendall" (ololourdes.org). One layer of the parish's multi-culturalism is Haitian, and over the years the Haitian presence at Our Lady of Lourdes has grown substantially enough to justify adding a monthly French-language mass and to compel the archdiocese to appoint a Haitian pastoral vicar to the parish, Fr. Patrick Charles.

That there are many Haitian parishioners at Lourdes but no Creole-language masses, and only a single monthly French mass reflects class distinctions between Haitian immigrants in Kendall and those in Little Haiti. For, unlike many Little Haiti residents, the middle- and upper-class Haitian immigrants in Kendall and similar neighborhoods are generally fluent in both English and French. One does hear a good deal of English spoken by Haitian immigrants in Little Haiti, but one does not hear learned French there very often. French—not Creole—is the language of choice, and of distinction, of the Haitian elite (Bébel-Gisler and Hurbon 1975; Hoffmann 1990). As such, Our Lady of Lourdes is catering to the tastes of its Haitian parishioners by holding services in French rather than in Haitian Creole. Jeanty and her family "love the French Mass" at Our Lady, "because it helps connect us to Haiti and it helps the kids keep up their French, so when we go to Haiti they can understand the Mass *properly*" (emphasis added).

One of the few other things that Notre Dame d'Haiti and Our Lady of Lourdes share in common is the abundance of cars in their parking lots on Sunday mornings. But unlike Notre Dame, which many parishioners walk to, very few arrive on foot at Lourdes. And, however they arrive, once inside the respective sanctuaries Haitian immigrants are in decidedly different places: one squat, cramped, and originally designed as a school cafeteria; the other a modern "Mediterranean style" church edifice with vaulted ceilings, a balcony, and abundant space and light. At Notre Dame, there are very few in attendance who are not Haitian and are not Black, whereas at Lourdes there are just a few Haitian families among the hundreds and sometimes thousands of White Latinos; some of those Haitian families are lighter skinned, and not all of the Black parishioners are Haitian but are Jamaican, Trinidadian, Bahamian, and African American. And, unlike Notre Dame, there is nothing that evokes Haiti in the sanctuary of Our Lady of Lourdes: no Haitian flag, no mural of boat people, no icon of Our Lady of Perpetual Help, no stained-glass window of Pierre Toussaint, and no Haitian choir. The style of worship, furthermore, is more typical of the many other middle- and upper-class White Latino Catholic congregations in Miami, decidedly modern and quite assimilated with "the American Church," with its music driven by acoustic guitars instead of Vodou drums.

In addition to the monthly French-language Mass, the Haitian congregants at Our Lady of Lourdes are also served by a Haitian parochial vicar in residence at the parish and by the Salva Regina Haitian ministry, a weekly prayer group "dedicated to prayer and evangelization by having retreats every 3 or 4 months" (www.ololourdes.org). The vicar, incidentally, had previously served as a novice at St. Ann Mission in Homestead, where his promotion of the feast day of St. Ann attracted hundreds of Haitians to the mission, whose predominately Mexican Catholics have made this the de facto Shrine of Our Lady of Guadalupe in Miami-Dade County (Báez, Rey, and Rey 2009). Prior to Fr. Charles's efforts, we had detected very little interest in St. Ann among the Mexicans at the mission, though she is tremendously popular in Haiti, where her feast day is the oldest in the history of Haitian Catholicism, dating since 1707 and centered at the Church of St. Ann in the northern Haitian town of Limonade (O'Neil and Rey 2012). Like hundreds of other Haitian Catholics in South Florida, Mirlène Jeanty brings her entire family to the feast of St. Ann each year: "In Haiti we always would go on pilgrimage for the Feast of St. Ann, so this is a tradition, but instead of going from Port-au-Prince to Limonade, we now go from Kendall to Homestead. Here it is a much shorter distance and the roads are a lot better!" We believe that Haitians who go to the mission out of devotion to St. Ann are invigorating veneration for this saint among Mexicans who more routinely venerate Our Lady of Guadalupe, a phenomenon that brings to mind Robert Orsi's (1992: 332) observations about Haitian immigrants at a traditionally Italian Catholic Church in New York City:

"The powerful and evident piety of the Haitian pilgrims, furthermore, which was there for everyone to see in the aisles of the church and the streets of the neighborhoods, deeply impressed and moved the Italian Americans, who openly expressed respect for Haitian spirituality during the event."

Among Haitian Catholics of whatever socioeconomic class, Mirlène Jeanty's religious life is fairly typical as it is so mobile and so deeply transnational. Like thousands of other Haitian Catholics in the diaspora, for instance, she travels to Haiti each April for the annual meeting of the National Convention of the Catholic Charismatic Renewal of Haiti (Congrès National du Renouveau Charismatique Catholique d'Haïti). (Her battle with breast cancer prohibited her from going in 2002 for the eleventh annual gathering of the convention, which was her first time missing the event since its inception.) Over the years her Catholic faith became increasing charismatic, especially when she learned of her cancer diagnosis, and she attributes the disease's remission to charismatic prayer and faith healing. As such, Jeanty is among the countless Haitian Catholics who turn to the Renewal for healing, making the movement "one of the most impressive developments in Haitian religion over the last few decades" (Rey 2010: 81). Because the Renewal has so radically changed the face of Catholicism in Haiti in recent years, the movement became extremely popular among Haitian immigrant Catholics in the United States, and this was indeed expected. As such, no discussion of Haitian religion can forego consideration of the Charismatic Renewal, which powerfully exhibits all of the hallmarks of the Haitian religious collusio.

Catholic Pentecostalism in Haitian Miami

Mirlène Jeanty was deeply disappointed that she could not travel to Haiti in 2002 for the annual gathering of the National Convention of the Catholic Charismatic Renewal of Haiti, but she found much consolation in the fact that the annual meeting of the Conseil du Renouveau Charismatique Catholique des Haïtiens d'Outre-Mer (CRCCHO— Council of the Catholic Charismatic Renewal of Haitians Overseas) was holding its own annual convention that year in Miami. She believed that to be providential: "God brought the Charismatic convention to Miami because I could not travel to Haiti that year, and I was even too tired to go anywhere far from home. But the Renewal came here, to Miami, and that is the work of the Holy Spirit, and it was a sign that I would be cured."

The 2002 CRCCHO convention drew several thousand Catholics from throughout the Haitian diaspora to the James L. Knight International Center in downtown Miami, the third time that the city had hosted the annual gathering since its inception in 1989. The theme of the 2002 event, which took place from August 16 to 18, was "All Generations Will Call Me Blessed," words derived from the Magnificat, the biblical prayer of the Virgin Mary (Luke 1:46), and much of the center's 4,600-seat theater was occupied during the three days. Over the course of the convention, the faithful participated in healing services, a Eucharistic procession, Adoration of the Blessed Sacrament, a recitation of the rosary, and Mass; witnessed re-enactments of the New Eve (Luke 1:27–56) and the Wedding at Cana (John 2:1–11); attended lectures on the Pentecost (Acts 1:13–14) and other biblical passages concerning the Virgin Mary. They listened to some dynamic preaching and danced with raised arms to lively praise music, some of it set to modern *konpa* rhythms more associated with Haitian nightclubs than Pentecostal revivals, performed by Jean-Robert Thémistocle, Gilbert Dabady, and Groupe Effusion. There was also a chapel for private prayer, priests available for confessions, and a special session for youth. It was a highly festive and deeply emotional experience. Especially during the times of prayer, some people would fall to the floor possessed by the Holy Spirit, and many others would speak in tongues, some chanting, screaming, and weeping, arms ever outstretched, with rosaries or photographs of loved ones held in many beseeching hands. Over the course of the three-day gathering, the faithful sang a total of seventy-seven hymns, fifty-two in Haitian Creole, twenty-five in French, and none in English. Highlights among the sermons were Fr. Jules Campion's, *"Faites tout ce qu'il vous dise"* (Whatsoever He Says Unto You, Do It), reflecting on a statement attributed to the Virgin Mary in the Gospel of John (2:5), and Msgr. Thomas Wenski's concluding homily, *"Marie, Mère du Nouveau Millénaire"* (Mary: Mother of the New Millennium). Despite the French titles (Wenski does not speak French), the sermons were all delivered in Haitian Creole.

Jeanty was especially excited about the convention because Sr. Claire Gagné, a French Canadian nun credited with having planted the

Renewal in Haiti in 1973, would be in attendance, along with Fr. Campion, the movement's most inspirational leader in Haiti (Rey 2010). Campion had traveled from Haiti to preach, say Mass, and participate in the healing service, wearing his trademark white robe with blue images of Our Lady of Fatima and a wooden rosary wrapped around his wrist. Arguably the most popular priest in the Haitian Catholic Church since Jean-Bertrand Aristide (who left the priesthood in 1994), Campion's healing services in Haiti are renowned for their holiness, exorcisms, and healing efficacy, and some consider him to be a prophet (see fig. 2.2). In fact, at a charismatic revival in Port-au-Prince on April 23, 2009, Campion perceivably prophesied the tragic earthquake of 2010, warning those in attendance that prayer and conversion were all that could inspire Jesus to prevent the catastrophe and that in order to move him to do so "we must turn away from the filth" of "sins" that "anger God," especially Vodou and homosexuality, or else "Port-au-Prince will be no more," crushed by the earthquake.[5] Jeanty was tremendously inspired by

Figure 2.2. The most influential Haitian leader of the Catholic Charismatic Renewal, a Pentecostal Catholic movement born in North America in the late 1960s, Fr. Jules Campion blesses the faithful at the annual meeting of the Charismatic Catholic Congress of Overseas Haitians in 2002 at the Knight Center in Miami. Photo by María Rey.

Campion's sermons at the 2002 convention, and though they weren't so dramatic as to warn that her hometown would be leveled by an earthquake and though she "was too weak to dance," she "was so moved by his sermons and felt the presence of God so powerfully. The Holy Spirit was so present, and I believe that was the moment I would be cured, especially when Father Campion blessed me with holy water."

Women were in the majority at the 2002 convention. They came from Boston, Paris, Montreal, Philadelphia, New York, Chicago, New Jersey, the Bahamas, and all throughout Florida. Representing all social classes of the Haitian diaspora, most were dressed in their Sunday best, which for some meant T-shirts with the silkscreened names of the charismatic prayer groups to which they belonged, like Groupe Charismatique Jésus Miséricorde (Mercy of Jesus Charismatic Group), Notre Dame du Perpétuel Secour Group Charismatique Grand Bahama (Our Lady of Perpetual Help Charismatic Group of Great Bahama), Groupe de Louange de Nyack (Nyack Worship Group), or blazoned with images of Jesus or the Virgin Mary. Some of them also carried colorful banners with the names and symbols of their respective groups, and no one could miss a large banner of Our Lady of Perpetual Help perpetually hoisted on high over the heads of one group. There were also a few small Canadian and Haitian flags waving above the flock.

In all, four priests, a nun, and several laypersons preached or lectured during the three-day convention, each scheduled for a forty-five-minute time slot. The Haitian priests who participate in the convention usually change each year, while the CRCCHO's moderator, Msgr. Joseph Malagreca, has been a fixture at the annual gathering since day one. The pastor of Sts. Joachim and Anne Catholic Church in Queens Village, New York, Malagreca is described by the *New York Times* writer Anne Barnard (2010a) as "a gregarious Creole-speaking Italian-American who built the church into a hub of New York Haitian life." Malagreca opened the 2002 meeting in Miami and delivered two lectures there, both reflecting on biblical passages about the Virgin Mary. All of the sermons and lectures were delivered in Haitian Creole. They were also quite stirring and were greeted with worshipful enthusiasm by the faithful, especially the one delivered by Fr. Campion.

Campion's frequent visits to Miami, to say nothing of his mesmerizing charisma and reputation for prophecy and healing, have earned

Figure 2.3. The Charismatic Renewal has changed the face of Catholicism in the Americas over the last forty years, nowhere more so than in Haiti and the Haitian diaspora. Here, the cover of the annual Charismatic Catholic Congress of Overseas Haitians depicts the Virgin Mary and the Congress's 2002 title, "All Generations Will Call Me Blessed." Photo by Terry Rey.

him a place of considerable importance in Haitian Catholicism in South Florida, especially among the throngs who are drawn to the Charismatic Renewal, and there are signs that the movement is actually growing in wake of the calamitous 2010 earthquake. In some Miami Catholic churches, news that Campion will be saying mass often causes a doubling or tripling of attendance, but not always. On one Sunday in 2000, for example, we attended Mass at Christ the King Catholic Church, a clean, bright, modest-sized, modern church in the middle-class Miami-Dade neighborhood of Perrine. We had been invited by several Haitian friends and relatives who were quite excited that Campion was to lead a healing mass there. Compared to the 2002 CRCCHO convention at the Knight Center, it was a minor gathering, with only a few dozen Haitians and Haitian Americans in attendance, and it was much quieter, but the depths of faith and charismatic spirituality were every bit as impressive. One attendee told us that this in fact had been planned, that Fr. Campion's visit to Christ the King had been "kept secret so that we could have him to ourselves." The Sunday Creole/French masses at this church are usually quite solemn and orderly, but on this day we witnessed several parishioners fall to the floor upon being anointed with oil, screaming out to the Lord ("*Seigneur!!!*"), while others were speaking in tongues. At one point, at least ten believers, including Mirlène Jeanty, were lying on the floor in religious ecstasy, possessed by the Holy Spirit.

To those of us who have observed the Haitian Charismatic Renewal over the years, it was not at all surprising to find that middle- and upper-class Haitians in Perrine would be speaking in tongues and possessed by the Holy Spirit in a Catholic church, for the Renewal first caught fire in Haiti among wealthy Catholics during the 1970s (Rey 2010). For the same reason, we fully expected the large middle- and upper-class participation in evidence at the 2002 convention in Miami. But as the Renewal grew in Haiti, and as liberation theology and its related base church movement began to decline in the late 1980s, the Renewal spread like wildfire among the poor Haitians. As Notre Dame d'Haiti is the Miami Catholic church most representative of these people, it also reflects this trend in Haitian religion, despite being absorbed in routine sacramental life and social ministries, as Mooney (2009: 77–78) explains:

> Charismatic prayer meetings can occur in small groups of eight to ten people in someone's home, or among much larger groups, sometimes reaching several hundred people at the weekly Charismatic prayer sessions at Notre Dame that end with Mass. During such meetings, people recite prayers together, such as the rosary. Some people pray in tongues, others then state their wishes out loud and ask for intercessory prayers. Some come forward to give testimonies and some recount how, through God's grace, they were able to overcome a serious problem.

Mirlène Jeanty is one such Haitian Catholic who attributes the Charismatic Renewal with healing her of a potentially fatal disease. Its success is, in large part, explicable in terms of the Haitian religious collusio, in that it is "pneumacentric" and calls upon unseen supernatural beings to effect healing. The Renewal thus transcends Haiti's stark class divisions—divisions that extend far into the Haitian diaspora—in ways that few other institutions in Haitian society do.[6] In preparing for publication an article on the Catholic Charismatic Renewal in Haiti the day before the earthquake of January 12, 2010, we concluded that, given

Haiti's many social, economic, and political problems, and given a repeated pattern of broken national promises, "It is thus not at all surprising that most Haitian Catholics are casting their gaze to the sky, the saints, and the Holy Spirit in search of miracles" (Rey 2010: 103). The next day the earth shook violently in Haiti, killing and maiming tens of thousands and devastating generations of human imagination and initiative. With a deadline of the very next day to submit the page proofs, there was only time to add to a list of social and political problems from which the Renewal offers solace and relief "—and now the tragic earthquake of 2010" and to dedicate the article to Msgr. Joseph Serge Miot, archbishop of Port-au-Prince and perhaps the most famous person among those who perished in the quake.

As the article predicted, the earthquake has driven even many more Haitian Catholics, rich and poor alike, toward the Charismatic Renewal, a development that Barnard (2010b) has also noted among Haitian Catholics in New York:

> The quake, too, is reshaping Haitian religion. It has demanded new resilience—not only from Haitians and Haitian-Americans, who often lay claim to a legendary, divinely inspired endurance, but also from faith itself, suddenly more vulnerable to doubt, disillusion and competition. And it has pumped new life into Haitians' version of charismatic Catholicism, which seeks direct contact with the Holy Spirit through uninhibited, even raucous prayer. This year, for many Haitians, the movement's embrace of raw emotion has seemed the only sensible response.

Most of our fieldwork and archival research for this book was conducted prior to 2010, and though we were no longer living in Miami when the quake struck in Haiti, our impression is that such a shift— a deepening and widening of Pentecostal spirituality—is also taking place among Miami's Haitian Catholics. That it is uniting Haitians in Miami and in Haiti inspires hope that it can more strongly unite Haitians across often contentious social and political divides. And this is what we have heard people pray for and preachers exhort time and time again in Haitian Christian gatherings throughout Miami. The Renewal promises, too, that the power to heal only further cements the movement as the present and future of Haitian Catholicism. Virtually every

Catholic congregation in Haiti has at least one charismatic prayer group, and soon every Catholic congregation with a Haitian ministry in Miami—and everywhere else in the Haitian diaspora, for that matter—will have one, too.

Conclusion

In one of the most influential recent studies of immigrants in the United States, Alejandro Portes and Rubén Rumbaut (2006: 157) argue that the immigrant experience, for Cubans and Mexicans at least, presents challenges that tend to efface class difference and spur a social effort that is more ethnically unified, "with ethnicity easily trumping class as the fundamental determinant of political mobilization." We have not found this to be the case among Haitian immigrants in Miami, where Little Haiti and Kendall are worlds apart, much like the seaside slums of Port-au-Prince and the leafy elite neighborhoods overlooking the Haitian capital are quite different social and economic worlds. There are signs, however, that the tragic 2010 earthquake could be changing that. Natural catastrophes commonly provoke solidarity, and the earthquake killed thousands in Haiti indiscriminately across social-class divisions, a truly unifying experience of devastation beyond any that Haitians had ever endured or imagined since the trauma of colonial slavery. Archbishop Wenski reflected this almost prophetically in an interview shortly after the quake:

> Almost every Haitian I've talked to in the U.S. since the earthquake has family members and friends in Haiti. Right now many are anxiously awaiting news of the fate of these loved ones. Haitians are a resilient people. They will survive, but the pain of loss—and the extent of loss—will leave a permanent mark on this community. Hopefully, even in evil God can bring about good . . . this tragedy has affected Haitians of all social and economic classes. Hopefully this tragedy will bring about a new national unity among the Haitian people who have been long divided over class and or political lines. (in Proust 2010)

Whether this recent change will endure remains to be seen, but it is the case, as Pè Reji observes, that "solidarity" and church attendance at Notre Dame d'Haiti grew after the earthquake, such that the church had to purchase chairs and speakers for the overflow crowd outside of the building during Mass. Since the quake, "we would have about thirteen hundred people coming to Mass" (WLRN 2010). Tragedy, of another form, in the homeland is what transformed thousands of Haitians into *botpipel* and drove them to Miami in the first place, many of them comprising the first generation of congregants who, along with the able leadership of priests like Wenski and Darbouze, and ample support from the local Catholic hierarchy, made Notre Dame d'Haiti the Haitian Catholic Church's home in Miami and made Little Haiti the center of Haitian Miami. Over time the geographic center of Haitian Miami has shifted northward toward the northern reaches of Miami-Dade County and on into adjacent Broward County as upwardly mobile first- and second-generation immigrants have made it out of the poverty of Little Haiti. Still many other wealthier Haitians have settled directly in upper-middle-class neighborhoods like West Kendall. This movement has created a variety and ever diversifying array of religious lives among Haitian Catholics in South Florida.

This diversification of Catholic religious lives in Haitian Miami could make the social unity reflected in the comments of Pè Reji and Monsignor Wenski even more of a challenge to achieve, but there are indeed clear signs that in the wake of the earthquake class antagonisms so endemic to Haitian society have lightened somewhat. For one rather stirring example, we turn to Holy Week of 2010 at Notre Dame, approximately three months after the catastrophe, when parishioners lined up outside the church to say confession to "a special visitor, former Port-au-Prince Archbishop François-Wolff Ligondé . . . sitting outdoors in a folding chair by an oak tree." At Holy Thursday Mass, a packed Notre Dame listened to Ligondé preach that "The people of Haiti have suffered. But today, we need to pray and show love for one another. We are a family. We have to stick together" (Kaleem 2010). So associated with the forces of oppression in Haiti is Ligondé that Aristide (1992: 45) calls him "a zealous servant of macoutism," and that angry mobs burned down the archbishop's residence in Port-au-Prince following a failed coup attempt against Aristide in 1991. Thus, the notion that Ligondé would one day be received without protest at Notre Dame, a place so associated with Haitian refugees fleeing the "macoutism" of oppressive Haitian dictatorships over the years, would have been altogether unimaginable in the 1980s and 1990s. Perhaps faith indeed can move mountains in ways more mysterious than they are sometimes moved by seismic faults.

Just as class distinctions make it difficult to foster Haitian unity, whether in Haiti or in the diaspora, so too do they make it difficult to theorize Haitian religion holistically. But, here is where our notion of the Haitian religious collusio proves effective, transcending, as it does, socioeconomic difference in addition to denominational difference. Haitian Catholics at Our Lady of Lourdes have socioeconomic backgrounds and immigration stories that are very different from their compatriots at Notre Dame d'Haiti in Little Haiti and from the Haitian Protestants and Vodouists (see chaps. 4 and 5). Nonetheless, they all tend to believe strongly that faith is a source of healing and of matchless protection against destructive supernatural powers and against the fallout from sin—a source of salvation goods.

In our efforts to theorize Haitian religion holistically, some of the academic literature has been suggestive in the cross-denominational or cross-traditional sense (Brodwin 1996; Corten 2001). But when it comes to conceptualizing across socioeconomic class divisions, the literature on religion and immigration is not very helpful; it focuses most of its attention on those classes of migrants that Max Weber would count among the "dis-privileged," in which "stories of unmitigated woe" are "the standard fare" (Portes and Rumbaut 2006: 170). Tuomas Martikainen (2005: 1) laments that there is a "lack of theoretical clarity in religious studies" due to an oversight of the important fact that "immigrants have highly different reasons to migrate and varying backgrounds." With very few exceptions (e.g., Rey 1999a), the literature on Haitian religion provides no insight into the religious lives of middle- and upper-class Haitians and Haitian Americans. Thus with little guidance from the literature, in this study we have found the Haitian religious collusio to be equally operative among these classes of immigrants, as is the joy and power of religious belief and practice that is generally otherwise quite evident in scholarship on Haitian religion. In higher income Catholic parishes in Miami where Creole or French-language masses are regularly said, such as Our Lady of Lourdes in West Kendall and Christ the King in Perrine, and among the thousands of middle- and upper-class Haitian Catholics in South Florida who participate in the Charismatic Renewal, we have been impressed over and again by the sincerity of Catholic devotion of wealthier Haitian immigrants, and with how they, too, believe profoundly in the intercessory and healing power of unseen spiritual beings, especially the Virgin Mary. As Terry Rey (1999a: 339) observes in his 1999 study of Marian devotion in Haiti, Haitian Catholics of whatever socioeconomic class, "the Virgin Mary is to them very real" in ways that force theory into the background:

> Class differences, legitimation, syncretism, "the psychological reassurances of legitimacy," "the opium of the people," and existential suffering aside, Haitians are, in general, unshakably convinced that the Virgin Mary intervenes in the world to help them through whatever trials they encounter on life's way . . . the sincerity of their devotion is unquestionable, and certain Haitian expressions of devotion to the Virgin Mary are as beautiful and moving as religion gets.

We have found that these observations about Haitian Catholicism in Haiti are equally true in Miami even across class divisions that also extend into the diaspora. Haitian Catholics are thus united spiritually in a Marian collusio of sorts, even if they remain divided materially, each possessing class-distinct religious habitus. In this sense, Haitian Catholicism has changed little transnationally on the other side of the water, and the Haitian religious collusio transcends not only religious difference and the Caribbean Sea but also Haitian class distinctions. And, on the Catholic side of the Haitian religious triangle of forces, the supernatural being who is believed to be most involved in the lives of believers and the history of their nation and its diaspora is the Virgin Mary, Mother of God and Mother of Haiti—Notre Dame d'Haiti. Even as Haitian Catholicism changes over generations and as it has been carried across seas, this is its most enduring feature, devotion to the Virgin Mary who fought for Haitian independence, who inspired the toppling of dictators, and who maternally guided thousands of Haitian immigrants in their crossing to and thriving in Miami.

3

Feting Haiti's Patron Saint in Little Haiti

The Feast of Our Lady of Perpetual Help

Overview

Key features of the Haitian religious collusio, such as service to invisible spirits and/or saints, the quest for healing from maladies and protection from evil forces, and pneumacentric spiritual embodiment, are nowhere more richly on display than during Roman Catholic feast-day celebrations. Dating to the early eighteenth century and taking place throughout the country, they are among the most storied and largest religious gatherings in Haiti, surpassed today in size only by the annual National Convention of the Catholic Charismatic Renewal, which draws upwards to 100,000 people during a three-day revival in Port-au-Prince. Even this convention is in some respects a Marian pilgrimage, patronized, as it is in Haiti, by Our Lady of Fatima and now annually held at the Our Lady of Fatima Biblical Center (Rey 2010). Most people go on pilgrimage to render cult to the spirits (*lwa*) with whom the feted saints are assimilated, and even if they do so primarily for this purpose and perform devotions to the lwa at a sacred waterfall, spring, or grove, a visit to the church to pray to and thank the saint is required of Haitian Vodouists. Though not as dramatic or syncretic as in Haiti, and far more about saints than lwa, the feast days of the most popular saints in Haitian Catholicism attract thousands of Haitian immigrants to certain churches in Miami, New York, and elsewhere in the Haitian diaspora that are consecrated to those celebrated saints (especially the Virgin Mary), where people pray and sing to the saints and commune so deeply with them that spirit possession sometimes occurs. Many of the pilgrims bring rosaries and believe that their capacity to protect them from evil is enhanced at such gatherings, while others bring photographs of loved ones in Haiti and believe that the saints see them and lovingly intervene in their lives "across the water"—where the deceased spirits reside. Religious ecstasy is common, as are afflicted people who come seeking the miracle of faith healing. And, though the feasts are adapted to local conditions in the United States, the Haitian religious collusio remains quite intact at the diasporic versions of the feasts.

In such ways as these, feast days for saints and their affiliated lwa have always have been the most popular form of communal devotion in Haitian Catholicism and Vodou, especially those for the Blessed Virgin Mary and St. James the Greater, who in Vodou are assimilated with the lwa Ezili and Ogou respectively. The leading Marian cults in Haiti witness some of the most vibrant and widely attended annual pilgrimage traditions, in particular those for Our Ladies of the Immaculate Conception (December 12), the Assumption (August 15), Mount Carmel (July 16), and of course Perpetual Help (June 27), Haiti's patron saint. With the exception of the highly syncretic week-long ceremonies that take place at the rural Saut-d'Eau waterfalls and the neighboring village of Ville-Bonheur, in Haiti's Central Plateau, and its Church of Mount Carmel for the feast of Our Lady of Mount Carmel, Marian feast celebrations in Haiti are usually limited to a single day in the Catholic liturgical calendar. These occasions share many chief characteristics: throngs of pilgrims; masses said throughout the day at churches consecrated to the particular Virgin cult figure being feted; myriad Vodouist ritual and symbolism; and impromptu marketplaces where one can purchase food, drink, and all kinds of religious paraphernalia.

In Haiti feast-day celebrations for Catholic saints and the extraordinary pilgrimage traditions that they inspire are as much Vodouist as they are Catholic, because of the two religions' being so deeply intertwined. In Miami, though, the presence of Vodou at such annual religious gatherings is comparatively weak. In keeping with our own observations of Haitian religious life in Miami, Margarita Mooney's (2009: 243–247) extensive research at Notre Dame d'Haiti Catholic Church demonstrates that despite what much scholarly literature about Haitian religion would lead one to expect, Vodou is not widely practiced among the faithful at Notre Dame. And, although one might anticipate things to be different during the feast of Our Lady of Perpetual Help in Little Haiti, we have not found this to be the case. Nonetheless, the quest for healing, magic, luck, salvation (understood etymologically and theologically), and spiritual fulfillment that is so central to the feasts in Haiti and to the Haitian religious collusio, do in fact carry over in the diaspora—they just do so with a lot less Vodou.

Haitians have long been among the most devout Roman Catholics in the world, although historically many, if not most, Haitian Catholics *in Haiti* have also practiced Vodou without any misgivings whatsoever. The Haitian Catholic hierarchy has had plenty of reservations about this over the course of its history, such that assailing Vodou has always been central to the Church's pastoral mission in Haiti, giving rise to its three "antisuperstition campaigns." The last of these campaigns, which took place in 1941–42, employed the Haitian army to demolish Vodou temples, drums, and all kinds of ritual paraphernalia. Alfred Métraux (1972: 343) recalls, "I was in Haiti in 1941 and remember seeing in the backyards of presbyteries vast pyramids of drums, painted bowls, necklaces, talismans—all waiting for the day fixed for the joyous blaze which was to symbolize the victory of the Church over Satan," a part of the Catholic Church hierarchy being "fixated . . . above all, on destroying, as systematically and also, it seems, as dramatically as possible, the material cultures and physical landmarks of 'superstition.'" (Kate Ramsey 2011: 200–201). One might therefore expect in diasporic Haitian Catholicism much clerical denunciation of Vodou and Vodouist syncretism. But, because there is actually a much lower percentage of Haitian Catholics who also practice Vodou in Miami than in Haiti, priests in the Archdiocese of Miami need not militate against the religion in any sustained or zealous fashion. In Haiti today, Vodou is not as widespread as it was during the antisuperstition campaign, although it remains a vibrant and majority religion. That said, there are Vodouists among the faithful at Notre Dame d'Haiti Catholic Church in Miami, but they seem to be a very small minority, as reflected in our field notes on the feast day of Our Lady of Perpetual Help, June 27, 2000:

There are many distractions throughout the Mass, mostly in the form of people coming and going. One of them is a thin, middle-aged woman dressed all in white, including the kerchief covering her head. Looking very much like someone at a Vodou ceremony somewhere in the Artibonite Valley, she holds an unlit glass devotional candle of yellow wax portraying an image of Our Lady of Charity, and she mumbles smilingly and animatedly while looking for a place to sit. Her gaze, as much as her candle and garb, makes her stand out in the, by now, large gathering. There are many hundreds of people in the church, the majority of them women and underclass, like her. If other people here are concealing their *vodouisant* [Vodouist] practice, however, she alone has taken no pains not to appear *vodouisant*: she wears a long white skirt to go with a white T-shirt, whereas most of the women in attendance wear dark skirts— even the many in white T-shirts with silkscreened images of the Virgin Mary or Jesus—and this woman's head is covered with a white kerchief, while most of the other women wear decidedly conservative and dressy hats. Her candle is also quite unique, one that she very probably purchased at anyone of the neighborhood's twelve botanicas. Seemingly everybody else in the church is carrying the small, thin white candles produced by a church supply company in China and purchased in the churchyard for a dollar each. This was in effect about the only moment that I had "a sense of Vodou" during the entire evening, making me feel light years removed from Bel-Air or Limonade.[1] Though the evening was a remarkable re-creation of Haitian Catholic devotion in the homeland, for whatever reason *vodouisant* [Vodouist] embellishments seem to have been either left back in the homeland or left down the street at home or in a botanica.

The two most important trends in Latin American Catholicism in recent decades have in some places caused a decline in the popular devotion to saints, although this has not been the case in Haiti. Daniel Levine (1995: 171) states that the emergence of liberation theology and the related base church communities in Latin America in the 1970s and 1980s weakened popular devotions associated with saint cults: "viewing saints as lawyers or agents has fallen into disfavor with group members. . . . As prevailing views of saints begin to change, traditional practices like pilgrimage or the making of specific promises (to bind

saints to their word) have lost popularity." The emergence of the Charismatic Renewal in many parts of the Catholic world, meanwhile, as
Thomas Csordas (2001: 65) observes, has resulted in saints becoming
"relatively superfluous as intermediaries in a religion that cultivates
direct person-to-person interaction with the deity." Although we have
no reason to dispute that this may indeed be the case in countries
where Levine and Csordas conducted their respective field work, there
is no indication that the meteoric rise of Haiti's version of the base
church communities in the late 1970s and early 1980s did anything to
dim Haiti's wildly popular saint cults. It may even be that liberation
theology's demise in Haiti was in part caused by its leadership's efforts
to redirect popular Catholic attention from the spirituality of saint
cults to the politics of street protests (Rey 2010). As for the impact of
the Charismatic Renewal on saint cults in Haiti, there are no clear signs
of their having been weakened. On the contrary, the Renewal has lent
considerable new force to several saint cults, such as the cult of Our
Lady of Fatima, for whom the national headquarters of the Renewal in
Haiti is named, the Biblical Center of Our Lady of Fatima, located in
Tabarre, just outside of Port-au-Prince and, incidentally, just down the
road from the National Monument to the Refugees (Rey 2006; 2010).
In Haiti, as elsewhere, the Renewal has also invigorated devotion to
St. Michael the Archangel. When Fr. Jules Campion assumed the pas-
torship there in the early 2000s, he made the Sacred Heart Catholic
Church in Port-au-Prince the epicenter of the Charismatic Renewal in
Haiti, adding numerous icons to the church and churchyard, including
a massive statue of St. Michael the Archangel. He also constructed a
small replica of Golgotha outside the church for the faithful to climb
up on their knees.

Thus, unlike developments elsewhere in Latin American Catholicism, the saints in Haiti are as popular as ever. To varying degrees, Haitians in the continental North American diaspora carry on the feast-
day traditions of their homeland. Dating to 1843, the feast of Our Lady
of Mount Carmel at Ville-Bonheur and Saut-d'Eau, for example, is Haiti's greatest pilgrimage tradition. The scholarly literature on the Saut-
d'Eau pilgrimage (e.g., Brown 1999; Herskovits 1938; Laguerre 1998;
Price-Mars 1928) generally suggests that for most Haitians who make
the pilgrimage to the beautiful waterfalls in the Central Plateau and the

Church of Our Lady of Mount Carmel in Ville-Bonheur each July, the experience is more about serving the Vodou lwa Ezili than the Virgin Mary. Leslie Desmangles's (1992: 136; emphasis added) observations are something of an exception to this, though, as he finds that religious practice in the village and its church during the pilgrimage is explicitly focused on the Virgin Mary, while up the hill and at the waterfalls is where pilgrims performs devotions for Ezili, a spatial juxtaposition that he refers to as "symbiosis by ecology":

> In my field research I found a marked change in the religious attitudes of the devotees as they travelled from the Vodou site to the village, and vice versa: in the countryside, they "served" the lwas by loud singing and by violent possessions, while at the church they showed more subdued devotion by quietly praying before the statues of the saints. *During the entire period of the Fête there were no Vodou ceremonies in the village.* The devotees attended the numerous masses during the day of the Fête, received communion, and lit their votive candles to the Virgin and to the other saints that adorn the church's sanctuary.

And so for most pilgrims at Saut-d'Eau, their service to Ezili notwithstanding, the "Fête" represents a highly important *Marian* feast day in Haitian religious life, and that some of the pilgrims in attendance are *katolik fran.*

Our observations in Miami and Haiti lead us to believe that the scholarly literature has exaggerated the reach and pervasiveness of Vodou in Haitian society and culture, whether during pilgrimages or more generally. Therefore, we refute the claim by Karen McCarthy Brown (1995: 35) that "Life in Haiti (and to some extent in the Haitian diaspora) is quite simply saturated with Vodou" and Claudine Michel's (2006: 119; emphasis in original) equally ambitious and unsubstantiated assertion that as a religion Vodou "is the cement that holds all Haitians together in times of crisis and during bouts of despair. *All* Haitians, we say, because despite appearances and a surface Catholicism, Haitians are Vodouists whether or not they are initiated, or at least they are crypto-Vodouists." Although Vodou does remain the religion of the Haitian majority, and although Vodou has been strongly influential on the reception and shaping of Christianity in Haitian history, there are very good reasons to believe that the number of practitioners of Vodou has been on the decline since the 1940s, a decline that may be accelerating in the wake of the tragic earthquake of January 2010, which many Protestant preachers have blamed on Vodou, and which was prophesied months earlier by Fr. Jules Campion as being punishment for the sins of Vodou and homosexuality (see chap. 2).[2] But the demographic decline of Vodou in Haiti was well underway long before the 2010 catastrophe, and its leading cause has certainly been the recent tremendous growth in Haiti of both Protestant and Catholic Pentecostalism. As Laënnec Hurbon (2001a: 132) explains, Pentecostalism in Haiti engages in "a permanent confrontation with the traditional symbolic system [i.e., Vodou]," which "ceases to be operative." Drexel Woodson and Mamadou Baro (1996: 54) add that in Haiti the "the mixture of *sèvis lwa* [Vodou] with Protestantism is rare."[3] In light of these trends, some observers predict that Vodou will soon lose its standing as the majority religion of Haiti and that Protestantism will one day count more followers in Haiti than Vodou and Catholicism combined. This is a very likely development that just a generation ago would have been unimaginable (Houtard and Rémy 1997: 34).

Nevertheless, Haitian Vodou, along with the Haitian versions of Catholicism and Protestantism, shares a collusio that emphasizes the integral, pervasive presence of spirits in everyday life. Rather than it being specifically Haitian Vodou, as Brown and Charles would argue, it is this collusio that unifyingly undergrids Haitians both in times of crisis and in times of celebration.

For Haitians in the United States and Canada, the most significant Mount Carmel feast-day celebrations take place in New York at the church in Harlem portrayed in Robert Orsi's already classic 1988 study *The Madonna of 115th Street*. In a later article, Orsi writes of the growing presence of Haitians at the mid-July feast in Harlem, which by the early 1990s had become so substantial that the Haitian national anthem was adopted to be played at the *festa* along with those of Italy and the United States. Masses for the occasion have since then been said in French and Creole, in addition to Italian, Spanish, and English (Orsi, 1992). In New York is seen a diasporic counterpart to the Saut-d'Eau experience in Haiti. Yet, whereas Italian worshippers at the New York *festa* have been deeply impressed by the Catholic faith of Haitians there, some anthropologists have observed that their Vodouist faith is either equally operative or that Vodou is the main reason why Haitians go to Catholic feast-day celebrations in the first place, with their acts of piety for the Virgin Mary being dismissed as little more than "a form of semipublic deception" (Brown 1999: 90). Elizabeth McAlister (1998: 137), for instance, states that with the exception of a few upper-class Catholics whom she admits know little or nothing about Vodou, the Haitians and Haitian Americans at both Saut-d'Eau and in New York "are addressing Notre Dame du Mont Carmel and Ezili Dantò *at the same time*." Also writing about Haitian immigrants in New York, Brown (1990: 6) more sweepingly generalizes that "Haitians, like their African forebears, operate from understandings of the divine and the virtuous that are markedly different from those of mainstream Catholicism. Bondye [God] does not get involved in the personal, day-to-day affairs of human beings." In addition to this latter assertion being certainly untrue for most Haitians who are Protestants and Catholics, we believe that many Haitian Vodouists, be they in New York, Miami, or Haiti, would not agree that God is as distant and indifferent as Brown suggests. We have found that most Haitians and Haitian Americans in Miami whom we have gotten to know personally over the last several decades quite simply do not practice Vodou, and many of them in fact know very little about the religion and even fear it.

It is of course possible that Vodou is more widely practiced among Haitian immigrants in New York than in Miami, Catholic saints' feast days in Miami being very much less infused with Vodou than they are in the homeland or in New York. One reason for this is provided by Karen Richman (2001: 17), who finds that significant numbers of Haitian immigrants in South Florida sever their ties to Vodou spirits as part of their integration into U.S. society, as many of them convert to the proliferating Haitian Pentecostal churches:

> Migrants are turning to conversion to resist their perceived domination by home kin and their spirits, and to take symbolic control of their remittances and the terms of their relationships with the home. They have rejected the lwa, withdrawn from the system of family ritual obligations, and joined Pentecostal churches. They blame the lwa for being

useless to them, for colluding with their families to exploit them, for turning a blind eye to migrants in need.

Adopting a function that historically has been served by Haitian Protestantism, today Charismatic Catholicism offers the same power of resistance to Vodou's sometimes taxing spiritual commitments. This represents a relatively new phenomenon in Haitian religion, since abandoning the Vodou spirits now no longer requires also converting to Protestantism from Catholicism, a trend that Métraux (1972: 351–352) noted in Haiti more than fifty years ago: "Many Voodooists have become Protestant . . . because they felt themselves to be the target of angry *loa* and saw in Protestantism a refuge. Hence Protestantism beckons as though it were a shelter, or more precisely a magic circle, where people can not be got at by *loa* or demons . . . . : 'If you want the *loa* to leave you in peace, become a Protestant.'" Whereas throughout Haitian history remaining Catholic kept the wavering Vodouist too close to the lwa to evade or ignore them, the Charismatic Renewal, *because it is Pentecostal*, offers the same "magic circle" to Haitians as Protestantism always has, and hence today one may remain Catholic while turning one's back on the ancestral spirits and safely keeping distance without fear of retribution (Rey 2010).

In Haiti, it often occurs in Charismatic Catholic healing services that the faithful witness to having been "liberated" from the lwa, the ancestors, and even from states of zombification. On February 19, 2002, for example, we observed one young man at a Catholic Charismatic revival at the grotto behind the Catholic Cathedral of Our Lady of the Assumption in Port-au-Prince publicly witness to how conversion to Charismatic Catholicism had saved him from a zombified state, during which time he had behaved like a cow, which he fully believed himself to be, having been transformed into one, as a *"zonbi,"* by a Vodou priest (*"yon gangan"*). His testimony was greeted enthusiastically by several hundred worshippers at the grotto. In rural Haiti, meanwhile, it has become common for Catholic Charismatic "missionaries" to exorcize demons from people who, in their judgment, have been harmed by Vodou, a religion that they strongly tend to demonize. Such exorcisms sometimes lead to equally dramatic conversion experiences. Similarly, we have had several Miami Haitian charismatics describe their "liberation" from the lwa upon their acceptance of the Holy Spirit in charismatic rite. This now represents a welcome strategy for many in the Haitian diaspora, as immigrants may now maintain the familiarity of Catholic practice *and* still distance themselves from (or in Hurbon's terms enter into "permanent confrontation with") the mercurial and exigent lwa. Accordingly, Catholic feast days in Miami are generally devoid of the Vodouist infusions and appropriations that so strongly characterize them in Haiti.

The Feast of Our Lady of Perpetual Help in Little Haiti

By the mid 1980s, Notre Dame d'Haiti had become the *axis mundi* for Haitian Catholics in Miami and all of South Florida. There is no greater illustration of this than the week-long celebrations surrounding the feast day of Our Lady of Perpetual Help. During the June celebrations, colorful flags adorn the foreboding black iron fence that, since 1998, surrounds the Notre Dame churchyard. The flags fly to remind passersby and communicants alike of the importance of this event in Haitian Catholicism: the patron saint of Haiti and *de facto* patron saint of Little Haiti. *"Pepetyèl,"* as she is affectionately called in Haitian Creole, is the most important symbol in Haitian religion; she is the saint most ardently prayed to by poor and wealthy Haitians alike, and by many Haitian immigrants in their journey to and settlement in the United States. For Haitian Catholics, this is Pepetyèl's church in the diaspora (see fig. 3.1).

Since its inception, Notre Dame d'Haiti Catholic Church has celebrated this feast day with special devotion. In 2002, for example, the feast attracted over fifteen hundred people daily over the course of eight days and nights of sacraments, devotions, procession, preaching, and song. Two particular events gave the festivities added importance in the eyes of the faithful: (1) the consecration of a Marian grotto in the southeast corner of the vast churchyard by Msgr. Wenski on Sunday, June 23; and (2) a Solemn Mass celebrated by Msgr. Hugh Constant, bishop of Fort Liberté, Haiti, which closed the ceremonies on Sunday, June 30. Here is the schedule for the entire duration of the feast of Pepetyèl as it appeared in the bulletin of Notre Dame d'Haiti Catholic Church, June 9, 2002 (authors' translation of Creole/French):

LEGLIZ KATOLIK NOTREDAM D'AYITI
[OUR LADY OF HAITI CATHOLIC CHURCH]

FETE NOTRE DAME DU PERPETUEL SECOURS
[FEAST OF OUR LADY OF PERPETUAL HELP]

MARIE, MODELE DE LIBERASYON
[MARY, MODEL OF LIBERATION]

Programme [Schedule]

Saturday, 6/22, 7:30–9:30: Spiritual Concert, Speaking Hands with Notre Dame Youth Group

Sunday, 6/23, 5:00: Consecration of the Grotto and Ceremony of Confirmation

Triduum

Monday, 6/24, 7:30–9:30: Lecture: "Mary, Model of Faith"

Tuesday, 6/25, 7:30–9:30: Lecture: "Mary, Voice of the Voiceless"

Wednesday, 6/26, Lecture: "Mary, Hope of the Poor"

Thursday, 6/27, 7:00–9:30: Feast of Our Lady of Perpetual Help,
    Procession and Consecration of the Virgin,
    Lecture: "Mary, Model for Families"

Friday, 6/28, 7:30–9:30: Stations of the Cross,
    Adoration of the Blessed Sacrament

Saturday, 6/29, 9:00–3:00: Health and Education Fair
    7:30–9:30: Inter-Parish Marian Concert

Sunday, 6/30, 9:30–: Solemn Mass, Cultural Revival

Following is a description of these events:

Sunday, June 23: Consecration of the Grotto

Over a year in the making by volunteers with financial contributions from parishioners, a large grotto housing a four-foot statue of Our Lady of Lourdes was added to Notre Dame d'Haiti's vast churchyard in 2002. Shaded by several dozen oak and banyan trees, the churchyard offers an beautiful natural sanctuary in the heart of one of Miami's poorest neighborhoods, a sanctuary that will largely be lost if the planned construction for a new church edifice moves forward. As if rising out of the earth in the shape of half of an enormous vertically split egg, the

Figure 3.1. Notre Dame d'Haiti has been the spiritual home to thousands of Haitian immigrants and Haitian Americans since its inception in 1982. Important religious gatherings,
such as the feast of Our Lady of Perpetual Help, patron saint of Haiti, require the faithful
to gather in Notre Dame's spacious churchyard, like this man here, deep in prayer. Photo
by Jerry Berndt.

concrete-and-stone structure stands roughly twenty feet tall and its
backside is covered halfway up with sod. In light of the great popularity
of Marian grottoes in Haiti (Rey 1999), the site quickly became popular
among Haitian Catholics in Miami, and it adds one more strong attrac-
tion to Notre Dame and the Toussaint Center.

In addition to thirty or so confirmation candidates standing near the
grotto in red (girls) or white (boys) robes, several hundred adherents
press together against a rope barrier that keeps them from approaching
within forty feet of the new holy site in the churchyard. Expectations are
especially high because Bishop Wenski is coming today to consecrate
the grotto. Shortly after 5:00 p.m. the bishop arrives, followed by several
Haitian priests. He is garbed in a white robe and a miter adorned with
the icon of Our Lady of Perpetual Help. Along with the miter, a staff
marks Wenski's stature as bishop. He is, as many claim, *their* bishop. At
Notre Dame it is not uncommon, for example, to see women wearing

T-shirts with Wenski's portrait on the front surrounded by the words "He Is Our Bishop—*Min Monseyè Nou*," while the back features an image of the Virgin Mary with the words "He is in your hands"—"*Li nan men ou*." Conducted in fluent Haitian Creole, the consecration of the grotto lasts for only about thirty minutes, after which the faithful follow the bishop, priests, and candidates into the church for the Sacrament of Confirmation.

Triduum: June 24–26

A Triduum is a three-day period of prayer during which Catholics prepare for particularly holy occasions, such as Marian feast days. Notre Dame has adopted this tradition for the feast day of Our Lady of Perpetual Help, thus on the evenings of June 24, 25, and 26 , from 7:30 to 9:30, the faithful gather for prayer, reflection, and song. A different Haitian priest based in South Florida delivers a sermon each evening: on the 24th Fr. Yves Jocelyn, of St. Bartholomew Catholic Church in Miramar, preaches on "Mary: Model of Faith;" on the 25th Fr. Ferry Brutus, of Holy Family Catholic Church in North Miami Beach, delivers a homily on "Mary: Voice of the Voiceless;" and on the 26th Fr. Robès Charles, of Sacred Heart Catholic Church in Homestead, delivers a sermon entitled "Mary: Hope of the Poor." Only the first evening includes a Eucharistic celebration. On the 24th and 25th, a layperson leads prayers from the pulpit in Haitian Creole while awaiting the entry of the priest. A Haitian nun performs this role on the final evening while sitting casually on the floor of the stage holding a microphone and offering reflections on the Virgin Mary. Between her meditations, she also leads the congregation in the recitation of the rosary.

The three nights of the Triduum are otherwise quite alike, featuring biblical readings, hymns, meditations, and prayers. A different choir sings at each service, and throughout the Triduum the hymns are driven by Vodou drums. Roughly five hundred persons fill the pews each night, many of them regular Notre Dame parishioners. In terms of social class, there is the usual tiny representation of upperclass Haitians in attendance. Women make up roughly an 80 percent majority, and most of them are forty years old or older. There are only a few dozen children and adolescents in attendance. As usual, people are

quite conservatively dressed, though many more than usual are wearing any one of the wide variety of silk-screened T-shirts with images
of the Virgin Mary, Bishop Wenski, names and logos of various church
groups (most of them charismatic), or commemorating various religious events either in Miami or in Haiti.[4]

Besides the striking displays of religious ecstasy in the pews and
aisles of the church, the highlights of the Triduum are the nightly sermons. With a different priest preaching each evening, one cannot help
but to perceive of the lecture series as something of a preachers' competition. One woman with whom we spoke later in the week reflected a
similar impression:

> All three of them [the priests] know how to speak and gave us beautiful
> sermons. But Father Brutus is the most inspirational. Now I want to go
> to his church in North Miami sometimes, because he really made me cry
> for joy to Mother Mary. The others are fine—in fact, when Father Jocelyn
> used to preach here at Notre Dame he was always so boring, but he has
> gotten better. This week he was actually funny.[5]

Since the mid-1980s, many Haitian Catholic priests have adopted the
dynamic "call-and-response" preaching style that was popularized by
Jean-Bertrand Aristide and other leaders of Haiti's Tilegliz movement.
This involves the priest's enunciating key points by raising his voice
before stopping between syllables of a given phrase's final word, which
invites the congregation to cry out the completion: e.g., Priest: "God
has given us through Mary the way to salvation and that is his one and
only son JÉ. . . " (priests halts his rising speech) – with the congregation
responding: ". . . SUS!!!" Generally speaking, however, older Haitian
priests do not employ such an antiphonic style of preaching, as evinced
by Fr. Jocelyn, who is senior to Brutus and Robès, on the first night of
the Triduum. He did nevertheless crack a joke at the beginning of his
sermon, sending the congregation into uproarious laughter.

The messages that were relayed in the Triduum sermons set a worshipful tone for the entire week; they frame theologically, for the faithful, the meaning of the feast of Perpetual Help. Fr. Jocelyn reflects on
the meaning of faith, denouncing hypocrisy among Christians, a common theme in Haitian sermons: "How many [prayer] groups are there

in our churches today? How many people are members of three and four groups, but really do not have faith? . . . So many carry around Bibles and rosaries, but really don't have faith . . . . Faith is about receiving the spirit of God, about knowing that Jesus is God. That's it."

Acknowledging the force of the Charismatic Renewal in Haitian Catholicism, Jocelyn suggests that while the Renewal is drawing new converts to the church, it is also obscuring important theological notions and causing some to lose sight of certain essential Catholic tenets:

> I am sometimes asked: "Father, when are you going to become a Charismatic?" And I answer "Listen, look! How dare you ask me that! How dare you! I have been Charismatic since the day of my baptism . . . I am confirmed, and well beyond that I have been ordained as a priest! So, how can you dare ask me when I will become Charismatic?!" Listen, there is need today to seek out the true meaning of "Charismatic." Do not confuse it with the Charismatic Renewal. . . . Many of those people do not even know what the Holy Spirit is!

Although a few congregants laugh and a few others shout "amen" in agreement, there is an unmistakable sense of shock over these comments among much of the congregation, which is obviously deeply influenced by the Charismatic Renewal. As if sensing this, Fr. Jocelyn abruptly shifts gears and uses the term "spirit" as a springboard for his brief denunciation of Vodou that follows: "Some believe in other spirits like the lwa, but they cannot really do anything for you." This proclamation is greeted with an enthusiastic chorus of "amen" from the faithful, surely because many among them conceive of evil as being something "persecutory" that is channeled through the Vodou lwa, and they conceive of their own religion, Catholicism, to be the producer and source of salvation goods that can best protect them from such supernatural threats (Corten 2001: 30).

The following evening's ceremonies, on June 25, 2002, are led by Fr. Ferry Brutus, whose sermon is "Mary: Voice of the Voiceless." In general, younger Haitian priests are the most open to the influence of the Charismatic Renewal. Brutus's preaching style, especially when contrasted with Jocelyn's, reflects this, though Brutus's own theology is still firmly rooted in concerns for justice, thanks in large part to the timing of his seminary training (Brutus is a member of the last generation of Haitian seminarians to have been trained by Fr. Gabriel Charles, one of the founders of Haiti's Tilegliz movement and the long time rector of Haiti's Catholic seminary). As Hurbon (2001: 121) notes, the Charismatic Renewal in Haiti has encouraged people to seek first personal rather than social transformation: "each individual in the movement believes he or she is responsible for his or her afflictions . . . the popular classes are seeking the amelioration of social and economic life through an inner, spiritual change." Brutus crafts his sermon in part to attempt to restore a social objective to this flourishing charismatic spirituality, wherein one considers personal sanctity her ultimate Christian responsibility; society can only benefit thereby, but as a fortuitous ramification rather than the central objective of Christian practice. His sermon is in large part a notable denunciation of those "who pray without acting; of those who pray but judge others; of those who pray while turning their backs on those in need of help." In effect, Brutus proclaims that genuine Catholic spirituality must inspire social action:

> A person who prays but does not perform acts for God is a liar and is actually offensive to God. . . . A true person of God learns in silence when to speak out, learns how to do good, learns how, like Mary, to serve God by acting for God and for justice; this is the whole point of the Magnificat. We must act in accordance with the Magnificat.[6]

The sermon winds down into a series of confessional prayers, wherein the priest raises questions like, "Have I driven all satanic forces out of my life, including the service of ancestors and idols?" The congregation responds emphatically, "Yes, I have finished with these things." Somewhat ironically, this denunciation of Vodou is immediately followed by two young men beating lively Vodou rhythms on tambours! The congregation then breaks out into a hymn vowing to follow the Magnificat, and a tremendous sense of joy sweeps the entire congregation. Women sway back and forth, hands outstretched, singing in worshipful ebullience. This "collective effervescence" and these "transports of enthusiasm" are interpreted by the classical sociologist Émile Durkheim (1995: 217) as amounting to "a sort of electricity," and they would carry throughout the entire week in ebbs and flows, though sometimes tempered by solemn reflections on sin and the desperate quest for miracles, especially on the evening of Friday, June 28.

Fr. Robès Charles leads the final evening of the Triduum on June 26. After a series of beautiful hymns accompanied by the tambours, the priest takes up the microphone and asks the congregation if he may step down from the pulpit into their midst. Cheerfully and resoundingly they answer, "YES!!!" Periodically Robès spontaneously begins singing a relevant and familiar hymn, and the entire congregation joins in for an impromptu verse or two. This has a tremendous effect on many congregants, who, while singing with outstretched hands, seem either in or on the verge of states of trance. Next the priest speaks condenscendingly of high-profile international political summits that seek to change the course of history. But ultimately, he says, such "great meetings" (*gwo rankont*) are capable of nothing, unlike the Annunciation of the archangel Gabriel to the Blessed Virgin Mary:

> A long time ago in a little town there was a small meeting that would change the history of humanity; a meeting between a poor young woman named Mary and the Archangel Gabriel. . . . Mary said yes to God and in doing so gives us Jesus. She is thus the future and hope for the poor. . . . We too, like Mary, should say yes to God; we always ask God for this and that, but we need to listen to God. He is asking all of us to say yes—and in turn to act to change the world, to change society. . . . This is the heart of the New Testament.

As a whole, the Triduum was a joyful, reflective celebration of Haitian Catholic spirituality and of the central role that the Virgin Mary plays in the lives of Haitian Catholics. Yet in preparing the faithful for the Feast Day of Our Lady of Perpetual Help, the content of the three priests' sermons also reflected some of the tension in the Haitian Catholic Church at this critical juncture in its history. In subtly attacking the Charismatic Renewal, a move that clearly shocked many congregants, Fr. Jocelyn was drawing attention to the movement's perceivably escapist tendencies and theological ambiguities.[7] It seems that one of the effects of the Renewal's remarkable success in Haiti is the popular Catholic Church's depoliticization, something decried by liberation theologians in Haiti and elsewhere in Latin America (Rey 2010; Cleary 2011).

Consequently, commitments to social activism and human rights concerns that were the hallmarks of Tilegliz have been replaced by a spirituality that emphasizes inward transformation and miracles. Reflecting this, and in an effort to rein charismatics in closer to the church's social mission in the hopes that it not be lost in the more abstract and ecstatic features of the Haitian religious collusio, the Triduum linked personal spirituality with humanitarianism. Or, as Fr. Brutus put it rather poetically: "We are to listen to God in silence and, like Mary, say yes to His call; then we will know how to act for justice—this is what it means to live a profound and dignified relationship with the Lord."

The Feast of Our Lady of Perpetual Help and Procession, June 27, 2002

Hundreds of people mull about the ten-acre Notre Dame d'Haiti churchyard in anticipation of the evening's procession. A few hundred more fill the pews and aisles of the church, listening to spontaneous sermons by parish lay leaders (usually women), praying, and singing. Prior to the procession there is a special theatrical performance of the Annunciation of the Blessed Virgin Mary, the biblical account of the archangel Gabriel announcing to Mary that she would be the Mother of God. It is given by three teenagers, one costumed as Gabriel, one as Joseph, and one as Mary. The narrative is spoken by a Haitian nun, while the actors recite the Annunciation dialogue from the Gospel of Luke (1:39–56). As is common in Haitian Christianity in general, the biblical passages are read or recited in French, while most of the rest of ritual life transpires in Haitian Creole and increasingly in English. The procession is scheduled to begin at 7:00 p.m., and things are only a few minutes late in getting underway. Then the vicar of Notre Dame, Fr. Reginald Jean-Mary makes his way to the pulpit to deliver a few animated announcements in Haitian Creole and stir up the faithful: "We are about to make procession with Pepetyèl, even if it rains . . . my brothers and sisters, we will process anyway and accept the rain as our Mother blessing us." Next he asks for silence in order to clearly explain the procession protocol: "There will be room for everyone, so please let us do this in an orderly fashion: four people to a row . . . just four by four, that is how we will process—four by four." Anyone at all familiar with Haiti could have predicted that Fr. Reginald's plea for order would go unheeded. It did however provide comic relief during the procession in one section when the occasional sarcastic proclamation of "four by four" by a few jocular women would provoke riotous laughter. To be sure, before even leaving the parking lot, any semblance of organization self-destructs, as an expectant gathering of nearly two thousand strong slowly spills en masse through the opening in the black iron fence and onto Martin Luther King Jr. Boulevard (see fig. 3.2).

Besides being an expression of genuine religious devotion, the feast-day celebration at Notre Dame is an attempt to re-create a sense of being Haitian and of being in Haiti. Moreover, just as La Virgen de la Caridad del Cobre is for Cuban Exiles in Miami, to use Thomas Tweed's (1997: 94–95) terms, Notre Dame du Perpétuel Secours is for diasporic Haitians a "translocative" and "transtemporal" religious symbol, transporting her flock across space and time to an idealized Haiti of yesteryear. By "trans-temporal" Tweed means that "Diasporic time is fluid, slipping from con-structed past to imagined future, and both the past and the future inform the experience and symbolization of the present," and by "transloca-tive" he means "the tendency among many first- and second-generation migrants to symbolically move between homeland and new land." These nostalgic visualizations are every bit as operative at Notre Dame as they are at the Shrine of Caridad del Cobre, just a few miles away, where Tweed first arrived at these important insights about symbolism and emotions among immigrant Cuban Catholics in the United States.

For all of the June Notre Dame celebration's Haitian-ness, however, there are radical differences between the patron-saint feast in Haiti and its diasporic counterpart in Miami. At the Church of Notre Dame du Perpétuel Secours in the Bel-Air neighborhood of Port-au-Prince, for example, vendors of ritual paraphernalia can be found near the church steps and surrounding sidewalks each June 27 (Rey 1999). Among their dizzying array of icons, candles, perfumes, rosaries, novena guides, scapulars, holy water, holy oil, candy, and crackers, the most striking items in their baskets are the colorful ropes that Haitian pilgrims tie around their heads or waists, which are chiefly employed to contain and intensify spiritual energy in their bodies (Rey 2001; Rey and Richman 2010), even though this practice is formally denounced by the Catholic hierarchy.[8] While chiefly associated with pilgrimage to Saut-d'Eau for the Feast of Our Lady of Mount Carmel, one can purchase ropes at any

Figure 3.2. For Catholics in Little Haiti, the highlight of each year is the feast of Our Lady of Perpetual Help. All generations of Haitian Catholics, whether born in Haiti or in the United States, gather for the festivities, highlighted by the procession, as pictured here. Photo by Jerry Berndt.

major Haitian pilgrimage site on feast days, especially on Marian feast days. At Notre Dame in Miami, however, we observed not a single person among the thousands over the course of the eight-day celebrations of the feast of Our Lady of Perpetual Help to be wearing any ropes.

To be sure, there were things for sale in the church parking lot and on the sidewalk along NE 62nd Street: small white candles (for the procession), squash soup (*soup joumou*), T-shirts bearing the image of the patron saint, a variety of prayer cards and novena manuals, framed icons of Jesus and the Virgin Mary and popular Catholic prayers, and small vinyl flags bearing the image of Our Lady of Perpetual Help. At one point it seems that practically everyone in the procession is waving them. Although it is certainly possible that some of these pieces of Catholic religious paraphernalia could be put to Vodouist purposes, during the feast they seem to have been employed toward solely

Catholic ones. However employed, such items are used in the Haitian religious collusio toward serving and communing with unseen super-natural beings and toward securing magic, luck, worthiness, or healing, which to *katolik fran* would be more accurately construed as blessings. To many Haitian Catholics, whether in Haiti or the diaspora, the salva-tion good of worthiness is obtained through the profound belief that Our Lady of Perpetual Help is the "Mother of Haiti," their mother, and that she has chosen to watch over them over and above all other people because they are somehow "worthy" of her attention.

The icon of Notre Dame du Perpétuel Secours, which is a large framed lithograph rather than a statue, measures about 3 x 4 feet and sits in the bed of a shiny new Dodge Ram pickup truck. It is adorned with garlands and large fresh-cut roses. A group of around two dozen people walk in front of the truck, which crawls along at five miles per hour. Several priests in white robes flank the procession at various junc-tures, one of them carrying an ineffective megaphone. He tries to lead the faithful in singing Marian hymns, but his weakly amplified voice reaches only so far, such that at one point there is a different hymn being sung at the same time in four different sections of the procession.

First we head east on NE 62nd Street and then turn right and south on NE 2nd Avenue. There are so many people now joining the proces-sion, perhaps three thousand in all, that by the time its tail end passes through the churchyard gates, its head is already now turning back west along 61st Street. Two Miami City police cars and four officers on foot provide clearance along the normally busy streets, and the procession manages to keep to one side and allow vehicular traffic to pass along the other. Along NE 2nd Avenue, the procession passes before Botanica Vierge Miracles, one of the neighborhood's dozen or so stores, called botanicas, that market Vodou and Santería ritual paraphernalia, and offer divination and sometimes healing services (see appendix 2). Two expressionless Vodou priestesses stand on the sidewalk in front of their botanica and quietly observe, demonstrating not the slightest hint of devotional interest. Many other observers, meanwhile, stop whatever it is they are doing to cross themselves as the icon passes by. Along NE 61st Street a group of five pre-teen boys begin playfully mocking the faith-ful from a front yard. Their disrespect angers one young woman, who breaks from the procession, approaches the boys, and angrily scolds them in Creole. This only eggs them on, however, and now they fall to their knees, cross themselves, and stretch out their arms in derision.

It is not until the procession has made its way back up NE 1st and turned eastward again onto NE 62nd Avenue back toward the church, that the sun has set enough for there be any point in lighting the candles that virtually everyone is carrying. As the procession finally returns to the churchyard, after taking over an hour to circle the block, unity of voice is finally achieved when everyone begins praying the Hail Mary aloud over and over. The pickup carrying the Virgin makes its way gently through the parking lot and turns right onto the lawn behind the church. Followed by the throng of pilgrims, it slowly rolls toward the grotto against the backdrop of a stirring Miami sunset, eventually parking adjacent to the stage. A solemn hymn to Mary fills the fading day as hundreds of pilgrims, most of them clutching flickering white candles and flags bearing the image of the Mother of Haiti, flow into the churchyard beneath the great oaks.

Following the arresting and meditative devotion of the procession, the icon is placed on the stage, and two worshipful lay women again lead the faithful in song and prayer. Emblematic of the central importance of Notre Dame to all Haitian Catholics, during one of the long hymns, priests praise God for those present from South Florida cities and towns with significant Haitian populations (e.g., Delray, Fort Lauderdale, West Palm Beach, etc.). And later in the same ad-libbed hymn, virtually every major town in Haiti is prayed for as well. Next, several priests take the stage to lead the prayers and offer further reflections on the place of the Virgin Mary in Catholic life. There is an obvious concern with orthodoxy, as again and again the faithful are reminded not to worship Mary but to venerate her. In the context of Haitian religious culture, this clearly connotes an attempt by the Roman Catholic Church to strip Haiti's Mary cult of Vodou influences. Likely this is more the product of certain priests' seminary training in Haiti than with any serious need for the Church to combat Vodou in Miami, as many migrants sever their ties to the lwa upon settling in the diaspora. There have been even more Haitians converting from Vodou to Protestantism since the 2010 earthquake, however, as "sin" of Vodou is widely blamed for the disaster, the latest interpretation of the "persecutory" conception of evil in the Haitian religious collusio.

Stations of the Cross and Adoration of the
Blessed Sacrament, June 28, 2002

A smaller but equally impressive gathering takes place on the evening of June 28. The Stations of the Cross is an exceptionally popular ritual in Haitian Catholicism, perhaps for all of its meditation on suffering, something that far too many Haitians know intimately. Hundreds of the faithful eventually squeeze into the church to hear the reflections of a laywoman on the ways in which one should relate to the Virgin Mary. She speaks in Haitian Creole. Moments of silent prayer follow each reflection, and she advises deep breathing as a technique to intensify prayer. She then turns her attention to the Stations of the Cross, connecting theologically the Virgin Birth to Mary's presence at the Crucifixion of Christ, interpreting this to mean that Christians should be there and present for others in times of suffering and need. After a half hour, a male layleader replaces her and greets the congregation by exhorting them to thrust their hands in the air and wave them back and forth. In due time, he transforms the gathering into a lively revival with arms and bodies swaying, and voices singing enthusiastically "Lord, hold my hand, hold my hand" ("*Senye, kembe men mwen, kembe men mwen*"), and "All my debts are paid; Jesus has already paid them" ("*Det mwen yo peye; jezi gen tan peye yo*"), two hymns that are quite popular in the Haitian Charismatic Renewal.

After roughly a half hour of such communal ecstasy so common in Catholic Charismatic ceremony, Fr. Jean-Mary takes up the microphone to explain how the event is to proceed: "When we arrive at each station we will pray together, *"Mama Mari, Ou La!"* (Mother Mary, you are here!). Next, the faithful assemble in the parking lot and begin to follow a group of two priests and about six child assistants who are dressed in white robes like the priests. The children take turns carrying the large wooden cross, forging its way from station to station.

The first two stations stand in the parking lot, while the rest meander their way chronologically through the churchyard. Each station in the churchyard is marked by a small wooden cross and a spray-painted number on a tree. The procession stops at each station, where Fr. Marc Presumé of Notre Dame offers reflections on the relationship between the station in question and the ongoing struggle for justice: "Jesus denounced hypocrites, and for this reason he was persecuted and sacrificed. Injustice still reigns in our world, in this society, and we as Christians are obliged to take up the cross like Jesus and speak out." Quite effectively, the priest relates the Passion to some of the grave problems faced by Haitian immigrants in the United States as part of their cross to bear: e.g., drugs, gangs, discrimination, restrictive immigration laws, and the like. Mention of each problem provokes enthusiastic chants of *"Mama Mari, Ou La!!!"*

Eventually the procession ends at the fourteenth station in front of a large oak tree near the grotto. More than a thousand worshipers now take seats in the rows of folding chairs before the stage. The cross is placed in a leaning position on the steps leading up to the altar, on which stands the monstrance. Soon enough, the transitional commotion subsides, and a prayerful air sweeps the congregation. After a few announcements, hymns, and prayers, the priests perform the liturgy of the Adoration of the Blessed Sacrament. In the Charismatic

Figure 3.3. Whether in Catholic, Protestant, or Vodouist form, healing is a prime mover of Haitian religion. Affectionately known by the faithful as Pè Reji, here, for example, Fr. Reginald Jean-Mary, pastor of Notre Dame d'Haiti Catholic Church, anoints the afflicted with oil. Photo by Jerry Berndt.

Renewal this rite is usually followed by a healing service, as is the case this evening. The quintessential features of Pentecostalism (speaking in tongues, possession by the Holy Spirit, laying on of hands, chanting, and faith healing) have been adopted in the Catholic Charismatic Renewal, reflective of the "strong preference for pneumacentric religion on the part of popular religious consumers" in the Haitian religious collusio, and these are forcefully present at Notre Dame this evening (Chesnut 2003: 6). Intermittently the prayers and hymns bring most of the faithful into trance states, as worshippers fall to their knees and stretch out their arms in devout supplication of the Lord. Women comprise the vast majority, many of whom have their heads covered.

Two lines of several hundred people each now form down the center aisle between the rows of folding chairs. All the while, personal prayers are invited and many are speaking in tongues. As the lines form, one of the priests reminds congregants over the loud speaker system to be prepared to catch the person in line before them while hands are being laid on her/him. On numerous occasions this advice is heeded, as several seekers fall into possession once being anointed with oil and/or having hands laid on their foreheads (fig. 3.3). Save one, all of the possession experiences that we witness tonight are of women. Though scheduled to run from 7:30 to 9:30, the healing service continues until well after midnight.

Solemn Mass: Sunday, June 30, 2002

Each year in February Haitian Catholic priests from throughout North America and several from Haiti gather for a retreat in Miami. At the 2002 retreat, Msgr. Hugh Constant, bishop of the northeastern Haitian diocese of Fort Liberté, suggested that patron-saint festivities in Miami should close with a Solemn Mass said by a Haitian bishop each year. His presence at Notre Dame d'Haiti in June 2002 thus inaugurates a new tradition for Haitian Catholics in Miami, much as Bishop Wenski's consecration of the grotto had on the Sunday prior. In spite of an intermittent subtropical downpour, there is a large turnout for the June 30 Solemn Mass, with a higher percentage of middle- and upper-class Haitians from Kendall, Pinecrest, and other suburbs in attendance today than on any other day of the Notre Dame celebrations. The arrival of religious leaders from Haiti often creates quite a stir among the Haitian community in Miami. We have found that Catholics, Protestants, and Vodouists alike often consider their homeland to be a place of exceptional spiritual power, and many return to Haiti for purely religious reasons. There is a tacit understanding that priests and pastors coming from Haiti embody something of that power, hence Bishop Constant's presence drew a substantial crowd to the 6:30 mass. Mass is said before an altar on a large wooden stage erected each June for the feast-day celebrations. The oak grove gives one the impression of being in a natural auditorium. On clear days the magnificent trees provide the faithful with ample shade from the hot Florida sun, but this day they do little to shelter them from the evening storms. A sea of several hundred umbrellas makes it difficult to estimate the number of people present, though there are easily over a thousand. Most are seated in the rows of metal folding chairs in front of the stage, while others sit in the distance under tents on the basketball court that remain standing from a health fair held there the day before.[9] Still a hundred or so more are cramped into "Restaurant Notre Dame," a open dining hall with picnic tables and a takeout window.

Bishop Constant arrives in procession with about sixteen children in white robes, each carrying a pink gladiola, and eight Haitian Catholic priests who are based in South Florida, including Les Cayes native and former Notre Dame pastor Msgr. Gérard Darbouze. The bishop wears a white robe bearing the icon of Our Lady of Perpetual Help on the front and back, and a cross adorns each side of his miter. He is tall, black, and wears large glasses. As the procession enters, Constant blesses the faithful with holy water, upon which they, already soaked from the heavy rains, cross themselves reverently.

By the time the bishop begins preaching, the rains have become torrential, and thunder and lightning, a literal electricity, drive dozens from their seats to seek shelter, recalling Pope John Paul II's abbreviated Mass in Miami in 1987. Most of Constant's homily is inaudible because the microphone malfunctions and the rain is loud. Undeterred, the bishop continues in stern fashion his denunciation of Christian hypocrisy in Haiti: "There are even people in Haiti calling themselves Catholic who never cross themselves! How can this be? This is very, very incorrect." The scene takes on a surreal air as the bishop preaches vehemently but inaudibly through the dysfunctional microphone, loud rain, and intermittent thunder claps, not to mention the clamor of congregants scrambling for shelter from the storm. Beneath the natural awning of the grand oaks, the torrential rain and bustling sea of umbrellas before the bishop's feet makes for a stirring scene. Eventually, and with the cooperation of the retreating storm, Mass is sped up and the long lines of communicants finally make their way to the bishop and priests to receive the Eucharist. And thus ends a remarkable week of collective religious fervor at Notre Dame d'Haiti Catholic Church in Miami.

Conclusion

The celebrations surrounding the feast of Our Lady of Perpetual Help at Notre Dame d'Haiti Catholic Church in Miami are certainly among the most significant forms of Haitian religious life in North America. If the Haitian presence at the feast of Our Lady of Mount Carmel in New York represents, as McAlister suggests (1998: 124), "the largest annual religious gathering of Haitians in North America," then the week-long celebrations each June at Notre Dame d'Haiti Catholic Church in Miami together represents the largest originally Haitian religious event in the Haitian diaspora.[10] By "originally Haitian," we mean one that takes place at a venue that was created by Haitians, such as Notre Dame d'Haiti, and not grafted on to established feast traditions and churches of earlier immigrant groups like at Mount Carmel in New York. Chicken-and-egg questions aside, the feasts of Mount Carmel in New York and Perpetual Help in Miami—not to mention the throngs of Haitian devotees of Mary who flock to the Shrine of Our Lady of Czestochowa in Doylestown, Pennsylvania each August—are impressive re-creations of some of Haiti's most important pilgrimage traditions, and they are powerful testimony to the endurance of Haitian faith in the diaspora.[11]

The feasts are also powerful testimony to the endurance of the Haitian religious collusio in the diaspora. Reading the feast of Our Lady of Perpetual Help in Miami in terms of continuity and change across the water, we find a foregrounding of an additional layer of gratitude to the patron saint in the sense that in Miami, where her devotees have an extra expression of thanks to make to her for having helped them arrive and survive in the diaspora . . . across the water. This inflects, furthermore, in the central feature of the Haitian religious collusio of serving unseen spiritual beings, because the Virgin Mary protected them in their journeys—as they so deeply believe and as reflected in the mural in Notre Dame d'Haiti Catholic Church—and fortified them to find the means to not only arrive in the United States but, in many cases, to secure green cards, find gainful employment, and make enough money to send their children to college. In Haiti, meanwhile, their loved ones who receive remittances from them are, on the very same feast day, bringing photographs of them to the Church of Our Lady of Perpetual Help in Bel-Air, Port-au-Prince, and saying prayers to their same Mother to keep their relatives in Miami safe and to ensure that they continue to send money back home to family in Haiti. So many salvation goods are exchanged in this entire transnational experience. Although the celebrations at Notre Dame in Miami are in many ways very different from those in Bel-Air, the Haitian religious collusio in which and according to which it unfolds remains unifying across the water and across religious difference and religious change.

Of the three sides of the Haitian religious triangle of forces—Catholicism, Protestantism, and Vodou—Catholicism has in many ways enjoyed the smoothest transition in its migration to and settlement in America, thanks chiefly to a strong and centralized American Roman Catholic Church. This is a religious institution with a rich legacy of aiding immigrants. In Miami it has added to this legacy by providing Haitian immigrants with the resources to make Notre Dame d'Haiti Catholic Church the most important single Haitian institution in South Florida, if not the entire Haitian diaspora. Central to this achievement has been the enduring faith in Our Lady of Perpetual Help and other Catholic saints, whose cults in Haiti have long and fascinating histories and have enjoyed the fervent participation of generations of countless devotees. Although the feast-day celebrations are perhaps unsurpassed in their size and duration in the Haitian diaspora, they are but one of many re-creations of homeland Catholic devotions that Haitian immigrants have realized in the United States. Haitian immigrants of Protestant faiths, meanwhile, have likewise benefited from the fact that in the United States, Christianity is by far the dominant religion, making the establishment of Haitian congregations, either in mainstream American Protestant denominations or independently, a promising opportunity that they have seized, as testified by the dozens of Haitian churches found today in Little Haiti alone. Not to discount the many challenges that Haitian Christians have faced in re-creating their faith traditions in the United States, we must nonetheless affirm that immigrant Haitian Vodouists have faced much greater difficulties in carrying their religious practice to Miami and growing it there and elsewhere in the diaspora. Their experience is the subject of the next chapter.

4

Vodou in the Magic City

Serving the Spirits across the Sea

Migration, Worthiness, and Beautiful Magic

Woody Marc Edouard followed the news from Port-au-Prince with keen interest as jubilant crowds in Miami greeted Cuban pilot Carlos Cancio Porcel as a hero. In December 1992, Cancio executed "a very complex maneuver, a year in the planning," drugging a co-pilot and commandeering a domestic flight out of Havana bound for the Cuban beach resort town of Varadero, and successfully diverting it to Miami. After being questioned by U.S. authorities, "Mr. Cancio later emerged from the customs office to inspect the plane and raised his arms in triumph." Despite having committed a blatant act of air piracy, Cancio was exonerated and, thanks to the "Wet Foot–Dry Foot" policy afforded to Cubans in the United States, won political asylum, thereby earning for himself legendary status in local Miami Cuban exilic lore (Rohter 1992).[1] Perhaps wondering "How hard can that be?" Edouard, a twenty-four-year-old with a low-paying job and fearful for his life because of his political activism against the junta regime then ruling Haiti, hatched a similar plan. In February 1993, he stole a handgun from his employer at a travel agency in Port-au-Prince and made his way to the northern city of Cape Haitian, where he forced his way onto a missionary plane preparing for takeoff from the city's small international airport. The plane's charted destination was West Palm Beach.[2] But, unlike the hero's welcome and eventual asylum that Cancio and his conspirators enjoyed, Woody was greeted on the Miami tarmac by six FBI agents wearing rubber gloves and pointing submachine guns at him. Indicted in due course on hijacking charges, Edouard later accepted a plea bargain by pleading guilty to lesser charges of interfering with a flight crew, a crime that carries a six-to-eight-year sentence in the United States.

The disparity between the ways in which Cancio and Edouard were treated upon arrival in the United States speaks volumes about the racism and other challenges that Haitian immigrants face in Miami, and it rightly caused outrage both in Haiti and in the Haitian diaspora. In Port-au-Prince, the incident was widely noticed and popularly discussed on the radio and in the streets. *"Woody pat gin bel maji,"* one woman was overheard proclaiming on an overcrowded public minibus (*tap tap*): "Woody did not have beautiful magic," a reference to a widespread belief among Haitians that migrating successfully to the United States, by whatever means of transportation, requires considerable religious investment. In the face of U.S. immigration policy, which considers Haitians, especially when compared to Cubans, as *unworthy* for admission into the country, Haitians often turn to religion—and often to Vodou—in a quest for a salvation goods such as *worthiness* for political asylum status and protection during the migratory experience itself. Take one teenaged seafaring migrant "named Pierre," for example, who recounted to Regine Dupuy-McCalla (1997) how he had survived a harrowing trip when the overloaded sailboat he was on nearly capsized off of the Bahamas: "'Two months ago I was in a boat with seven hundred people that was going to Miami, but ended up in Nassau when the boat began to sink. Many people died that night but since I left with my own magic to protect me, I was able to survive and return home.'" It is quite possible that prior to leaving Haiti, Pierre had received the life-saving magic (*maji*) from a Vodou priestess (*manbo*) or priest (*oungan*), and that he had participated in one of the communal ceremonies for Agwe, the chief Vodou spirit of the sea, that are commonly orchestrated by passengers prior to embarking on such risky voyages.

For many Haitians, to be successful in the quest for legal settlement in the United States requires *maji* for a safe journey and luck (*chans*) to obtain worthiness in the eyes of U.S. immigration authorities, and Vodou is believed to have the capacity to augment one's *chans* of gaining asylum or a green card, of being deemed *worthy* to stay. This explains why so many Haitian migrants, historically speaking, have probably spent as much money on Vodou as on airline tickets or on places in leaky wooden sailboats in their attempts to reach Miami. In the minds of some of his religiously oriented compatriots, Woody Marc Edouard wound up being arrested because he hadn't spent enough on the spirits, because he hadn't acquired the necessary salvation goods: he just didn't have the beautiful magic to make it in the Magic City.

Vodouist visual culture in Miami also reflects such beliefs. For example, some of the work of Edouard Duval-Carrié, one of Haiti's greatest living artists, whose studio is located in Little Haiti, celebrates the lwa's protection of Haitian *botpipel*, as do certain exhibits at the Jakmel Art Gallery, where opening receptions sometimes morph into Vodou ceremonies, orchestrated by an artist/oungan named Papaloko. Such extra-temple venues as the Tap-Tap restaurant in South Beach and the Libreri Mapou bookstore in Little Haiti, which is adjacent to the replica of the Port-au-Prince Iron Market and across the street from both Brave Guede Botanica and Notre Dame d'Haiti Catholic Church, also help raise awareness of Vodou's role in helping refugees survive and in the creation of the Haitian diaspora. Add to this the city's two dozen other botanicas and ritual offerings or amulets found in streets, courthouses, and schools, the visual presence of Vodou in Miami is as variegated as it is assured. For everything else that these powerful reflections of Vodou in Miami are, they also represent expressions of gratitude to the lwa and the ancestors for sustaining *botpipel* in their crossing of the water and in their seeking new lives and making new homes in the Haitian diaspora, for making magic to make it to and make it in the Magic City.

Overview

People who are quite knowledgeable of Vodou in Miami tend to speak of it as a "worldview," over and above its being a "religion." Jude Thegenus, a local *oungan* known as "Papaloko" who oversees one of Miami's few quasi-public Vodou temples on the eastern edge of Little Haiti, asserts that "Vodou is more than a religion. It's a way of life" (Taft 2003).[3] One of Miami's leading Vodou priestesses, Ingrid Llera, who also oversees a temple in the back room of her botanica in Little Haiti, is of the same mind: "It's a way of life. It's a religion. It's how people live every day, day by day, minute by minute. It's who we are" (in *BBC World News* 2011). Miami's Catholic archbishop, Thomas Wenski, who has long and deep ties to Haitian religious life in Little Haiti, puts it: "Besides being a religion, voodoo is a worldview that permeates Haitian culture just as secularism permeates American culture. All Haitians are influenced by that worldview" (in Taft 2003). That is to say, the Haitian religious collusio is in large part shaped by Vodou.

In this chapter we offer an ethnographic glimpse into Vodouist life and worldview in Miami, arguing that Vodou's traditional raison d'être in the Haitian homeland, namely healing, protection, serving spirits and the dead, and the enhancement of life and luck (*chans*), endures in the Magic City. Because their religion is so maligned and misunderstood in America, however, Vodouists have faced many more challenges to carry on their faith traditions here than have Haitian Catholics and Protestants; some Vodouists almost immediately convert to Christianity once reaching Miami. But the religion does survive and in some cases thrives here, thanks in large part to its legacy of overcoming some of the most foreboding tragedies in human history, like chattel slavery, brutal dictatorships, and catastrophic earthquakes, but also thanks to the creativity, calling, knowledge, and entrepreneurship of its priests and priestesses. Like the Haitian churches of Little Haiti, moreover, Vodou communities in South Florida are profoundly transnational—in some respects even more so because of the deep belief in Vodou that the spirits are tied to the land in Haiti—and Vodouists have artfully adapted their religious practice to maintain generations worth of commitments to spirits, "practicing long-distance worship, anchored in the sacred landscape of the family land back home," as Karen Richman (2005: 24–25) writes of immigrant Haitian Vodouists in Broward, Palm Beach, and St. Lucie Counties, and they often do so through the "creative uses of cassette tapes and, increasingly, video recorders" and sending money to Haiti to feed the lwa.[4] Unlike the Christianity of their immigrant compatriots, Vodou is quite unfamiliar to most people in the United States, where the word "voodoo" is more likely to conjure notions of malevolent sorcerers sticking pins in dolls and of cannibalistic zombies than of the complex and beautiful religion that it really is. Hence a very brief word on just what Vodou is.

Vodou emerged as a religion among African and African-descended slaves in the French plantation colony of Saint-Domingue (1697–1804), which at one point was the most lucrative European colonial project in the Americas, at its height producing 40 percent of all sugar and 60 percent of all coffee consumed in Europe. Despite the colonial administration's formal prohibition of African religions, both on plantations and in Maroon settlements of escaped slaves, African and Creole slaves extended and re-created ancestor and spirit cults from the mother continent, most influentially from Fon and Kongo religious cultures, mixing in some Catholicism for good measure, and hence Vodou was born. Initially clandestine and variegated, Vodou has no founder, no unifying doctrine, and no formal organizational network. To this day, neither these nor any Vodouist scripture has ever developed.

Africans who were enslaved and forcibly brought to Saint-Domingue from West and West Central Africa during most of the eighteenth century were usually baptized Catholic upon arrival and given minimal religious instruction by Dominican, Capuchin, or Jesuit friars. Religious syncretism thus immediately resulted, as slaves identified Catholic saints as new (to most of them) manifestations of African spirits, and adopted crosses, holy water, and rosaries as powerful religious trinkets to be used in conjunction with the amulets that they reconstructed from African religious memory. The Catholic "pantheon"—with its single high creator God, Virgin Mary, and host of dead individuals (the saints) who intervene in the world of the living—lent itself to assimilation with the traditional African community of spiritual beings, which likewise has a single distant creator God (called *Bondyè* in Vodou) and numerous spirits and ancestors, who, much like the Catholic saints, are perceived of as accessible and with whom the greatest amount of human/divine collaboration and commerce transpires.[5]

Spirit possession, divination, song, dance, and prayers are the main forms of communication with the dead (*lemò*) and the lwa in Vodou (which are collectively referred to as "the mysteries"—*mystè*) and together form the religion's communal ritual focus. Put simply, when one's relationship with the *mystè* is in harmony, life is full and pleasurable, whereas when this relationship is discordant, sickness, some other hardship, or even death may result. Upon the occurrence of such misfortune, *manbo* or *oungan* are consulted. Through divination and/or the orchestration of lively drumming ceremonies aiming to provoke spirit possession (which in Haiti most often take place either in temples [*ounfò*], near sacred topographical features, at family burial compounds, or in public cemeteries), the *manbo* or *oungan* establishes communication with the *mystè* in order to discover the cause of the illness or discord and to determine a means of reestablishing harmony and/or of effecting healing. The maintenance and the reconstitution of this harmony often require offerings and sacrifices in various forms and/or communal drumming ceremonies in which spirit possession occurs, while healing often involves herbalism and ritual baths. And, because sorcery is often blamed for sickness and misfortune, one of Vodou's primary functions is to defend people against, or undo the effects of, "black magic."

As with Cuban exiles who brought to Miami the African-derived religions of Santería, Lukumi, and Palo Monte, so too have Haitians brought Vodou to the Magic City. We estimate that some 25,000 Haitians in Miami, or 10 percent of the total Haitian population in Miami-Dade County, regularly practice Vodou, while thousands of others occasionally consult a *manbo* or *oungan* for spiritual guidance, healing, protection, or empowerment. Our estimation assumes similar religious demographics among Haitians as among Cubans in Miami and rests upon the clearer picture of Afro-Cuban religions in the city. Jose Antonio Lammoglia (2001) concludes that there are roughly one hundred Cuban botanicas in Miami that serve a community of 100,000 practitioners of Afro-Cuban religions, meaning 1,000 practitioners for each botanica. There are roughly twenty-five Haitian botanicas in Miami-Dade County, so if we grant that there are 1,000 Vodou practitioners per botanica, we arrive at the figure of 25,000. Doubtless, some will dispute this figure as being either too high or too low, but any estimation of the number of Vodouists in Miami (or anywhere else in the Haitian diaspora or in Haiti, for that matter) would depend on one's definition of "practitioner," in the case of Vodou, by which we mean an individual who is initiated and/or regularly practices devotions to the lwa and ancestors (many Vodouists in fact never actually undergo initiation). That debate aside, this chapter discusses the nature of Vodou in Miami, with four particular foci: (1) changes that the religion has undergone in the Haitian immigrant experience; (2) the use of Catholic churches and shrines for ritual Vodouist purposes; (3) the complexities that Vodou has forced upon Miami's criminal and immigration courts; and (4) the transnational dimensions of Vodouist life in Miami.

Vodou across the Water

Since emerging in the face of prohibitions as a Creole religion in Maroon communities and on slave plantations in Saint-Domingue, Vodou has at times been forced to negotiate its existence underground. Yet, over the last thirty years the religion has become increasingly open in Haiti: the 1987 Haitian Constitution afforded Vodou "official religion" status along with Catholicism; in 2003 President Jean-Bertrand Aristide granted legality to its baptisms and marriages; and now very public Pentecostal style "Vodou churches" have recently opened in Port-au-Prince (Hurbon 2008). Having arrived in Miami with the first significant waves of Haitian refugees in the late 1970s and early 1980s, however, Vodou would once again negotiate its existence, at least initially, largely underground, in spite of the supposed religious freedom that the United States might have safeguarded for Haitian immigrants, who have encountered many obstacles and much racism in their "searching for life" (*chache lavi*) in South Florida. This was especially true for the first generation of Haitian immigrants in Miami, as Alex Stepick and Alejandro Portes (1986: 335) explain:

> Haitian refugees arrived in a city that did not expect or desire their presence. They suffered frequent incarcerations and, when finally released, lacked the support of strong family networks. They sought refuge in ethnic neighborhoods which gave them access to cheap but deteriorated housing. These severe initial difficulties combined to make economic problems their central concern in the United States.

Because it has always been "a religion of survival, and it counsels what it must to ensure survival," as Karen McCarthy Brown (1991: 254) puts it, Vodou would therefore serve as a resource for empowerment among Haitian refugees in Miami. Or, in Archbishop Wenski's words, "It has helped them cope with great turbulence in their lives. Sometimes the Haitians think that rather than put all their trust in prayers, they'll hedge their bets. They'll do a little voodoo too" (Doup 1987).

Just as in Haiti, where the religion's adherents have time and again found creative ways to respond to sometimes foreboding challenges, so too in Miami and elsewhere in the Haitian diaspora have Vodouists adapted their faith to preserve devotions to the spirits that many of them had inherited in Haiti. Over the last two decades, however, a considerable number of Vodouists, both in Haiti and in the Haitian diaspora, have converted to Protestantism and thus abandoned their ritual devotions to the *mystè*. Many underlying causes of religious conversion are common to homeland and diasporic Haitians alike, such as healing effectiveness (Conway 1980: 14), yet there are additional factors that suggest more widespread apostasy among Haitian immigrants. The sometimes taxing financial expenses of Vodou devotions in the homeland factor centrally in the decisions of some Haitian immigrants in South Florida to sever their ties with the *mystè* and join Protestant churches for their spiritual sustenance, thereby gaining more control over remittances that they send back to Haiti (Richman 2008: 253). This is not surprising when one considers that even in Haiti, people leave Vodou because of the material expenses that the religion sometimes requires (Métraux 1972: 354, 357). To these understandable reasons for conversion we would add (for Haitians in Miami) racism. It may be that Haitians face more racist discrimination in the United States than most other immigrant groups ever have (Stepick 1998: 115). Keenly realizing this, in their struggle to gain acceptance in the United States and to assimilate, Haitian immigrants often dissociate themselves from Vodou, fully aware of how maligned their traditional religion is in the "host" society. There are some signs that this attitude is beginning to change as part of a resurgence of Haitian pride in Miami, which we have noticed over the last ten years or so (Rey and Stepick 2010: 246–247).

Local noise ordinances and a lack of space are realities in Miami that also hinder the practice of Vodou among Haitian immigrants and force the religion to adapt. With few large temples or other venues to gather the faithful, and faced with the threat of visits by police responding to the complaints of unsympathetic neighbors, it is very difficult in Miami for Haitian Vodouists to re-create the festive and dramatic communal drumming ceremonies that are a hallmark of their religion in Haiti. But, as one Haitian *manbo* in Paris explained to Lilas Desquirons: "The mysteries understand that we are far from home" (in Hurbon 1995: 165). Likewise, in New York the lwa have allowed for significant changes in how the religion's boisterous musical processions known as *rara* are conducted, as Elizabeth McAlister (2002: 185) explains, for "unlike

Haiti, there were no queens, and the women on the scene were mostly relegated to the sidelines. Lifted from its Lenten context to fit the summer weather, Rara in the United States is a secular affair, and the lwa have not (yet) demanded libations, trips to the cemetery, or mystical seven-year contracts."

As far as we know, over the last twenty years, there have been at least five quasi-public temples (*ounfò*) in Miami: one in the backyard of Jude "Papaloko" Thegenus's Jakmel Art Gallery; Papa Paul Noel's Botanica Halouba; Manbo Carol de Lynch's Lakou Hounto; another at a different venue overseen by Manbo Ingrid Llera; and Societé Linto Roi Trois Mysteres, located in North Miami and overseen by Manbo Michelet Tibosse Alisma, a highly trained priest and native of Gonaives. The efforts of these *oungan* and *manbo* are to be lauded for helping to dispel pernicious myths about Vodou in Miami and to remind or educate Haitians and non-Haitians alike of the religion's integral place in Haitian history and culture. Instead of being a source of shame, Vodou is a rightful source of Haitian pride, having helped inspire, among other truly admirable things, the only successful national slave revolt in human history and a national artistic culture that has been acclaimed throughout the world. Papa Paul is the spiritual godfather to numerous other priests, priestesses, and lay initiates in South Florida. His Botanica Halouba sometimes draws upwards of three hundred worshippers for ceremonies in its sanctuary (*peristil*). Halouba has become especially noted for its annual first-harvest ceremony (*kouche yam* or *manje yam*), which takes place on or around November 25. As Manbo Margaret Armand explained, the ceremony

> is done after the harvest of Yam. They are placed in the hounfor [temple] on white sheets and leaves and prayed over. The ceremony lasts two days because the next day they are cooked and served with salted fish. The ceremony is very beautiful as all the hounsi [novices] and mambos carry over their head those kwi [pots] filled with yam and fish that have been blessed by the ancestors (lwas).[6]

In Haiti the scheduling of communal Vodou ceremonies is often synchronized with the Catholic liturgical calendar, with major celebrations for the lwa occurring on the official feast days of the Catholic saints with whom they are conflated, sometimes resulting in the effusive and syncretic pilgrimage celebrations that occur throughout Haiti, especially from June through September (Cosentino 1995; Rey 2005; Rey and O'Neil 2012). Vodouists in Miami have to be more selective in choosing which feast day celebrations to re-create in the diaspora, however, and some of them are per force largely abandoned, at least as far as communal gatherings (as opposed to personal devotions) are concerned. One glaring exception is of *Fet Gede*, the feast of Gede, the chief spirit of the dead, which takes place during the Catholic feast days of All Souls and All Saints. Fet Gede is arguably the most important religious holiday in Vodou and exemplifies the religion's remarkably creativity and adaptability. Usually requiring ceremonies both in temples and in cemeteries, Fet Gede emerged out of the trauma of the transatlantic slave trade when Africans, who had been torn from their homelands and taken against their wills across the Atlantic Ocean from the burial sites of the ancestors where important ancestral devotions were performed, appropriated All Souls Day and All Saints Day as the occasion to venerate all of the dead in Saint-Domingue. And, both in Haiti and in the Haitian diaspora, the feast of the dead has taken on even greater importance as a means of serving the tens of thousands who died in the January 2010 earthquake and never received proper funerary rites, provoking tremendous anxiety for many Haitians and prompting one leading *oungan* in Port-au-Prince, Max Beauvoir, to lodge a complaint with President René Preval about the mass graves on the outskirts of the city (Delva 2010). Ingrid Llera and Erol Josue, for instance, both conduct Fet Gede services annually in Miami; Llera in her botanica temple, and Josue in his home: "Artists and advocates for Haiti have been doing relief concerts to bring money for Haiti, which is good," explains Josue, "but as a priest, as a spiritual person, I think first of all we have to pay respect for our brothers and sisters, for those souls who have died." Adds Llera, "When you do Gede, it's like therapy" (in Kay 2008).

Another Vodouist feast tied to the Catholic liturgical calendar is *Fet Danbala*, the Feast of Danbala, the serpent spirit who in Vodou is assimilated with St. Patrick, an identification that is largely due to the snakes that appear in this saint's hagiography—snakes that, as legend has it, Patrick drove out of Ireland in the fifth century. Danbala has particular relevance for migrants and pilgrims in general because he is, as Leslie Desmangles (1992: 125) explains, "identified . . . with the eternal motion of human bodies," a lwa that Brown (1991: 306–308) herself spiritually married in New York in 1980. The oldest and the purest of the lwa, Danbala's great importance in Vodou is attributable in part to the fact that he "connects Haitians to their lost African ancestors and, at the same time, shows them how to be flexible enough to adapt to whatever the future may bring" (ibid., 275). One of the most remarkable examples of such flexibility and adaptation inspired by Danbala was on display at the feast for this lwa at Societe Linto Roi in North Miami in 2012, on St. Patrick's Day, when the temple was adorned with shamrocks for the occasion and most of the participants were dressed in kelly green! Lest one wonder whether this innovation might be as much a deviation from Vodouist tradition, we should point out that Oungan Alisma, who oversees the Societe Linto Roi temple at his home, is one of the most impressive Vodou priests or priestesses we know. A native of Gonaives, an epicenter of Vodou where he maintains close ties to some of Haiti's most respected temples, like Soukri, Badio, and Souvenance, Alisma was initiated as an *oungan* at the age of seven, in 1983, and sent to West Africa by his father as a teenager to study Vodun traditions there. Benjamin Hibblethwaite, a Haitian Creole linguist and author of *Vodou Songs* (2011), tells us that Alisma possesses mastery over hundreds of Vodouists hymns and rhythms.[7] This notice of the approaching Fet Danbala at Societe Linto Roi was posted in advance on Alisma's Facebook page:

> Societe linto roi trois mysteres vous invite dans une priere pour Saint-Patrick (Papa Dambala aida wedo) a 1425ne 136th Street North Miami Florida, qui aura lieu le samedi 17 mars 2012 a 8:00pm . . . pour plus information contactez-nous au 786-287-0754, ou le 786-379-3078, merci. . . . (King Linto Society of the Three Mysteries invites you to a prayer service for Saint Patrick (Father Dambala aida wedo) at 14245 ne 136th Street North Miami Florida, which will take place on saturday at 8:00pm . . . for more information contact us at 786-287-0754, or at 786-379-3079, thank you.)

Much of the ceremony took place outside in the temple yard, and it began with a woman leading a series of hymns. After some twenty minutes of singing, she addressed the congregants: "Now we will listen to the good *oungan* read from the Gospel for us, John 3, verses 3 to 11. You should remain standing for the Gospel reading because this is the word of God." Alisma took the microphone and addressed the faithful, much like a Catholic priest or a Protestant pastor would, in succession: "The Lord be with you" (to which they responded, "And also with you"), "Blessed be the Eternal!" ("Blessed be the Eternal!"), and "Allelujah!" ("Allelujah!"). There were about forty people present when Alisma opened the prayers, which went on for quite some time. Several congregants took turns leading the prayers over a microphone; they were all in French and Haitian Creole, including the Lord's Prayer, the Hail Mary, and the Apostle's Creed. Other prayers normally reserved for the Virgin Mary, Jesus, or God the Father were adapted by way of giving thanks to St. Patrick and, by extension, to Danbala. One of these prayers had St. Patrick speaking the words attributed to Jesus in the Bible "I am the way, the truth, and the light," while another had St. Patrick "who art in heaven," and another still proclaimed the saint as "he who created everything on earth as it is in heaven."

This early part of the ceremony seemed very much like a liturgical service in a Catholic or Episcopal church or a worship service in a Protestant church. The person leading the prayers stood behind a lectern facing the congregation, who were alternately seated and standing before rows of chairs. Almost everyone wore something in kelly green, including shiny top hats that one might see at the St. Patrick's Day Parade in New York City, some of them adorned with the words "Happy St. Patrick's Day!" About half of the congregation wears green T-shirts made especially for the occasion, silk-screened with the name of the temple and the occasion in white. Banners of green adorned the temple yard, which was strewn with a series of shamrocks, a unique adaptation to Fet Danbala in Miami that we had never observed in Haiti.

Anything remotely Protestant at the service ended when we saw the altar that was mounted for the occasion: a miniature palace made of wood that closely resembled one vertical half of the large gingerbread houses for which Haitian cities and towns are famous. The palace/altar has two floors. Upstairs is a statue of St. Patrick, and he, too, is dressed in green and draped in green Mardi Gras beads. Next to him is a plate of salt, one of the most common offerings to Danbala in Haitian Vodou because a lwa eats only white food. The lwa's house rests on the edge of a tub built in masonry and tile in the ground that serves other ritual purposes, as does an adjacent smoldering fire pit. In front of the house are several tall votive candles, all adorned with St. Patrick's lithograph, whose flames flicker and reflect off the surface of the water. The lower floor of the house appears to contain a statue of St. Lazarus, who, as already noted, is not very popular in Vodou in Haiti but who is of great importance in Cuban Santeria, especially in Miami. As such, this is another interesting adaptation in diasporic Haitian Vodou. And to top it all off, Danbala's palace is crowned with a large green shamrock. Vodou in the Magic City has thus become a bit Cuban and a bit Irish.

Alisma founded his Miami temple in 2000, naming it after his personal patron lwa, Linto Roi, and since 2008 sixty-seven people have undergone initiation there (*kouche kanzo*). As such, Societe Linto Roi is a most welcome and reinvigorating addition to South Florida's Vodouist landscape—it already holds a position of prominence there, in fact, having gained the respect of most or all of Miami's leading *oungan* and *manbo*, some of whom regularly participate in ceremonies there, especially the annual *fet kay* (house feast), which takes place from December 31 to January 4.

Societe Linto Roi is served by several talented *oungan*, in addition to Papa Alisma, and has initiated many people into the religion, with initiation ceremonies usually held each summer. The Societe's inner sanctuary is part of Alisma's house, and it is abundantly ornate, with dozens of lithographs of Catholic saints on the walls, a mural of the lwa Lasyrenn, a *poto mitan* in the middle of the space, which is decorated with a painting of Danbala, flags and kerchiefs draped throughout the *perestil* (sanctuary), and bottles and statues of saints on shelves in one corner. Ceremonies inside the temple look a great deal more like Vodou ceremonies that we were accustomed to seeing in Haiti over the years than the Fet Danbala described earlier: women dressed in white, depending on the occasion; *oungan* and *manbo* salute one another with ritualized dance steps and handshakes, their *asson* (rattles) in hand; drummers seated against a wall, and their drumming drives the motion of the occasion and summons the lwa; some people dance with lighted white candles and small plastic bottles of *Agua Florida* (Florida Water) perfume, saluting the drums; antiphonic singing for the lwa; offerings placed on the *poto mitan* for the lwa; spirit possession; and, occasionally, animal sacrifice. Some differences were noticeable, too, like the large flat-screen television on one wall that broadcast the ceremony as it was being filmed, and the silk-screened "Societe Linto Roi Trois Mysteres" T-shirts that several participants wore. In this fashion, in addition to Fet Danbala, Societe Linto Roi orchestrates a range of ceremonies throughout the year for other important lwa like Ezili, Ogou, Ayizan, Loko, and the Simbi.

Societe Linto Roi brings energy, expertise, and the wherewithal to invigorate feast day and initiatory traditions that have sometimes wavered in Haitian Miami. We know of no major gatherings for the feast of St. James the Greater in South Florida, for instance, or for Our Lady of Mount Carmel, which are among the most important Vodouist occasions in Haiti (see chap. 3). This wavering in the Haitian diaspora of adherence to the Catholic/Vodouist liturgical calendar that structures much communal ritual life in Haiti is in large part explicable by the spatial restrictions that Vodouists confront in Miami; however, we feel that this is also symptomatic of a decline in Vodouist devotion among Haitians in Miami in general. Even on the feast days of the major Catholic saints in Haitian religion (e.g., St. James, St. Ann, St. Philomena, Our Lady of Perpetual Help, Our Lady of the Assumption), the syncretism that marks those feasts at churches consecrated to the relevant saints in Haiti is quite rare in Miami. For instance, we have never seen Haitian attendees at Catholic saint feast celebrations, whether at Notre Dame d'Haiti, St. James Catholic Church, or the St. Ann Mission in Homestead, in Miami-Dade County, wearing the colorful ropes that adorn the waists of Vodou practitioners at such gatherings in Haiti.[8] Margarita Mooney (2009: 246), who conducted extensive fieldwork among Haitian Catholics in Miami, Montreal, and Paris, likewise observes that "Vodou practice at my field sites was relatively weak."

A concerted effort to invigorate the religion in Miami occurred in 2004, when Max Beauvoir, Vodou's most public leader in Haiti, visited Miami for the first annual "Vodou-Fest," which was inaugurated during the bicentennial of Haitian independence.[9] For Beauvoir, participation in the event was an opportunity to demonstrate that Vodou "carries with it a vision of the human at the center of the universe, among stars, animals, plants and among each other"; it is a religion through which believers "solve their daily problems" (in James-Johnson 2004).

Beauvoir, who led the ceremonies at Botanica Halouba on this occasion, is the most recognizable figure in the religion, overseeing Temple Yehwe in Mariani, Haiti, while residing much of the year in Washington, DC. On other occasions, *oungan* and *manbo* rent out space to hold communal ceremonies. Manbo Margaret Armand describes one such gathering in the Fort Lauderdale Women's Club: "To see all these *manbo* dancing around beneath the portraits of Confederate women must have had them rolling around in their graves!"[10]

Manbo like Armand have recently made efforts to educate the local community about Vodou and to combat popular American misconceptions about the religion. Manbo Carol de Lynch for instance, opened a public temple in 2004, Lakou Hounto in Little Haiti, "to encourage our fellow compatriots, as well of the citizens of the world's interest in the sacred art of Voodoo as well as Haitian culture in general" (de Lynch 2003). To celebrate the Haitian bicentennial, de Lynch and Llera launched "Vodou-Fest," with the hopes of holding it annually. Following a panel discussion entitled "Holistic and Traditional Healing" and a large ceremony at Botanica Halouba in Little Haiti, Vodou-Fest culminated with a celebration and concert in downtown Miami's Bayfront Park. For this occasion, a section of the picturesque park, nestled between downtown Miami and Biscayne Bay, was transformed into a veritable *abitasyon* (lit. "habitation"). An *abitasyon* (sometimes called *lakou* [yard], or "family compound") is an expanse of land consisting of various sacred trees, each one the dwelling place of a particular lwa, complete with offerings placed at their trunks. A number of tables offered a variety of Haitian crafts, and *manbo* were on hand for readings. For Llera, the point of Vodou-Fest is to demonstrate that:

> Vodou is an everyday way of life. It's a very promising way of life. To me, this is the only thing we have left after so many centuries of misery. You have everything you need in this culture . . . . We're going to do a special ceremony for Agoueh [Agwe], who is the god of the ocean. Because most of the Haitians came here by boat, it's symbolic to thank the ocean. After all, this passage . . . was so hard for everyone who took it. (Sick 2004)[11]

Aside from Vodou-Fest and the few quasi-public temples in the city, Vodou in Miami is largely a home-based religion, with altars erected in practitioners' houses, where *oungan* and *manbo* visit to preside over occasional ceremonies. Often *oungan*'s and *manbo*'s homes double as makeshift sanctuaries for small communal ceremonies, like Alisma's does for Societe Linto Roi. Jacqueline Charles (2003) richly describes the home of Little Haiti Oungan Clotaire Bazile:

> The door swings open, and for a split second, the living room resembles a blessed sanctuary. Flowers, flaming candles and various depictions of Jesus and the Virgin Mary adorn an altar. A child-size statue of St. Lazarus greets you at the threshold. As you stare at St. Lazarus, a kindly old man with crutches, something catches your eye. Just below the table bearing the Catholic saint, like an oversized Smirnoff bottle, partly shrouded in a flaming red rag. Inside is the Haitian moonshine, *kleren*, steeped with weeks-old red peppers.

Because the Magic City is built on a swamp, Bazile's house, like most houses in Miami, has no basement. Compared to other cities in the Haitian diaspora, this is something of a disadvantage for Vodouists in Miami, as basements serve well as temples for Vodouists in places such as New York and Paris, where Vodou also thrives in the devotion of many Haitian immigrants, often quite literally underground (Béchacq 2010; Brown 1991).

As with Santería in Miami, which functions in exile largely without the *casas de santo* (spirit houses) that serve the faithful as temples in parts of Cuba, Vodou's lifeline in the Magic City is the botanica, or religious goods store. In a real sense, Cuban Santera/os (practitioners of Santería) blazed trails in Miami that allowed Vodou to take on a more public face in the diaspora, as Haitians adopted the botanica culture from Cubans, much as they have adopted the storefront church culture from African Americans. Most Haitian botanicas are either run by or are affiliated with a *manbo* or *oungan* who offer divination services, in addition to retailing a plethora of herbs and ritual paraphernalia. Generally botanicas also feature a small room in the back that serves as a divination chamber, and a few actually have fonts for ritual herbal baths or contain sanctuaries for communal drumming ceremonies.

Catering to Miami's estimated 100,000 *oricha* (spirit) devotees and 25,000 Vodou practitioners, whether Haitian or Cuban, botanicas are the most visible testimony to the growth and vivacity of African-derived religion in Miami and elsewhere in the United States. In them one can purchase anything from cowry beads and statues of Catholic saints to herbs and aerosol cans of perfume that, once sprayed on the body, are supposed to strongly attract desired lovers or ward off evil or reverse its effects. Lammoglia (2001) has demonstrated that there are more than one hundred Cuban botanicas in Miami, and that their pro-liferation has been consistent with the growth of the Cuban exile com-munity. This is even more striking when one considers that until the Castro regime recently opened a botanica in Havana geared to tourists, such stores were nonexistent on the island. Likewise, such stores are relatively unknown in Haiti (we know of only one in Port-au-Prince), although in Miami there are roughly twenty-five Haitian botanicas, half of them in Little Haiti. Thanks in part to this proliferation of Hai-tian and Cuban botanicas, Miami has emerged as an important "nodal point," to use Kamari Clarke's (1999) term, in the globalization of tradi-tional African religious culture. Historically, cities like Havana, Cuba, Port-au-Prince, and Salvador da Bahia have served as the geographic rudders and motors of this remarkable transformation of once-local tribal African spirit and ancestor cults into a world religion, despite its practitioners' having faced some of the most brutal persecution in history (Olupona and Rey 2008). And over the last twenty-five years, Cuban and Haitian botanicas have been instrumental in Miami's emer-gence as such a nodal point.

Testimony to Vodou's central concern with healing, and tits cen-tral place in the Haitian religious collusio, herbs are the most popular products retailed in Miami's Haitian botanicas. Nadine Louissaint, a health services coordinator at a prominent Haitian community-based organization in Little Haiti, Sant La (The Center, santla.org), has doc-umented more than thirty herbs that are commonly used by Haitians with whom she works: *fey langichat*, for instance, is used for colds, *fey korosòl* and *fey pwa kongo* for stomach aches, and so on (Louissaint 2002). Many immigrants are wary of approaching medical clinics or hospitals out of fear of deportation; many are uninsured and unable to afford clinics, so undocumented immigrants—whether Vodou practi-tioners or not—turn to botanicas for herbal remedies and for mental health services. Mercedes Cros Sandoval (2006: 143) notes that among

Cuban immigrants in Miami, "eliciting supernatural guidance for the diagnosis of illness and the prescription of treatment" and functioning "to assist in the solution of life's problems, such as the resolution of family conflicts, job-related struggles, preserving or restoring health, and providing help in making decisions about weddings, journeys, business ventures, love affairs, and other matters" parallel this trend.[12] The contrast in the receptions in Miami for Woody Marc Edouard and Carlos Cancio Portel illustrates that legal immigration makes a difference for Cuban Santero/as, whereas one must include the difficulty of attaining a legal immigration status on any list of struggles facing many Haitian Vodouists in the United States. That said, health concerns, along with the quest for *chans* and seeing to inherited devotional obligations to the *mystè*, remain the principle reasons why many Haitians in Miami practice Vodou. And healing remains the main draw for occasional incursions into the religion among other Haitians who do not consider themselves to be Vodouists.

Wagner St. Pierre's story is a case in point. A thirty-two-year-old undocumented Little Haiti resident, St. Pierre became terribly ill with fever and weight loss in February of 2001, causing him to lose his "under-the-table" job as a dockworker. Recalling the successful cures of his grandmother, a *medsin fey* (lit. leaf doctor;/herbalist) in rural Haiti, Wagner took the advice of a neighbor and visited a botanica for a reading, which prescribed a series of baths and teas. "I was very sick, I got no insurance, and I don't trust doctors in Miami," he explained. "So I went to an *oungan* on NE 2nd Avenue, who took pity on me because I was so sick, and he told me I could pay him when I found another job." After four cleansings in the botanica's back room, along with a month of drinking teas made by the *oungan*, not to mention a steady diet of boiled fish and white rice, Wagner felt well enough that he landed a new job washing dishes at a local chain restaurant. When asked if he considers himself a Vodouists, Wagner replied philosophically, "Only God can heal you; God empowered the leaves and the *oungan* learned from Vodou traditions in Haiti, so God is in Vodou. I'm not into Vodou, I just respect God wherever he functions."[13] Even though he is neither a regular churchgoer nor a registered parishioner, when he does attend Mass, Wagner finds himself in the pews of Notre Dame d'Haiti Catholic Church.

"You Have to Be Catholic to Serve the Lwa"

There is a Haitian proverb that "You have to be Catholic to serve the spirits" (*"Fòk ou katolik pou sevi lwa yo"*). Though nowhere as widespread as in Haiti, the phenomenon of Vodouists performing devotions to the lwa at Catholic churches does occur in Miami. Sometimes divination will prescribe such devotions at churches consecrated to saints conflated with relevant lwa, and other times the lwa themselves request Communion, which their *sevitè* (devotees) can receive for them by carrying one of the requesting lwa's sacred stones in a pocket while attending mass (Métraux 1972: 332). On other occasions, Vodou rituals are scheduled according to the Catholic liturgical calendar, a tradition that extends into the diaspora and dictates when vows to particular lwa should be fulfilled both communally and personally (see chaps. 2 and 3). Guerda Joseph, for instance, is a North Miami Vodouist who attends Mass at Our Lady of Perpetual Help Catholic Church in Opa Locka, in northern Miami-Dade County every year on June 27, the Feast of Perpetual Help. She thanks the lwa Ezili Freda for helping her make it to Miami on a leaky wooden sailboat more than twenty years ago: "It is thanks to Freda that I am here; and I will never miss a chance to thank her and Perpetual each year at her feast. It is they who were with me on the boat, and I owe my life to them."[14]

Thus, for several decades, Santeros and Vodouist have occasionally made ritual use of some of Miami's Catholic churches, cemeteries, and shrines, though much more discreetly than they had done in their respective homelands. This is especially true of ornate churches or ones dedicated to saints who are assimilated with popular oricha or lwa, where devotees sometimes render homage and offerings to the originally African spirits (although some Catholic priests and even ushers do eject from their churches anyone wearing *eleke*, devotional beads for the oricha). Behind the Shrine of La Virgen de la Caridad del Cobre, for instance, one can often find Santeros casting yellow flowers into Biscayne Bay as gifts for Ochun, the water orisha with whom Caridad, Cuba's patron saint, is so strongly assimilated. On September 8, Caridad's feast day, Santería initiates dressed entirely in white can be found among the multitude of the faithful either at their patron saint's shrine or at the American Airlines Arena.[15] Yellow flowers and garments are in also abundance at the Shrine and the Arena, adorning even those who don't realize this to be Ochun's and not Caridad's color.

While researching Cuban devotion at the Shrine of Caridad, Thomas Tweed (1997: 59) noted the occasional Haitian visitor, rightly explaining their presence in terms of both Catholic and Vodouist devotional service:

> Haitians have their own official day at the shrine too . . . and have a small but noticeable presence inside the shrine and, especially, at the annual festivals. That makes sense for two reasons: first, there are direct connections between Our Lady of Charity and the creole religion of Haitians, and second, as one form of Mary, the Cuban Virgin invites all Haitians with Marian devotion to petition her in their need. . . . Haitians connect Our Lady of Charity, and the African orisha with whom she is associated, with several female spirits who belong to the group called the Ezili. Practitioners of Vodou . . . associate Ezili with fertility and love, just as Catholic Cubans view Our Lady of Charity and followers of Santería imagine her African counterpart, Ochún.

Missing from Tweed's account is any mention of the long-standing devotion to Our Lady of Charity in Haiti, a popular cult there and which has a history of over one hundred years, especially at her church in the Port-au-Prince neighborhood of Carrefour-Feuilles, one of the Haitian capital's most popular Catholic churches (Rey 1998). Although it is perfectly feasible that Haitians visit the Caridad Shrine in Miami to perform Vodouist devotions for Ezili in her form as Lasyrenn (the maritime/mermaid representation of the lwa Ezili with whom Caridad is often assimilated in Vodou), it is more likely that it is Catholicism rather than Vodou that draws most Haitians to the shrine. For years Archbishop Wenski, while serving as pastor of Notre Dame d'Haiti, organized bus trips to the shrine every September 8 for the feast day of Caridad. And the Cuban Catholic priest who is most identified with the shrine, Msgr. Augustín Roman, has long included outreach to Haitians as part of his ministry.[16] We need to stress that *Catholic* devotion draws at least as many people to Catholic churches in Haiti as Vodouist devotion, and this is even more so the case in Miami. Tweed's speculation that some Haitians at the shrine must be Vodouists is certainly plausible, but whether their address is "to the Virgin herself or to the loa which to him the statue of the Virgin evokes or represents," as Laënnec Hurbon (1974: 104) notes more generally about Haitian Marianism, would be very difficult to say. The one Haitian quoted by Tweed refers to Mary, at any rate, and not Lasyrenn or another of the Ezili lwa. The question of devotional intent aside, we have known quite a few *botpipel* over the years who made a point to visit Caridad's church in Port-au-Prince before embarking on their journeys, whether they perceive of her as Lasyrenn, the Virgin Mary, or both, and it would make perfect sense for them to go to her shrine in Miami to say thanks for aiding them making it across the water.

Another of Haiti's most popular Catholic churches is the Shrine of St. Philomena in the northern coastal village of Bord de Mer de Limonade, an hour's drive east of Cape Haitian. It is also is one of the most openly syncretic Catholic religious sites in Haiti, as the saint for whom the shrine was built, a third-century virgin martyr, is assimilated with Lasyrenn (as is Caridad, coincidentally). Since the construction of its latest iteration in 1953, the Shrine of St. Philomena in Bord de Mer, which was first established in 1873, has become a top-choice destination in Haiti's thriving pilgrimage culture. A brackish lagoon behind the shrine serves as a natural baptismal fount and a bath for ritual purification. While masses are being celebrated biweekly in the shrine, *manbo* and *oungan* orchestrate Vodou rituals on the edge of the lagoon, right where the ruins of a retreat house stand. All that remains of the edifice are its foundation and parts of two walls, one of which runs into the water. Candles burn in their nooks and crannies, and all kinds of offerings in zinc bowls to the saint and the lwa are left on the banks just below. People strip down to their underpants to undergo purification baths performed by Vodou priestesses, while others sacrifice chickens and goats, and leave other offerings for the *mystè* in the churchyard. Once mass ends, the drumming begins beneath a tree near the beach, which has served as a sacred site for local in Vodou for as long as anyone can remember. These festive scenes repeat themselves twice weekly, as hundreds of people flock to the village to keep vows to the feisty saint. Around September 5, the main pilgrimage event draws tens of thousands to the normally sleepy village, many of them from Miami and elsewhere in the Haitian diaspora (O'Neil and Rey 2012).

Much to their delight, some Vodouists would discover in Miami a Shrine of Saint Philomena, a Traditionalist Catholic church not recognized by the Archdiocese of Miami (see chap. 2). Most of the faithful who gather at the shrine are either unaware of or unconcerned with this fact, for they are quite fond of the shrine's pastor, Fr. Timothy Hopkins, who takes his role as exorcist seriously and who frequently grants requests to bless Haitians' homes and cars. Vodouists also find a mysticism relative to their own in the Latin of the Mass and the abundance of statues in the shrine, as many Vodou ceremonies open with Catholic prayers (sometimes said in Latin), and most Vodou temples are replete with images of Catholic saints. A former Episcopal priest who was later ordained a Catholic priest in Rome, Hopkins served for several years as a missionary in Tanzania, which imbued in him a sincere appreciation for the vivacity and depth of African spirituality. He would discover this anew in his Haitian congregants in Miami, some of whom practice Vodou and appreciate the relatively blind eye that he turns to the occasional signs of Vodouist rituals in and around the shrine. Hopkins once described for us a service during which two Haitians gradually undressed in a pew, changed into white garments, and doused themselves in oil. It is not uncommon, he added, to find all kinds of ritual offerings for the lwa and oricha in and outside of his church.[17] Perhaps unbeknownst to Father Hopkins, a Vodou priest named Max has performed a protective ritual (*pwen pwotèj*) for the shrine's main statue of its namesake to protect it from sorcerers or other individuals with sacrilegious intent. As Deborah O'Neil and Terry Rey (2012: 179) explain, Max arrived to his devotion to St. Philomena after she had appeared to him

> in dreams and called him to worship at her church in Miami. He found the Shrine of St. Philomena in the phone book and has attended Mass there regularly ever since. Max splits his time between Miami and Port-au-Prince, where he keeps a temple, and each September he makes a pilgrimage to Bodmè for the annual Feast Day of St. Philomena.

Thus have certain Catholic churches and shrines in Miami become spiritually desirable sites for personal Vodouist devotions, paralleling a phenomenon that is integral to Santería in the Magic City as well. And, although the copious infusion of Vodou at Catholic feast-day celebrations at churches is absent in Miami, Catholic sacred sites in the diaspora are indeed important sanctuaries where Vodouists quietly leave offerings to the *mystè* to bolster their *chans* in life in general, or in the American legal system in particular.

Vodou Trial: The Lwa in Miami Courts of Justice

Ignorance about Vodou abounds in the United States, where the religion is widely misunderstood, misrepresented, and maligned. Equally to blame for this are sensationalist Hollywood films, such as *White Zombie, I Walked with a Zombie*, and *The Serpent and the Rainbow*, and the high-profile use of the word "voodoo" as an adjective intended to imply stupid, diabolical, and wrong, as in George H. W. Bush's derision of Ronald Reagan's national financial plan as "voodoo economic policy" (Shogan 1980).[18] Vodou is *not* about cannibalistic "zombies" and or pins stuck in "voodoo dolls," but it is primarily about empowering people, enabling them to commune with divinity, healing them, defending them against sorcery (black magic), and influencing supernatural forces to increase the likelihood of favorable outcomes to events and/or situations, be it the lottery or hearings in immigration court—salvation goods of the highest order indeed! It is thus no surprise that Vodou, though to a lesser extent than Santería, has made its way into Miami's courts of law.[19] Just as the American judicial system itself uses a Bible or requires witnesses raise their right hands in order to supernaturally influence them to speak the truth, so too do Vodouists seek the support of the spirits, ancestors, and charms to help assure what Vodouists more broadly refer to as *chans*; for the lack of *chans*, as Brown (1991: 296) notes, is "the broadest diagnostic category in the lexicon of the Vodou healing system."

Janitors at certain Miami courthouses regularly scour the premises to remove a variety of ritual objects left by Santera/o or Vodouist plaintiffs and defendants or their supporters to spiritually influence verdicts. Carcasses of sacrificed chickens, bundles of leaves, statues of saints, and all kinds of bowls, plates, candles, foodstuffs, coins, and bottles of perfume are among the daily intake. Haitian and Cuban workers generally recuse themselves from such cultic cleanup duty, though; having been reared in lands where sorcery abounds, they are loath to come into contact with such items for fear of falling victims to some rene-gade hex. At the downtown Richard Gerstein Justice Building, the jani-torial crew responsible for picking up such offerings is known as "the Voodoo Squad," as Larry Libowitz (2003) explains: "Black magic [*sic*] is rarely found at the federal courthouse, but is more common outside the Richard Gerstein Justice Building, the state criminal courthouse. A janitorial crew dubbed 'the Voodoo Squad' regularly removes sacrificial chickens, roosters and goats from the grounds." Even at Florida Interna-tional University it is not uncommon for offerings to oricha and lwa to be found in the library during exam week. A 2001 exhibit of altars from African and African diasporic religions at the university art museum, meanwhile, attracted some Vodouists who were sent there by *manbo* or *oungan* for devotional purposes (Rey forthcoming).[20]

There are occasions in Miami when Haitians take advantage of the ignorance and fear of Vodou as sorcery in the city's broader Caribbean community. For example, on February 28, 2002, and on several days prior, Marie Jean-Philippe, a middle-aged Haitian woman and union organizer who frequently appears in public with a rosary tied to her wrist, allegedly placed glasses of water and pennies in ritual fashion in the room where workers at a the St. Francis Nursing Home were to vote on whether to join the Service Employees International Union (SEIU). Although a few years earlier, in 1995, these tactics had failed to gain an electoral victory for the SEIU, this time they would be successful. After carefully studying the circumstances and being convinced that union representatives were indeed manipulating Vodou to frighten employ-ees to vote pro-union in the 1995 case, Leslie Desmangles testified as an expert witness:

> The woman was a union organizer and a recognized *manbo*. Her hus-band was thought to have extraordinary powers and could inflict evil on people. During the time that there was a campaign to join the union, he would stand on the other side of the street and watch the workers go in and out of work at different shifts. Some workers said that they each found a coin on their cars which they considered a *wanga* [hex] that warned them of impending danger to their persons or to members of their family if they did not vote to join the union. On the day that the workers went to the poles, he was seen standing all day across the

street. Moreover, the workers also believed that he could see through walls or faraway places without actually leaving his actual location. When the time came from them to vote, many claimed that they felt intimidated and voted against their will to join the union. . . . The workers had been coerced, even threatened by the union, before and during the time of the election. If you recall, the union organizer's husband was reputed to be a fierce *boko* [sorcerer] who frequented the parking [lot] of the facility and stood across the way from the entrance of the facility, watching the employees at the end of every shift.[21]

In the 2002 case, meanwhile, many employees at the St. Francis Nursing Home indicated that they had seen ritual paraphernalia, such as stacked coins, shells, and glasses of water, in the days leading up to the vote, and several indicated that they felt intimidated and thought it best to vote for the union rather than risk supernatural retribution from the *manbo*. As one Jamaican woman claimed, "You don't mess with Haitians when they do Vodou."[22]

The union won the election, which the nursing home disputed, claiming that the SEIU used employees' fears of Vodou as part of its intimidation tactics to influence the vote. The National Labor Relations Hearing Board found enough credence in the nursing home's complaint to hold a hearing in Miami in April 2002. But despite the testimony of several employees claiming to have indeed been intimidated to vote for the SEIU by Jean-Philippe's machinations, the board sided with the union. An appeal was later rejected in federal court.

In a much graver example, Marie Jean-Baptiste likewise hoped to exploit local ignorance about Vodou to contest an attempted murder charge filed against her by federal prosecutors. A fifty-year-old Haitian immigrant and life-long practitioner of Vodou, she so feared being the target of a hex (*wanga*) that she was driven to kill—or so she and her attorneys claimed in a Miami federal court in 2003. As she had evidently explained to her attorneys, Jean-Baptiste believed that her ex-lover's new mistress had cast a *wanga* on her, so she hatched a plan to have the woman killed and her ex-lover's tongue cut out, a plan that was not disputed at the trial. Jean-Baptiste allegedly had been receiving, free of charge, substantial amounts of cocaine from her erstwhile boyfriend, a high-level South Florida drug dealer, which she in turn retailed at a handsome profit. Now shunned out of romance and free cocaine because of his new flame, Jean-Baptiste was not about to go down without a fight, and a particularly gruesome one at that. To set the scheme in motion, she reached out to her daughter's boyfriend, himself a convict serving jail time for dealing cocaine, to put her in touch with someone who could carry out her plan to put a definitive end to the love triangle. Unbeknownst to her, however, the convict happened to be keen on buying the good graces of federal prosecutors in order to have his sentence shortened. And so, thanks to his subsequent cooperation, detectives surreptitiously recorded their phone calls, thus producing hours upon hours of taped conversations in which Jean-Baptiste thought she had successfully arranged to hire a hit-man to murder the woman and sever her former boyfriend's tongue. In lieu of a cash payment, the hit-man was to keep all but one of the more than twenty-five kilos of cocaine that he was sure to find in her ex-boyfriend's house; the other kilo would be for her. The hit-man was in reality an undercover police officer, who duly arrested Jean-Baptiste at their first meeting in person. In all of several hundred pages of recorded conversation between the two, there is not a single mention of Vodou.

There was a great deal of discussion about Vodou at Jean-Baptiste's trial, however, as her defense hinged upon the novel argument that her boyfriend's new lover had cast a *wanga* on her. This, she claimed, drove her to such irrational fear that she did not know what to do, in part because she could not find a reliable *manbo* or *oungan* in Miami to defend her from the *wanga*. Adding even more drama to the affair, during one pre-trial hearing Jean-Baptiste, dressed in an orange prison jumpsuit and handcuffed, either feigned or genuinely went into spirit possession, hissing and writhing on the floor as if "mounted" by Danbala, the serpent lwa. The hearing was postponed after paramedics strapped her to a gurney and wheeled her off, treating her for a seizure.

In the end, prosecutors managed to establish convincingly that individual Vodouists are not routinely driven to murder those whom they suspect of sorcery, and that that there are in fact very reliable *manbos* and *oungans* in Miami who could have helped Jean-Baptiste negotiate a truly traditional ritual response to protect herself from the alleged *wanga*, and that the defense argument hinged on numerous fallacies. The jury was convinced that this story was truly about cocaine and jealousy, not sorcery and Vodou, and on June 20, 2003, Marie Jean-Baptiste was found guilty of attempted murder and several other charges.[23]

On a lighter though still stressful legalistic note, many Haitians in Miami find themselves distressingly entangled in complex immigration proceedings, making the threat of deportation foreboding, to say the least. It is common for Vodouists to seek assistance from the spirit world to gain *chans* in their quests to establish that they are *worthy* of residency or citizenship in the United States. For one example, Luckner Thomas's adolescence was beset by difficulties since arriving in Miami as a nine-year-old in 1984.[24] Born in Haiti and brought to the Bahamas at a very young age, he is one of a growing Miami community of Haitians born and raised in the Bahamas who speak Creole poorly, if at all, and who have never even been to Haiti. Unfortunately, as an adult Thomas found himself a member of another growing Miami immigrant community: detainees at the Krome Detention Center facing deportation to Haiti for criminal offenses.

Raised by an illiterate aunt, herself an undocumented immigrant, Thomas never went through the process of applying for citizenship, even though he is a longtime legal resident in the United States. By the age of fourteen, he had become involved with a violent Little Haiti street gang and eventually began dealing crack cocaine. Before the age of twenty he developed severe epilepsy and schizophrenia. By 2001 Thomas had been in and out of the criminal justice system but was acquitted of the most serious charge leveled against him: grand theft auto. In March 2002, agents from the U.S. Immigration and Naturalization Service arrested him and brought him to Krome, where he spent more than a year before facing deportation. His attorney, Mitchell Cohen, filed an appeal, thus extending Thomas's stay at the infamous detention center in the Everglades for another few months.

Vodou would play a decisive role in Thomas's appeal. Although Thomas spoke no Creole, had no family in Haiti, and suffered from a serious mental illness, the U.S. government aggressively sought to deport him. Cohen argued that episodes triggered by his epilepsy and schizophrenia might be misinterpreted in a Haitian prison either as some kind of threatening spiritual possession or belligerent behavior and lead to his torture at the hands of prison guards, something that Thomas himself indeed feared greatly. In a landmark ruling, the

U.S. Department of Justice's Board of Immigration Appeals ruled that Thomas's deportation should be overturned on the basis of the UN Charter against Torture, to which the United States is a signatory:

> The respondent was born in Haiti and fears that if he returns to Haiti he will be subject to an indefinite detention due to his prison record. He further fears that he will be viewed as demonic on account of his epileptic condition. . . . We find that the respondent has satisfied his burden of proof in these proceedings for a grant of deferral of removal. . . . We believe that the existence of the respondent's mental condition makes it more likely than not that he would be severely punished for non-standard behavior, and may likely result in a longer period of incarceration. Moreover, we believed, based on the evidence of conditions in Haitian prisons in general, that it is more likely than not that the treatment that the respondent would experience in Haiti would constitute torture. . . . There is sufficient evidence in the record to establish that it is more likely than not that the respondent will be subjected to torture on his return. (U.S. Dept. of Justice 2003)

Terry Rey testified at the hearing as an expert witness on human rights in Haiti, on Haitian prisons, and on Haitian religious culture, recounting a number of cases from his fieldwork in Haiti in the 1990s of lynch mobs attacking and sometimes killing people suspected being possessed by demonic spirits, over and above his observations of conditions in Haitian prisons. This background information helped the board reach an informed and, in our estimation, just decision to remove Thomas's deportation order and indicate that he was *worthy* of political asylum in the United States.

Transnational Maji: Vodou Rebounding from Haiti to Miami and Back

In one of the most celebrated books about Vodou, Karen McCarthy Brown sheds helpful light on certain ties that Mama Lola, a Haitian Vodou priestess in Brooklyn, New York, maintains in Haiti. For Mama Lola, like many Haitian Vodou priests and priestesses in the diaspora, an occasional trip to the homeland is required to "take care of some ritual obligations" and especially to acquire herbs and other items needed for her practice in New York (Brown 1991: 169). Alourdes, as the priestess is also called, had already been living for quite some time in New York before returning to Haiti for her initiation. Yet, despite the fact that "Alourdes' commitments to the family of spirits are grounded in commitments to a human family, most of who still live in Haiti," Mama Lola actually returns quite infrequently (ibid., 180), at least up until the early 1990s before Brown's book made her the most famous Vodou priestess in the world. The only trip to Haiti described in the book, incidentally, was one suggested and financed by the Brown herself. During that trip, moreover, "For the first time in a decade, Alourdes' family spirits were awakened and called to the table" (ibid.). Karen Richman's research (2005: 24), meanwhile, indicates that Haitian Vodouists in South Florida, being much closer to the homeland, return more frequently for ritual purposes than their diasporic compatriots in northeastern cities like New York and Boston. Therefore, Vodouists are not obliged to establish alternative or replacement shrines for the lwa in South Florida, and our own research in Miami concurs with this. In any case, whatever the frequency or occasion, the effectiveness of many forms of spiritual work, to Haitians, is more promising if done in Haiti than anywhere else.[25]

The proximity of Miami to Haiti also allows for some priests and priestesses to reside chiefly in Florida while overseeing temples in Haiti. One prominent Vodou temple in Leogane, for instance, Sosyete La Deesse De La Mer (Society of the Goddess of the Sea), is run by a forty-two-year-old *manbo* named La Deesse De La Mer, with help from a Miami-raised Haitian *oungan*, Loray Gronde Bon Hougan. According to her Facebook page, La Deesse De La Mer was born in Leogane but currently lives in Miami, where she was educated at Central High School, class of 1983, and Miami-Dade Community College. Founded by the *manbo* in 1997, Sosyete's mission is one of teaching and service to anyone wishing to learn about "Traditional Haitian Vodou," and it offers spiritual assistance in solving problems and matters pertaining to "Love, Marriage, Business, Luck, Health, Court matters, Kanzo (Initiation into Vodou) Spiritual Wedding, Prepare Altar for your Ancestors. . .." The Facebook page also includes many photographs of the Sosyete's temple, altars, and ceremonies, along with video clips of rituals. Of the iconography representative of the lwa, those of Lasyrenn are posted most often, giving the indication that she is both Goddess of the Sea and the patron lwa of the Sosyete. Sosyete's emblem includes an image of the Candomblé orisha Yemaya, the Brazilian incarnation of the West African Mami Wata divinity (a mermaid spirit who in Vodou is Lasyrenn), standing before a rainbow of colors beneath the name of the congregation. Its "CEO," the *manbo*, joined Facebook in July 2011; judging by the relatively large amount of content now on the page, one can say that she has been very active on the Internet ever since. Meanwhile, at least one Vodouist who was initiated at Sosyete La Deesse De La Mar has gone on to found another Vodou temple in New Zealand (kiwimojo.com).

Marie-Carmel Fontus is another Miami-based Haitian *manbo* who oversees a temple in Haiti.[26] She also owns a botanica in North Miami, Botanika Mawu-Lisa, to which the temple is closely tied. Living in Miami as opposed to New York or Montreal makes the return to Haiti more affordable, which is certainly one reason why Marie-Carmel is in Haiti as often as three weeks out of every two months. Her reasons for returning are similar to those of Mama Lola, although more often Marie-Carmel is sent to Haiti on behalf of a client to perform some *maji* there instead of in Miami, where it would certainly be less effective. While in Haiti, she also tends to ritual obligations at her family's Miragoane temple and at shrines on family land in the surrounding plain and hills.

Like many Haitian botanicas in Miami, Botanika Mawu-Lisa bespeaks an important form of adaptation of Vodou to the Miami religious field. Although virtually unknown in Haitian Catholicism or Vodou, the largest statues in Marie-Carmel's botanica are of St. Barbara and St. Lazarus. These saints are conflated in Santería with the orichas Shango and Babaluaye respectively, among the most important orichas in that religion, and their statues are found in prominent places in every Cuban botanica in Miami. Haitian botanicas also retail soup tureens, which likewise feature centrally in Santería but not in Vodou. But these symbols and ritual items are far more than mere guises to make Vodouist botanicas more palatable to the Miami public; many *manbos* and *oungans* in Miami count Cubans and other Hispanics among their clientele, and the presence of these saints in Haitian botanicas lends both legitimacy and spiritual power to the premises and their clerics. It may be that the immigration experience of Haitian practitioners will one day produce new lwa cults in Haitian Vodou, if it hasn't already. Or, at

Figure 4.1. A Vodou priest stands next to a statue of St. Lazarus in a North Miami botan-
ica. Largely unknown in Vodou in Haiti, St. Lazarus, who is central to the longer-standing
Miami religion of Santería, has recently become integral to diasporic Haitian Vodou in
Miami. Photo by Jerry Berndt.

the very least the experience will add new features to old cults, such as
the shamrocks for Danbala at Societe Linto Roi.

In August 2001, Sylvain, a twenty-eight-year-old Haitian American
man, visited Botanika Mawu-Lisa on the advice of a friend. A lapsed
Catholic who knew very little about Vodou, Sylvain was madly in
love with his girlfriend, to whom he was soon hoping to propose. He
became encouraged to have some *maji* done to ensure her acceptance,
and so he went to see Marie-Carmel and paid her to divine for him.
He was invited to sit in the small divination chamber in the back of
Botanika Mawu-Lisa, across a small table from the *manbo*, who sat
beneath a number of old photographs of her ancestors, including one
faded portrait of a rather dignified-looking Haitian military officer, and
lithographs of Catholic saints. She said a series of prayers and incanta-
tions, asked Sylvain a number of questions about his and his girlfriend's
background, and began to lay in four rows a series of playing cards on

the table. After about thirty minutes of meditating on the cards, chain-smoking all the while, Marie-Carmel reached the verdict that she could do *maji* to help Sylvain, but that it would be most powerful if done in Miragoane rather than in Miami. Sylvain paid her $50 for the divination and made an appointment with Marie-Carmel to return the following week to further discuss the matter. On his way out the door, Marie-Carmel reminded him to leave an offering in the plate at the foot of the statue of St. Lazarus and implored him to pay very careful attention to his dreams.

Over the ensuing nights, Sylvain dreamt repeatedly of a large tree and the sound of roosters. Marie-Carmel explained to him that she knew the tree in his dreams and that Sylvain's family spirits were using roosters to summon him to Haiti to make the *maji* work. Finally convinced of this, he arranged to travel to Miragoane with Marie-Carmel, a trip that Sylvain financed entirely. Marie-Carmel told him to be sure to bring his favorite photograph of his girlfriend, or the one that was the best "reflection of her spirit."

The curvy dirt road that leads to Marie-Carmel's Miragoane temple is flanked by powerful expressions of Vodou. Colorful flags (*drapo vodou*) hang from tree limbs indicating the presence of the lwa and the proximity of the temple. There are family tombs on one side, quite large and well kept. Just beyond them looms a huge *mapou* tree (*Ceiba pentenda*) that "belongs to" Marie-Carmel's mother, herself a highly respected Miragoane *manbo* who actually owns Botanika Mawu-Lisa.[27] At the very moment when Marie-Carmel pointed to the tree and told Sylvain that it was the one that had appeared in his dreams, a rooster crowed.

The entire temple compound is surrounded by a cement block wall roughly twelve feet in height, and a foreboding red-iron sliding gate is the only way in and out. The compound is spacious, roughly 150 x 150 feet. There are some small trees and herbs growing along a cement path that leads off to the right to the tombs of several ancestors. Off to one corner is a large wooden cross, painted black, and near the very center of the yard stands the *poto mitan*. Inside of Marie-Carmel's Miragoane temple are three rooms: the front smaller room is mainly a shrine to Ezili-Kawoulo (her family's most important inherited lwa). In another corner sits a large icon of Our Lady of Mount Carmel, above which hangs ritual clothing worn whenever Ezili appears in the body of a possessed devotee. There is a bottle of rum on the altar, along with plastic flowers before a statue of the Virgin Mary and a machete wrapped in a Haitian flag behind her. Another room, adorned with a multitude of lithographs and statues of Catholic saints, consists only of a bed, where Sylvain would sleep during his three-day stay. The third small room is for ritual baths, containing a square tub built into the floor with cement blocks. The tub is about three feet deep, three feet wide, and five feet long. There is no bed in this room nor are there imagines or icons of saints, only shelves holding an abundance of jars with powders, herbs, and potions, along with plates holding offerings and forms of *maji* in the works.

As reflected in the five reasons outlined below, Marie-Carmel visits Haiti for "spiritual obligations" similar to those of Mama Lola, although for a variety of reasons (Miami's geographic proximity to Haiti versus New York's being one of them) Marie-Carmel comes much more frequently:

1. To tend to the temple and its clients during her mother's extended stays in Guadeloupe, Martinique, or France, where she has many clients and followers (her mother was in France during our visit);
2. To perform ritual offerings and ensure the upkeep of shrines on family land in and around Miragoane;
3. To get herbs and ritual paraphernalia to bring back to the Miami botanica for sale and for her practice there;
4. For special feast day celebrations or services for people close to her, like her goddaughter's approaching baptism;
5. And to do *maji* for clients in Miami who either come with her to Miragoane or ask her to do "work" for them in Haiti, which is more likely to be effective there than if performed in Miami.

As retailing herbs, and healing with them, is the backbone of her botanica in Miami, reason #3 features in all of Marie-Carmel's trips to Haiti. Some of the herbs she grows herself in the Miragoane temple yard, and some she pays people to purchase or forage locally, but the majority are bought either in the Carrefour-Dufort market, near Leogane, or in the Port-au-Prince Iron Market. Marie-Carmel listed and summarized the functions of the following herbs that she brought from Haiti to her Miami botanica during this trip in October 2001:

- *Ròv*—for cleansings and for "pwen"
- *Zo devann*—for cleansings
- *Twa Pawòl*—used in baths that bring luck
- *Kapabre*—for healings
- *Wònt*—makes someone else give you something out of shame
- *Simik*—heals various illnesses
- *Bwa Kaka*—makes people recognize their faults
- *Bouziyèt*—makes a wayward lover return to you
- *Rale mene*—makes you attractive to a particular person
- *Respekte Kapitin*—inspires others to respect you
- *Ver-Vin*—used to make a tea that brings calm
- *Presipitè wouj*—used to make a powder for a variety of magical ends.

She then explained that there were many other herbs incorporated into her sacerdotal practice, but these were the ones that are most in demand in Miami, adding, "You can do *maji* with anything."

Reason no. 5 was of course what brought Marie-Carmel and Sylvain to Haiti on their trip together in October 2001. Each day while in Miragoane Marie-Carmel administered Sylvain's bath and made him teas, but the climax of his stay was her creation of *maji* for him. Two days before his departure the *manbo* focused her efforts on this alone, explaining to Sylvain that "this *maji* will make her crazy for you; she will never be able to live without you and will want you like never before . . . with a burning heart." Since several ingredients for this ritual were missing, Marie-Carmel dispatched her sister to acquire more herbs, some stove gas, and three bottles of three-star Barbancourt rum (*twazetwal*). The three hundred dollars that Sylvain had paid for this ritual would remain on an altar until she received signs of positive results. The *manbo* either invests these profits in her practice or donates them to the poor.

Creating the love potion in question was an extremely arduous task: "*Maji sa* [Marie-Carmel sucks her teeth], *l'ap prann tout fòs mwen*" ([Making] this magic [charm, potion, amulet, powder, herbal remedy] is going to take all of my force.)[28] She insisted that photos not be taken of the ritual and that the anthropologists not write about it in too much detail. Obviously, we complied, though, with her blessing, we offer this briefest of descriptions of what was an elaborate and masterful ritual performance: One bottle of rum is left unopened on an inside altar, while some of the other two are poured on the ground for the ancestors. After taking a few swigs from the bottle, Marie-Carmel spits some on her client, pours some into her ears, and then pours the rest into the pot, along with a host of herbs, powders, and other things. She stokes a fire in the temple yard over wood and charcoal, and places the pot thereupon, where it heats for several hours under her careful, prayerful concentration. She chants softly during the entire process, smoking the occasional cigarette. At sunset Marie-Carmel brings the pot into the house, where it will pass the night on the stove simmering over a low flame.

Two days later, Marie-Carmel displays the results, which fizzled inside a Gerber's baby food jar, explaining that "this is what it is going to do to her heart: make it burn for you." She instructs Sylvain to take it back to Miami with him, place it under his bed, and to chant several times his girlfriend's name and say one Hail Mary with her name replacing "Mary" right before going to sleep. She remained in Haiti to tend to other temple business, keeping the photograph to "finish the *maji*."

Figure 4.2. *Maji*, in various stages of development, idles on a shelf in a Haitian botanica in North Miami. Photo by Terry Rey.

Two weeks later Marie-Carmel returned to Miami and called Sylvain to invite him to the botanica. Inside the divination chamber was his girl-friend's photograph leaning against a statue of Our Lady of the Assumption. Sylvain was instructed to leave $75 for the lwa Ezili-Kawoulo and then to take the picture home. It had a series of X's marked on the back with ashes from the fire that had cooked the *maji* in the temple yard back in Miragoane. Before he left, she indicated the precise time and day that he should propose to his girlfriend. He did. They are now happily married with two children.

Besides such situational visits to Haiti to effect *maji* or to heal, sometimes Vodouists must also go there either for initiation or ordination into the priesthood. Over the past twenty years that she has served as a *manbo* in South Florida, Margaret Armand has accompanied "about a dozen" initiands to Haiti. The main purpose of these trips is to locate and visit the *lakou* (temple compound) of the initiands' ancestors. This terrestrial/spiritual transnationalism reflects one of the deepest roots of the religion. As Ira Lowenthal (1985: 275–276) writes about Vodou in rural southern Haiti:

> the land stands as a repository of the past, and provides a vast amphithe-ater not only for ritual performances directly related to that past, but for the playing out, generation after generation, of more mundane, day-to-day existence as well. . . . The very landscape becomes a spatial represen-tation of the past, of the living's relationship to it, and their ties to the gods.

In a word, Vodou's depth of attachment to its homeland is surpassed in world religion perhaps only by Judaism's attachment to Jerusalem and Islam's to Mecca. Because of this, Vodou's evolution in the Haitian diaspora is and will always be decidedly transnational, with people like Sylvain, Marie Carmel, Margaret, and Mama Lola often returning to the earth of the ancestors and spirits in ways that their own enslaved ances-tors never could have returned to *Ginen* (Africa)—physically, at least, for there has long existed in Vodou the belief that upon death part of one's soul can return to Africa.

Vodou in Miami is thus a thoroughly transnational religion, and the lwa are understood to be equally important agents in processes of transnationization, which is perhaps most powerfully reflected in

Duval-Carrié's masterpiece *Migration of the Beasts*, a painting that represents Haitian migrants as Vodou spirits. Surely this is thanks in large part to the remarkable adaptability that the lwa have exhibited across generations of devotees and to their reflection of the lives of their children, their devotees—two realities that have been underscored by some of the most influential scholars of Haitian Vodou. Reflecting upon "the mirroring that goes on between a people and their gods," for instance, Brown (1979: 110) writes of how devotional relationships to the lwa create "a very special sort of language, one especially well suited to handle existential situations" and to "provide the categories of thought that make people and the situations that arise between them thinkable." For thousands of Haitian Vodouists, immigration to Miami has been the central existential situation to which such a language must speak, as reflected here by Richman (2008: 24–25):

> Although they are characterized as ancient, immutable repositories of "African" tradition, the lwa have shown that, like their children, they, too, can adapt to changing conditions of global reproduction. With so many of their children now living "over there" (*lòt bo*), these mobile, transnational African lwa, who have always been travelers in the Haitian imagination, are busier than ever. I once had the opportunity to interview a spirit about her protection of migrants. The female spirit possessed a male ritual leader, who was conducting a healing rite for an absent migrant in the presence of the migrant's parents and me [in Leogane, Haiti]. The spirit, whose name is Ezili Dantò/Our Lady of Lourdes, said to us, "Every three days I am in Miami. I have to keep watch over everything that goes on. Miami is where the core is."[29]

Conclusion

Even as the percentage of Haitians who practice Vodou, whether in the homeland or the diaspora, declines, the religion's appeal as a source of salvation goods, particularly worthiness, healing, *chans*, *maji*, and protection, assures for the religion a healthy future, and it will always remain a cornerstone to the Haitian religious collusio and a side to the Haitian religious triangle of forces, however shortened that side might have recently become. Over the centuries, Vodouists have demonstrated time and again an impressive ability to draw strength from the spirits and the dead to overcome extraordinary challenges, to empower people, and to derive meaning and pride from a national identity to which the religion is undeniably an integral part. For many Haitians in Miami, the migration experience has been fraught with such challenges, which extend far beyond the crossing of the water and the quest for a green card. And yet, many of them have surmounted the challenges, usually inspired and empowered by some form of religion, often Vodou, to contribute to the growing and increasingly secure Haitian community of Miami. As such, Vodou sounds very much as one of the faith traditions that Tweed (2006: 54) might have had in mind when crafting his recent definition of "religions" as "confluences of organic cultural flows that intensify joy and confront suffering by drawing on human and suprahuman forces to make homes and cross boundaries."

We also note that in recent years there has been a resurgence of Haitian pride in Miami, and Vodou has been an important part of this encouraging development, as have the arts, often inspired by the religion. In a city where some Haitian youth once felt such shame of their cultural heritage that they became "cover ups," attempting to pass as African Americans or Jamaicans, a reality that actually drove one adolescent male to suicide upon being "outed" as Haitian, the importance of this shift can hardly be overstated (Stepick 1998: 1). And, though in Haiti Vodouists have been newly targeted for persecution by Evangelical Christians who blame them for the tragic earthquake of January 2010 (McAlister 2012), in Miami the religion, though practiced only by a minority of Haitian immigrants, is at the heart of a Haitian cultural renaissance. As important, Vodou is a wellspring of salvation goods for immigrants in their assertion of worthiness to belong and to thrive in the Magic City.

5

Storefront and Transnational Protestantism in Little Haiti

Harvesting the Gospel in the Haitian Church of the Open Door

Overview

By the mid-1980s, already 40 percent of all Haitian immigrants in Miami were Protestant, sparking an impressive proliferation of storefront churches in Little Haiti. It is likely that today the majority of people in the Haitian diaspora in general are Protestant. Because the religion incorporates far less ritual paraphernalia than either Catholicism or Vodou, and because it venerates far fewer spiritual beings than the other sides of the Haitian religious triangle of forces, the Haitian religious collusio might seem less pronounced among Protestants than Catholics or Vodouists. Upon more careful investigation, however, Haitian Protestantism is every bit as concerned with the central features of this collusio, especially in seeking to utilize unseen supernatural forces to effect healing and to protect its practitioners from persecutory forms of evil. The leader of one of the churches featured in this chapter, for instance, teaches that "the Devil has no power over those who are cloaked by the Holy Spirit" (Valéry n.d.). Across the range of varieties of Haitian Protestantism, these are consistently central facets of belief and practice among the faithful, and while the Haitian religious collusio underlies all three sides of the triangle, the interpretation and negotiation is what is contested and varied. In this chapter we employ a modified form of market or field theory of religion to help understand the growth of Protestant Christianity among Haitians, both in the diaspora and the homeland, as this side of the triangle is every bit as transnational as the other two. In doing so, we trace the histories of two of Little Haiti's Protestant storefront churches and take a trip to a Baptist church in a northern Haitian village, which has close ties to Miami's largest association of Haitian clergy. We also offer ethnographic descriptions of these churches and biographical sketches of people in their pulpits and pews.

Did Ronald Pierre-Louis Rationally Choose His New Church?

We first met Ronald Pierre-Louis in Port-au-Prince in 1992. A thirty-seven-year-old father of four with limited job prospects, Ronald decided to do what so many of his compatriots have done in despair over the last forty years, joining the ranks of *botpipel* and searching for life in Miami. He sold virtually everything he owned to pay for a spot on a *kantè* (wooden sailboat), which left from the southwestern Haitian town of Pestel early one morning in November 2003, once hurricane season had passed. After a few days at sea, the *kantè*, with roughly forty people aboard, made it to the Bahamas, where Ronald had a few contacts in the swelling community of Haitian immigrants there. In due time, he found work cleaning up construction sites and over a few months saved enough to pay for the last leg of his journey, an outboard speedboat ride at night from Bimini to Florida, just fifty miles away.

It was about two o'clock one Sunday morning in March 2004 when, some seventy yards from shore, Ronald and the other *botpipel* were instructed to jump off the boat and swim for shore. The tide was low and the surf was flat, and after a few strokes Ronald found that he could stand. He managed to reach the beach in no time and then sprinted for some bushes he saw near a parking lot. From this vantage point, he waited about two hours and witnessed several other *botpipel* get arrested. When a flashlight was shone on him, Ronald thought that he too had been caught. Instead—and this Ronald attributes to Jesus—a voice called out to him in Spanish: *"¿Eres Haitiano?"* (Are you Haitian?). It was a Cuban American police officer, who, rather than arresting Ronald, directed him to a taxi cab just around the corner, driven by another Haitian immigrant. The cabbie brought him to a storefront Baptist church in Little Haiti where his uncle pastored. The pastor allowed Ronald to sleep in the pews for a couple weeks, and as such the church also became his spiritual home in Miami, for a while, anyway. Given the events that brought him to this church—finding the right bushes on the beach in which to hide; a sympathetic Cuban American policeman directing him to a cab whose driver knew in advance that the boat from Bimini was on the way; the cabbie's uncle being a pastor of a church that sometimes housed newly arrived *botpipel* for free and helped them get their feet on the ground—Ronald Pierre-Louis can hardly be said to have chosen his church. In due time, however, he changed churches, becoming a member of a nearby Pentecostal Haitian congregation, even though he remains grateful to the Baptist church that helped to make his search for life in Miami successful, and to which, whenever possible, he still tithes, eight years later. Obviously, *choice* was involved in this Ronald's change of churches, but we wonder how *rational* that choice was, and how *calculating.*

Ronald secured new lodging arrangements with a cousin in North Miami, which allowed him to leave the Baptist church and seek out a new church with greater resonance with his Pentecostal worldview and dispositions: his Pentecostal habitus. Ronald was spiritually unsatisfied in a Baptist church where no one got possessed by the Holy Spirit, no one spoke in tongues, and where healing services happened only once a month instead of several times per week. These were, after all, the hallmarks of his church in Haiti, Eglise de Dieu (Church of God), one of the many Pentecostal churches in Haiti that make up *l'Armée Céleste* (the Celestial Army), an informal and unstructured group of congregations known for their use of militaristic language and symbolism (uniforms, flags, titles, even imitation sounds of machine-gun fire) that teach "a diabolical reading of reality" and "make daily life a quest for security" against the persecution of an "omnipresent Satan" and other "fallen angels," as Nicolas Vonarx (2007: 118) observes. To Ronald, the lack of "heat" and what he saw as an unacceptably relaxed campaign against Satan in this particular Baptist church meant that he didn't feel as secure there as in the Church of God back in Port-au-Prince. It was thus time to find a new church, and there were many in Little Haiti from which to choose. But what, really, were his choices? Once he made them, could we soundly label his choices "rational"? How, furthermore, were they defined and limited, and what could a sociologist expect and/or say about his search and negotiation thereof? Raising the question more broadly, as does Rex Adhar (2006: 50), "is choice really possible in religion? To the extent that the individual is 'embedded' or 'situated' . . . her faith may reflect little real 'choice' on her part."

Conceptual terminology derived from economics has gained considerable currency in the study of religion over the last twenty-five years, especially among proponents of rational choice theory. The notion of "religious capital" is central to this theoretical development. However, definitions of the term are sometimes elusive and/or dislodged from its original intellectual architecture, and two streams of thought on the term have emerged without much confluence or conversation: one largely European sprung from the work of Max Weber (1962) and Pierre Bourdieu (1971); the other, largely American, from the work of Laurence Iannaccone (1990; 1992; 1997) and Rodney Stark and Roger Finke (2000), among others. In brief, microeconomic theory of religion holds that the religious field functions according to the logic of economics; that is, that religious institutions are engaged in competition over adherents, much like *real* marketing enterprises are engaged in competition over consumers. Those that succeed and grow do so because they accumulate rich stores of religious capital that promotes a sense among the laity that the "salvation goods" that they produce and market are legitimate and thus worthy of pursuit and consumption, while those of their competitors are not. In this chapter we reflect upon the utility and some of the limitations of this approach to the study of religion, with substantive examples from Little Haiti, in the heart of Miami, and Dolval, a rural village in northern Haiti with strong ties to Haitian Protestant churches in Miami.

The enthusiasm with which the sociology of religion has embraced "market theory of religion," most identified with Iannaccone and Stark and his collaborators (e.g., Stark and Finke 2000), is far from universal, and its critics make some very important points. The analytical power of such a paradigm is certainly enticing, but people's personal motivations and inspirations to practice religion are not as rationally calculating as the leading "rational choicers" would have us believe, one's religious practice being far more determined by tradition, socialization, mysticism, habitus, and collusio than by the measured estimations characteristic of cost-benefits analyses. All the same, we do not think that economic theory of religion is as "beyond redemption" as Steve Bruce (2002: 182), its leading critic, argues, or that it is little more than "the malign influence of a small clique of U.S. sociologists of religion" (Bruce 1999: 1). We would certainly agree that rational choice theory of religion has some serious limitations; yet, rather than suggesting that the approach be abandoned altogether, we would instead promote engaging it in a kind of Hegelian dialectic toward adapting, improving, and extending it, thereby fleshing out a more fully synthetic theory as to why people believe in and practice religion. In this chapter, in addition to profiling two Haitian Protestant storefront churches in Little Haiti, we seek to do so by taking seriously both economic theory of religion and some of the valid criticisms thereof made by Bruce, Roland Robertson (1992), and others (e.g., Adhar 2006; Chaves 1994), with an eye toward infusing it with Bourdieu's concepts of habitus and collusio, and grounding it in Weber's discussion of religious needs and his original articulation of the notion of salvation goods.

It is curious that leading proponents of rational choice theory of religion almost never cite Bourdieu, despite their adopting economic terminology in the study of an extra-economic social field in ways that strongly evoke him (e.g., "capital," "market," "interest," "consumer," "profit," etc.), and despite the fact that, like them, Bourdieu (1971) sees competition as integral to the nature of the religious field or religious market (Maduro 1982; Rey, 2004; 2007). Furthermore, Bourdieu is the most widely cited social scientist of our time, so why the absence of incorporation of his theory of practice in so much rational choice theory of religion? One possible answer is that Bourdieu himself is quite opposed to the radical subjectivity and freedom of individual choice that rational choice theory assumes to be a given. In one sense, Bourdieu developed his pivotal notion of habitus to counter the kinds of subjectivist assumptions underlying rational choice theory: "Thus, against the scholastic illusion which tends to see every action as springing from an intentional aim, and against the socially most powerful theories of the day which, like neomarginalist economics, accept that philosophy of action without the slightest questioning, the theory of habitus has the primordial function of stressing that *the principle of our actions is more often practical sense than rational calculation*" (Bourdieu, 2000: 63–64, emphasis added). In other words, "most actions are objectively economic without being subjectively economic, without being the product of rational economic calculation" (Bourdieu, 1990: 90–91).

Robertson (1992: 151) helpfully suggests how Bourdieu's theory of practice, despite a structuralist rigidity that many scholars have assailed, can help counter the "complete absence of constraint on consumers" in rational choice theory of religion. Such a Bourdieuian adjustment guides inquiry into how "choices are formed by circumstances" (ibid.: 155), being neither freely individualist and subjective nor the unalloyed products of circumstance and social structure, though for Bourdieu the latter are resoundingly more influential than the former on the production of religious practice and the forms that it takes. Haitian immigrants' "choices" of churches in Miami, for instance, are generally restricted by language and by material factors such as poverty and an unreliable public transportation system, and they are framed by the triangular Haitian religious collusio.

We are motivated by a conviction that the sociology of religion could benefit from a critical conversation between the two streams of thought on religious capital, the European, which is dominated by the influence of Weber and Bourdieu, and the American, dominated by rational choice theory and "the new paradigm" (Warner 1993). This conversation has already been initiated by European sociologists like Robertson, Jean-Pierre Bastian (2006), and Jörg Stolz (2006), and we seek to further it in this chapter by engaging Stoltz's (2006) reminder that Weber actually developed a similar concept to religious capital, "salvation goods," very early in the history of the social scientific study of religion, and by orienting this reminder with another excavation of the key notion of "worthiness" in Weber's *Sociology of Religion* (1956: 106). In addition to offering an historical and ethnographic portrayal of Haitian Protestantism in Miami and some of its transnational realities, this chapter purports to contribute to recent academic debates over the microeconomic theory of religion.

Little Haiti's Religioscape[1]

Metaphorically and sociologically, it is easy to think of Little Haiti as a religious marketplace. More than one hundred churches grace its roughly six hundred square blocks, botanicas retailing Vodouist ritual paraphernalia abound, murals of Catholic saints adorn grocery stores, and on any given Sunday throngs of well-dressed, Bible-toting

Christians shuffle about neighborhood's streets. Little Haiti's boundaries are unofficial and hence disputed, but generally U.S. Route 1 delineates its eastern border, NW 7th Avenue its western, the Design District its southern, and Miami's Catholic Cathedral of St. Mary its northern. Within these boundaries lies an approximately 50-x-12-block swath of one of the poorest neighborhoods in Miami, which is one of America's poorest cities. Many Little Haiti residents thus "struggle to survive, bouncing between regular jobs in the formal sector, unemployment, and small-scale self-employment in the underground economy or informal sector" (Stepick 1988: 33). Jobs might be hard to come by in Little Haiti, but churches surely are not. Just twenty-five years ago there were merely a dozen or so Haitian churches in the neighborhood. In the interim this number has multiplied tenfold, while the city's Haitian population has "only" tripled since then (Vaughan 1983a).

With so many churches, Little Haiti could well be one of the most religious inner-city neighborhoods in the United States. On NE Miami Avenue, for example, just two blocks north of Notre Dame d'Haiti Catholic Church, one of the most significant "ethnic parishes," there are four other Haitian churches. Clustered within three blocks, they are all freestanding and hence not of the storefront variety: Grace United Methodist Church, Eglise de St. Paul et les Martyrs d'Haiti, Eglise du Christ de North Miami, and the First Haitian Free United Methodist Church. Fanning out a few blocks in any direction, one finds several other churches, most of them storefronts, an approach to physical church establishment that Haitians in the United States have borrowed from African Americans.[2] Although we steer clear of his portrayal of storefront churches as "revitalization movements," for the most part it remains the case since Ian Harrison (1966: 160) opined over forty years ago that "the data on how they begin, what kinds of activities prevail within these churches, and the differences among various types of storefront churches are not always clear." In agreement with Frances Kostarelos (1995: ii), meanwhile, we would reject the portrayal of the black storefront church—whether Haitian, African American, or other—"as a capitulation to white economic power structures or as an otherworldly escape from the ghetto," opting instead to view such religious gathering place as "the embodiment of solidarity" and the "visible vehicle for sharing . . . identity and collective action." In addition to demonstrating their crucial function in providing Haitian immigrants with a sense of "worthiness," more generally, we also fill in some of the gaps in the literature alluded to by Harrison, at least as concerns the storefront churches of Little Haiti.

South Florida received a massive influx of Haitian immigrants beginning in the late 1970s and early 1980s. By 1980, two churches in the neighborhood of Lemon City had absorbed so many Haitian Christians that they sought out clerics with relevant linguistic and cultural expertise to pastor the swelling immigrant flock from "*la Perle des Antilles*" (The Pearl of the Antilles). These two churches happened to be among the most significant churches in the city: the Roman Catholic Cathedral of St. Mary and Grace United Methodist Church. Erected in 1958 and consecrated as a cathedral in 1965, St. Mary's is the epicenter of Catholic life in Miami, while Grace United is the city's oldest church, founded in 1893. These two churches predate the influx of Haitians into Miami. In the interim, however, they have both become predominately Haitian churches, and are the oldest "mainstream" Haitian congregations in the city, though anteceded as Haitian churches by the independent Pentecostal congregation Eglise de Dieu Sanctifiée Haïtienne (The Haitian Church of God Sanctified), the city's first Haitian-founded congregation, and by the First Interdenominational Haitian Church and Eglise Baptiste Emmanuel.

Two years after Eglise de Dieu Sanctifiée Haïtienne was founded in 1969, a second Haitian congregation appeared in downtown Miami, the First Interdenominational Haitian Church. Typical of today's leading independent Haitian churches in the city, First Interdenominational grew and stabilized, and its members gradually raised enough funds to purchase their own building in 1976 in the heart of Little Haiti on NE Second Ave. Now counting more than five hundred members, this is one of the largest Haitian storefront churches in Miami, which generally count fewer than one hundred members.

"When something called the Haitian Church of the Open Door puts up a sign and has someone who speaks Creole, where's the Haitian going to go?" Msgr. Thomas Wenski raised this rhetorical question when a local reporter asked him in 1983 to explain the recent appearance of several Protestant storefront churches in Little Haiti. An astute ecclesiologist, Wenski offered two other reasons for the spread of such independent churches: (1) Until 1983 the only Catholic Church in the neighborhood was the Miami Cathedral of St. Mary, whose "English signs and wood paneled rooms scared away many Haitians"; and (2) "These congregations, because they are smaller, tend to offer that sense of community that attracts many of these people who are new to the country" (in Vaughan 1983a). Both of these reasons ultimately are rooted in the notion that religion plays a key orienting role in the immigrant experience in urban America, offering to new immigrants an immediate space where a sense of homeland cultural identity is rediscovered or maintained. This is obvious in the second reason, while it is implied in the first: that is, the need for a sense of self and belonging in a new and strange world is so great that should the Catholic Church provide no culturally resonant reception to Haitian Catholic immigrants, they will convert to the Haitian Church of the Open Door, which in Little Haiti usually takes the form of independent Pentecostal or Baptist storefronts. Churches like these, writes Margarita Mooney (2009: 5), furnish "individual immigrants with a moral community in which they can nourish their faith and affirm their dignity." Weber (1963: 106) states that churches like these provide their congregants with "a worthiness that has not fallen their lot . . . the world being what it is."

This reflects one of the quintessential statements on immigrant religion in America, one made long ago by the sociologist Will Herberg (1960: 28) in his classic 1960 study *Protestant, Catholic, Jew*:

> [The immigrant's] becoming an American did not involve his abandoning his old religion in favor of some native American substitute. Quite the contrary, not only was he expected to retain his old religion, as he was not expected to retain his old language or nationality, but such was the shape of America that it was largely in and through his religion that he, or rather his children and grandchildren, found an identifiable place in American life.

Though Herberg was commenting on the waves of immigrants in the late nineteenth/early twentieth century, scholars writing about the religious experience of "new immigrants" in the United States, like Raymond Williams (1988: 29), explain the strength of immigrant religion in similar terms: "Immigrants are religious—by all counts more religious than they were before they left—because religion is one of the important identity markers that helps them preserve individual self-awareness and cohesion in a group." We have found the case of Haitian religion in Miami to be consistent with the findings of Herberg and Williams, but at least three other factors must be taken into account here: (1) that Haitians attend church more frequently than any other immigrant group in the United States (Stepick and Portes 1986); (2) that Haitian religious leaders have been adept at adopting both the ecclesiological and sometimes the homiletical approaches and entrepreneurial spirit that are typical of successful urban African American churches; and (3) that Haitians are subjected to more racism and ostracism than most other immigrant groups in the United States and therefore find in religion an especially rich source of "worthiness," or of "pride against prejudice" (Stepick 1998). The second factor, though not as exclusive to Haitian immigrants as either the first or the third, will emerge as relevant in our comparison of two Little Haiti storefronts.

In 1980, thousands of Haitians fleeing abject poverty and the brutal persecution of the dynastic Duvalier dictatorship took to sea in rickety sailboats in the desperate hope of reaching *"Miyami,"* a city that has taken on mythic proportions as something of a promised land in popular collective consciousness in Haiti.[3] Responding to the needs of this ample and devout new addition to its flock, the Archdiocese of Miami established a Haitian apostolate, eventually converting a girl's high school into Notre Dame d'Haiti Catholic Church and the Pierre Toussaint Haitian Catholic Center in 1982, and several local African American pastors stepped up to advocate for and support the Haitian refugees. That same year, Bishop Calvin Scofield of the Episcopal Church likewise acted to reach out to Miami's Haitian refugees, transferring the Haitian cleric Rev. Fritz Bazin from a parish in Jamaica to shepherd St. Paul's Episcopal Church on North Miami Avenue. Bazin modified the name of his church to St. Paul et les Martyrs d'Haiti (St. Paul and the Martyrs of Haiti) as a reflection of solidarity with the downtrodden of his homeland. "I chose this name for the Holy Innocents, the Haitian children who were killed in the DR (Dominican Republic) by Trujillo. But beyond that, every Haitian who has ever died in the name of freedom, from rebel slaves to boat people, they too are the martyrs of Haiti. The church stands for all of them."[4]

Bazin is one of a handful of well-educated and talented Haitian religious leaders who were called to serve Miami's swelling population of refugees from their country in the 1980s, and whose tireless and invaluable efforts are most praiseworthy. Fr. Gérard Darbouze was sent from Haiti by the archbishop of Port-au-Prince to minister at Notre Dame d'Haiti. Rev. Jonas George also arrived around that time to establish outreach programs for the Presbyterian Church. Meanwhile, from New York, where he had been in political exile since the early 1970s, Fr. Gérard Jean-Juste came with the hopes of gaining an appointment as pastor of a Catholic parish in Miami. Jean-Juste's leftist politics and outspokenness, however, made the local diocesan hierarchy uncomfortable, so they ostracized the charismatic and controversial priest despite the dire need of Creole-speaking clergy. Instead, Jean-Juste would use his directorship of the Haitian Refugee Center as his springboard to influence both religious and political life in Little Haiti over the next ten years.

By 1983, Haitians had established around a dozen Protestant churches in the neighborhood now called "Little Haiti," most of them independent Baptist and Pentecostal storefronts. Gradually the number of churches increased as more and more Haitians settled there upon successfully fleeing Haiti's perpetual economic and political crises. In the thirty years since the 1980 massive wave of Haitian refugees arrived in Miami (estimated to have been a total of some ten thousand), Little Haiti has witnessed an impressive proliferation of churches: from approximately twelve in 1983 to more than one hundred in 2000. Of the ninety-five churches that we have identified in Little Haiti,[5] independent storefronts of either Baptist (twenty-six) or Pentecostal (sixty) orientation predominate, as reflected in the following sampling of their names: Eglise Baptiste de la Renaissance (Baptist Church of Rebirth); Eglise Missionaire Trompette de Sion, Inc. (Missionary Church of the Trumpet of Zion, Inc.); Eglise Evangélique Maranatha (Maranatha Evangelical Church); Eglise Baptiste de la Régénération (Baptist Church of the Regeneration); Eglise de Dieu du Temps de la Fin (Church of God of the End of Time); Première Eglise Universelle du Seigneur (First Universal Church of the Lord); and Eglise de Dieu l'Arche de Déliverance (Arch of Deliverance Church of God). With one known exception, the independent Pentecostal church Temple de l'Eternel, Inc. (Temple of the Eternal, Inc.), which was established on NW 2nd Avenue by Sr.

Thérèse in 1976, all of Little Haiti's Protestant storefronts were founded by male pastors. At least five of the Baptist churches and eleven of the Pentecostal congregations are not exclusively Haitian, being led by African American, Bahamian, or Jamaican pastors. Additionally, there are three Seventh Day Adventist churches, one Kingdom's Hall of Jehovah's Witnesses, an Elks lodge, a Masonic Temple, two Islamic mosques, and a substantial new Mormon ward, not to mention two of Miami's largest Catholic churches.[6] About twelve botanicas, a couple of Vodou sanctuaries, and an African American orisha temple, Ile Orunmila, round out Little Haiti's extraordinary religioscape, as do the numerous murals of Catholic saints or Haitian revolutionary heroes, as well as private shrines and grottoes. Many of the churches are located on the main commercial arteries of the neighborhood, e.g., NE 2nd Avenue, NW 7th Avenue, NW 54th Street, and N. Miami Avenue.

The typical trajectory of Haitian storefronts in Miami is the following: A pastor arrives from Haiti and establishes a church either in a private home, a restaurant, school gymnasium, or the like, and attracts an initial following by word of mouth or by radio advertisement. Once enough funds are secured, the congregation rents a small building and recruits members. This is a critical phase in any congregation's life, and numerous churches in Little Haiti have folded or merged with others at this stage. Fund-raising becomes crucial toward making the next step in the Haitian storefront course, which is the purchase of a building. Typically, churches that rent their space count fewer than seventy-five members, whereas the most successful Protestant churches in Little Haiti all own the buildings that they occupy and count roughly ten times more members than congregations that rent their places of worship. For example, Rev. Devil Legrand, senior pastor of Nouvelle Eglise Baptiste Bethanie (New Bethany Baptist Church), recognized the importance of such ownership, which he made a priority upon founding the Miami branch of his church in 1986; he managed to purchase the congregations present location on NE 2nd Avenue four years later.[7] Legrand's church in Little Haiti, which is an extension of a church, Eglise Baptiste Bethanie (Bethany Baptist Church), that he founded in the town of St. Michel de l'Attalaye in Haiti's Artibonite Department in 1970, today counts 250 members. The largest independent storefronts in Little Haiti, meanwhile, are Eglise Baptiste Emmanuel (Emmanuel

Protestant Churches in Little Haiti

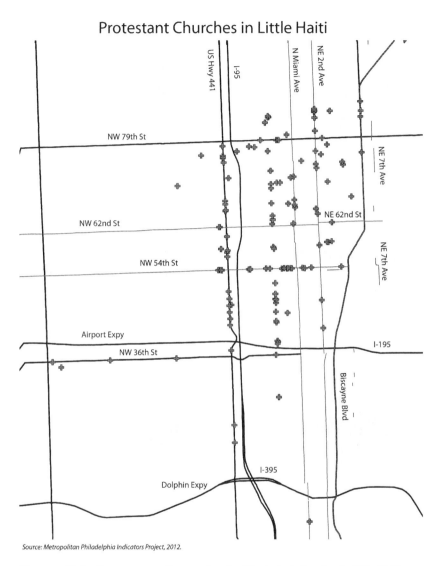

Source: Metropolitan Philadelphia Indicators Project, 2012.

Figure 5.1. Today there are more than one hundred Protestant churches in Little Haiti, the vast majority of them Haitian and of the storefront variety. See appendix 3 for a list of these churches, among which Baptist and Pentecostal congregations predominate.

Baptist Church), founded in 1973 and now with 1,300 members; Nouvelle Eglise Evangelique Baptiste Bethel (Bethel Evangelical Baptist Church), founded in 1975 and now counting 650 members; and the First Interdenominational Haitian Church, founded in 1971 and now counting 500 members. The actual construction of a church edifice is something to which few Haitian congregations aspire, often because they deem that the required funds for such a project would be better spent helping sister congregations in Haiti, or contributing to relief and reconstruction projects in the wake of the January 2010 earthquake. Some Haitian Protestant storefronts, furthermore, have move out of Little Haiti and into North Miami or Broward County; the Miami Baptist Association (mbachurches.org), for example, counts one hundred Haitian churches in its membership roster of three hundred churches, and only fourteen of them are located in Little Haiti. One of the association's leaders and the director of its Haitian ministry is Rev. Dr. Scott Nelson, a former missionary in France and Haiti who is fluent in French and Haitian Creole. Nelson has also established the Institut Biblique Logos (Logos Biblical Institute), both online and at the Premiere Haitian Baptist Church in North Miami, where weekly Bible classes are held each Monday evening (institutbibliquelogos.com).

A Tale of Two Churches

To illustrate the nature and trajectory of storefront Protestant Christianity in Little Haiti, we focus comparative ethnographic and historical attention on two of the neighborhood's storefront churches: Eglise de Dieu Sanctifiée Haïtienne (EDSH—Sanctified Haitian Church of God), founded in 1968, and Mission Evangelique du Christianisme (MEC—Evangelical Mission of Christianity), founded in 1993. The oldest Haitian church in Miami and one of the oldest in America,[8] EDSH typifies the Haitian American storefronts that have recently proliferated here in several ways: for instance, its membership is fewer than one hundred and shows no signs of increasing, it is independent and transnational, and it is decidedly Pentecostal. Conversely, MEC counts thousands of members in two dozen congregations in five different countries, its Miami membership is over three hundred, and it is not Pentecostal. In addition, MEC also represents a unique phenomenon in Haitian

Christianity in being indigenously Haitian; that is, its mother church in Haiti had no affiliations with any foreign missionary group, and much of the mission's understanding of Christian practice derives from the mystical experiences and healing ministry of its Haitian founder, the missionary Salomon Sévère Joseph (1891–1973). His independence from any form of mission Christianity, we hold, is fundamental to MEC's appeal and a wellspring of the church's religious capital and salvation goods.

Eglise de Dieu Sanctifiée Haïtienne, Inc.

Before the massive 1980 exodus of *botpipel* from Haiti, some Haitian immigrants had already settled just to the north of downtown Miami, in a neighborhood then known as Lemon City. One of them, Rev. Pascal Duclair, had enjoyed a long career as a pastor of Eglise de Dieu de la Prophétie (Church of God of Prophecy) in his hometown of Les Cayes, the largest city on the south coast of Haiti, prior to immigrating to Miami in 1968. The present pastor at Eglise de Dieu de la Prophétie is Rev. Pierre Joseph, who at times visits Miami to preach at EDSH. The two churches maintain a close affiliation. Because of limitations in material resources, besides its fund-raising for its mother church in Les Cayes, EDSH has never developed extensive local social programs, save for support to some of the Little Haiti's elderly and orphans. It also has a modest Sunday school program, which today is conducted entirely in English.

Upon his arrival in Miami, one of the first things that Duclair did was to open a Pentecostal storefront church on NW 14th Avenue, where his small Haitian flock re-created the lively worship and healing services that drew hundreds to his church in Haiti. By 1973, the congregation had raised enough funds to purchase a small abandoned commercial building in Lemon City on NW 2nd Avenue near NE 54th Street. Duclair and his nascent congregation could not then have known that this would become the very heart of Little Haiti in the early 1980s. To the EDSH faithful, this was nothing short of providential.

For more than a decade EDSH remained one of the only Haitian churches (if not the only Haitian church) in Miami, and it eventually established an informal relationship with a local African American chapter of the Church of God. Definitively Pentecostal, Duclair fashioned his Sunday worship services to inspire "gifts of the spirit:"

speaking in tongues, baptism in (or possession by) the Holy Spirit, faith healing, and the like. With the sudden infusion of ten thousand Haitians in 1980, Eglise began holding Friday night healing services called "The Cry of Midnight" ("*le Cri de Minuit*"), and word soon spread of all kinds of miracles performed there: from curing illnesses to exorcising *move zespri* (evil spirits). Usually it has been newly arrived Haitian immigrants who come to EDSH to seek healing. On one evening in 2004, for example, a family who had just arrived from Haiti brought their young-adult daughter to the healing service. She had not spoken a word since arriving in Miami some three months prior. After much prayer and laying on of hands, a Vodou spirit allegedly responsible for her muteness was exorcised, and the young women began to speak: "She had been possessed by an evil spirit and had lost the ability to talk," explained one pastor after the miraculous event. "We laid hands on her, prayed, and she went home, where the Holy Spirit touched her and enabled her to talk again."[9] Stories like these abound in Miami's Haitian Pentecostal community, reflective of a key facet of the Haitian religious collusio—the quest for healing of protection from illnesses or disorders caused by evil spirits or sorcery.

EDSH is housed in a white two-story building on a large corner lot. To the south of the building toward the corner is an unpaved parking lot surrounded by a relatively new chain-link fence. There are usually very few vehicles in the lot, including a yellow school bus and a large white passenger van. Most of the church's sixty members live within a short walking distance. Evidently the building was originally designed for some kind of small manufacturing enterprise. The sanctuary makes up about two-thirds of the ground floor, behind which are two small bathrooms and a classroom where Sunday school and Bible study are held. Presently there are twenty students enrolled in Sunday school, which is taught by a 1996 graduate of Florida International University named Nadege, whose mother has been a member of the church for decades. The second floor is not used.

Measuring approximately 75 x 125 feet, the sanctuary is white, walled with two columns of ten pews each, which are separated by a red-carpeted aisle leading to the pulpit. The pews are wooden and well upholstered with red cushioning. A series of support buttress stands in the middle of the aisle; there are donation boxes chained to two of them.

The pulpit sits atop a stage that is about two feet higher than the floor. On it are the large lectern from which the sermon is delivered and four leather chairs. The stage is adorned with artificial flowers in large vases. Styrofoam plates adorned with yellow ribbons also are hung about the church. Except for a large sign hanging crookedly on the south wall that reads "Israel," there are no religious symbols in the church; nor do any congregants visibly wear crosses. On the stage sits an electric organ, and just beneath that is a drum set. They are seldom played during Sunday worship services.

Just to the front of the stage and off to the left is a table draped in white cloth. There is a filing cabinet located to the left of the stage, and a large speaker is affixed to the ceiling off to its right, protected from theft by iron bars and a padlock. It is very loud and can be heard during hymns and sermons and prayers from a couple of blocks away. The door is kept open throughout the service for this purpose, and one congregant testified to us that he first was drawn to this church while walking nearby in the streets and hearing from afar "something about salvation"—a rather chance event, one hardly driven by rational calculation, as it were. Several window air conditioners and six ceiling fans cool the sanctuary.

Generally about forty people attend Sunday worship services, which are scheduled to begin at 11:45 a.m., as in the vast majority of Haitian storefronts in Miami. Most of the adults who attend are middle-aged or elderly, and roughly three-fourths of them are women. The drummer is a teenage boy who usually arrives with four younger children in tow, three boys and a girl. He is not entirely successful in keeping the boys under wraps, who are sometimes rambunctious to the point of fisticuffs during services. But no one seems to mind. Of the adults, seldom are any in attendance between the ages of twenty and forty, and often no more than six adult men attend, three of whom are the church leaders. Most of the women are middle-aged and a bit on the heavy side. They are always well dressed and wear either hats or veils to cover their heads in gestures of pious respect to the Lord. The majority of the women sit on the left side of the church, where sometimes one or two men also sit, while a few women usually sit with the rest of the men on the right side.

Routinely, Sunday morning services at EDSH open with a benediction, followed by several minutes of spontaneous communal prayer, led on the microphone by "the evangelist," François Duclair. Neither he nor anyone but the day's preacher—normally either Rev. Jacques Clotaire or Rev. F. F. Duclair—ever mounts the stage. Everyone prays softly aloud, mostly in Creole, though as the fervor builds several people begin speaking in tongues (glossolalia is very common at EDSH, although we have heard no evidence of polyglossia). Then the evangelist leads the congregation in a series of hymns from *Chants d'espérance* (Chants of Hope), which the adult congregants seem to know by heart.[10] These hymns are all in French. Another period of spontaneous prayer much like the first follows, and then the evangelist leads a reading from the Psalms. More hymns follow, and then another period of very moving spontaneous communal prayer, when gifts (charisms) and sometimes "deliveries" (*komisyon* or messages) from the Holy Spirit are received. This is followed by a reading from the one of the Gospels. Intermittently during all of the service, the evangelist cries out *"Lapè Bondye ave nou"* (The peace of God be with you) or *"Beni soit l'Eternel"* (Blessed be the Eternal), to which the congregation responds *"Amen!"* or *"Allelujah!"* all in antiphonic cadence.

Pascal Duclair died in 1999, leaving the leadership of EDSH in the hands of his brother, Evangelist François Duclair, his wife, Rev. F. F. Duclair, and Rev. Jacques Clotaire, a former Catholic who converted to Protestantism in 1975 and who has been serving EDSH for more than twenty years. François leads the hymns and communal prayers, while Madame Duclair and Clotaire alternate as preachers. Their sermons usually begin at around 12:00. Invariably, the sermon opens with expressions of thanks to the Lord for bringing the congregation together, and then any visitors present are asked to introduce themselves. They are always very warmly received with applause and shouts of *"Allelujah!"* and *"Beni soit l'Eternel!"*

Often the preacher then breaks into a series of prayers for peace and unity in Haiti, which is perhaps the most common exhortation one hears from Haitian pulpits throughout Miami, and then for peace throughout the world. Reflective of a typical theme in Pentecostal theology, EDSH sermons are firmly rooted in the conviction that our prayers can bring the wisdom of God into the hearts of the world's political leaders, and the love for God into the hearts of people everywhere. The sermons are thus interspersed with prayers and spontaneous call-and-response cries of "*Lapè Bondye ave nou*" (The peace of God be with you) or "*Wi, Jezi Sove*" (Yes, Jesus saves!). Although spontaneity is a hallmark of preaching in this church, there is at least some structure in the sermons' being grounded in biblical readings. Repentance is a regular theme. The preaching usually lasts for about forty-five minutes, and the homiletics are quite effective and provide the congregation with abundant food for religious thought for the new week. More spontaneous communal prayers and a final hymn follow the sermon, and the service finally ends at around 1:00 p.m.

On the first Sunday of each month, EDSH celebrates the Holy Communion. On these occasions, the normal sequence of prayers, hymns, and sermon is shortened somewhat to allow time for the special rite. In a ritual gesture reminiscent of the Catholic Mass, the pastor first blesses the "bread" and the "wine" and recites from memory Jesus's words from the Last Supper, then exhorting the congregation to repent seriously and deeply in order to take Communion with a pure heart, "a heart whiter than snow." The women then take the plate and pass it among themselves, each silently praying before eating the broken crackers, and then the men do the same. The cup, which was not a gold chalice with wine but a Tupperware jug filled with grape juice, is then shared in the same gendered sequence.

Communion culminates with some of the deepest religious ecstasy seen at EDSH, surpassed only by the Friday evening healing services. Some women go into possession upon placing the bread into their mouths, crying out sharply and incomprehensibly, yelping, and convulsing. This lasts for several minutes and recurs when they drink the wine. Once Communion ends, Rev. Clotaire and the evangelist wash the feet of each male, one by one, in a large zinc basin; Rev. Duclair does the same for the women and girls, hymns being sung all the while. The church leaders all then dry off everyone's feet with a white towel.

Indeed, EDSH has been quite an influential congregation, if not for its size then as a model, as a leading healing sanctuary, and as a "*pepinyè*" (tree nursery), which since its inception has seeded Miami with faith in Jesus Christ and the gifts of the Holy Spirit. Several other Little Haiti and North Miami churches have been founded by former EDSH members, including Miami's largest storefront, Eglise Baptise Emmanuel (1974), whose founder, Rev. Wilner Maxy, had his conversion experience at

EDSH years prior. Healing and spreading the Christian faith are thus the raisons d'être of EDSH, over and above the growth of its own membership. In many ways, such as size, economics, ecclesiology, and programming, EDSH is representative of the dozens of Haitian storefront Pentecostal churches that dot Miami's religioscape. Because of its local primacy, EDSH possesses a unique form of religious capital, however, which accrues for its follower a salvation good in the form of worthiness.

Mission Evangelique du Christianisme

If EDSH's claims to uniqueness among Little Haiti's Protestant storefront churches lies in its local primacy, its healing prowess, and spawning of other Haitian churches in Miami, then that of the Mission Evangelique du Christianisme (MEC) lies in its absolute Haitian-ness; or, as its leaders explain with pride, in its being "the only truly indigenous form of Haitian Christianity."[11] Whereas all other Protestant Christian churches in Haiti and in the Haitian diaspora are either parts of mainstream mission churches, offshoots of mission churches, or inspired by and/or modeled on North American forms of Pentecostal churches,[12] MEC's origins lie in the mystical experiences and healing ministry of its remarkable Haitian founder, The missionary Salomon Severe Joseph (Le Missionaire). His fascinating story is well worth summarizing here.[13]

Salomon Severe Joseph was born on December 12, 1891, in Jonc d'Audin d'Aquin on Haiti's southern coast about twenty miles east of Les Cayes. His father was a military officer and a devout Roman Catholic, hence Salomon received a good formal education and was baptized and raised Catholic. One of twelve children, he was very pious, and was an altar boy and a member of the choir of the local parish. In 1918 he began studying law, and in 1920 he founded an elementary school for peasant children in his hometown. He also married and soon fathered the first of his own twelve children. His life changed radically when in 1930 he began to have tremendous mystical experiences, in particular receiving visions and hearing voices. The first vision was brief and occurred out in the fields one day while working with his father. Joseph saw a radiant angelic figure robed in white and alerted his father, who saw nothing. A few nights later Joseph saw three similar figures approaching him. The youngest one said to him, "Do not fear, my child." The oldest one said nothing but kissed him three times on the cheek. The third one said to him: "And I will kiss you not three times but 3,399 times. And these kisses will be multiplied fourfold so that only the spirits will know the depth of our friendship."[14] The tree beneath which Joseph received these initial visions is greatly revered by MEC members; it is also the site on which the first MEC church was constructed in 1934.

Joseph's healing ministry began soon after the visions and would continue for the remaining forty years of his life. One of the first people he healed was a young woman who was believed to have been pregnant for two years but was unable to give birth. The missionary successfully delivered her child, whose own son, Rev. Fandor Saint-Felix, is today one of the MEC pastors in Miami. In one sense, faith healing was a kind of supernatural offshoot of the de facto infirmary that his large and charitable family had earlier established on their homestead. With no formal healthcare available in the area, *"lakou Joseph"* (the Joseph homestead) attracted many sick peasants from the surrounding hills. In addition to providing free of charge whatever medicine the Joseph family had in stock, they also conducted communal prayers for healing and employed the service of one family member who was a well-respected herbalist, a *medsin fey*. In this milieu, Sévè, as he was called locally, began healing the sick by laying his hands on them, exhorting them to repent, surrender to Jesus Christ, and commit to fervent and regular prayer to the Lord. Any monetary donations that he and his family received were quickly turned over to the local Catholic parish.

From then on, word spread throughout the region that Sévè possessed the gift of faith healing. From near and far people brought to him loved ones who were possessed by evil spirits, who were blind, and who were impotent or barren. Once under Sévè's care, he implored the afflicted to abstain from using graven images, from sacrilege, from superstition, from consecrating meals to idols, from Vodou ceremonies, from harming their neighbors, and the like. He always asked them if they had faith in God, to whom he usually referred as *"le Très Haut"* (All High) *"Père de Miséricorde"* (Father of Mercy) and *"Adorable Providence"* ("Adorable Providence"), and in God's power to heal. The rejection of all things associated with Vodou was de rigueur requisite to healing. Furthermore, those who were healed were henceforth exhorted to love their neighbors and to be just to everyone around them.

In time, some members of the Joseph family grew resentful of Sévè's popularity, such that by 1934 a schism developed at the homestead. Those who remained faithful to Sévè proclaimed themselves to be the *Mission du Christianisme* (Mission of Christianity), while the dissenters, who accused Sévè of being an egocentric magician, took the name *"Selon nos plans"* (According to our plans). Most members of the second group soon converted to the Baptist Protestantism that had been planted in the region in the late nineteenth century by the Baptist Missionary Society of London, and the Jamaican Baptist Missionary Society (Romain 2004: 41). Those of the first group were the original MEC congregants.

Sévè's visions eventually compelled him to read the Bible, which he then did for the first time ever, despite being a lifelong Catholic. Through his readings and meditations he began to doubt the truth of Catholicism. His healing ministry, meanwhile, led to conflict with the local Catholic priest, Fr. Ricodel. Things escalated between the priest and the missionary after Sévè cured a gravely ill woman for whom Ricodel had already said last rites and prepared a funeral. Outraged, the priest railed against the missionary: "How could a Haitian man possibly undo what I have done?" In turn Ricodel arranged to have Sévè ex communicated, along with any Catholic who took part in his ministry (MEC: nd).

Not to be undone, as his conviction of the falsehood of his former church strengthened and his confidence as a healer grew, *le Missionaire* incorporated the burning of Catholic icons and other ritual paraphernalia into his healing ministry. At one point, Sévè actually emptied the contents of a local Catholic church, placed them in a heap in the churchyard, and set them ablaze. This act of divinely inspired iconoclasm led to the first of his three arrests, making Sévè one of a number of Protestant religious leaders to be victimized by the anti-superstition campaigns that the Haitian Catholic Church, in collaboration with the state and the army, conducted to eradicate Vodou from Haitian society, with Church leaders and "lay supporters," as Kate Ramsey (2011: 103-104) demonstrates, viewing "the campaigns against *le vaudoux* and against Protestantism as closely interconnected."

Over the ensuing decades, Sévè was credited with having performed countless miracles, usually in the form of healing sick humans and even animals, including the resurrection of his own dog, Mégarde, who followed the missionary wherever he went. Some attest that he even raised the human dead. People from throughout Haiti flocked to his church, and Sévè's mission flourished, even after his death in 1973. Eventually MEC would become not merely a transnational church but a well-organized international network of twenty-four congregations. Besides its fourteen churches in Haiti, there are five in the United States (four in Florida and one in Brooklyn), and one each in Canada, France, St. Martin, and French Guyana.[15] MEC members in Connecticut recently established the Salomon Severe Joseph Foundation, a nonprofit 501c(3), "to cooperate collectively in an effort to bring high quality education, healthcare and community service to the Haitian Community in the United States and Haiti. The overall goal is to build a solid foundation for those less privileged in the Haitian community by providing schooling, basic healthcare and essentials for basic living" (www.myspace.com/ssjfinc). Like so many other missionary efforts in Haiti, the foundation's focus shifted to relief work in the wake of the 2010 earthquake, soliciting contributions for medical supplies on its blog and noting that it senior pastor, Jude Valéry, had helped more than six hundred earthquake refugees at his home in Port-au-Prince, which was transformed into a refugee camp and emergency medical center (http://www.myspace.com/ssjfinc), somewhat reminiscent of the healing center into which his grandfather, Sévè, had transformed *lakou Joseph* about a half a century earlier.

Reasons for MEC's remarkable success are of course varied and complex, though the mission's adoption in Miami of African American homiletics is, we believe, key among them in that it helps retain especially younger members who might otherwise leave for African American or Bahamian churches where only English is spoken and where preaching is usually dynamic. In addition, MEC succeeds for the very reasons cited by Paul Brodwin (2003: 85) for the success of Haitian Protestant churches in Guadeloupe:

> In particular, self-consciously upholding scriptural edicts . . . has become a strategic rebuttal of the denigration of Haitians by the majority society. Migrants memorialize the Haitian homeland and articulate the collective sentiments of loss . . . and . . . thus, invest the divisions in their social world with theological significance, and they validate their theology

through the everyday details of marginalization . . . . [As such] religiously based moral schemes become social operators in the improvised and unfinished zones of transnationalism.

Finally, the mission's stress on being originally Haitian and having never relied on any larger church association or foreign mission quite effectively appeals to Haitian pride. Several congregants noted to us that MEC's uniquely Haitian origins were what most attracted them to its pews. In a "host" society that is not exactly warm to Haitians, MEC thus processes a trove of religious capital and a wellspring of salvation goods, worthiness being paramount among them.

There are other features of MEC belief and practice that are also refreshingly original and hence appealing. For one, MEC members refer to themselves as *"christianistes"* (Christianists), as opposed to the usual term in French *"chrétiens"* (Christians). And although born in large part out of Séve's anti-Catholic iconoclasm, the typical MEC service includes the peace greeting from the Catholic Mass, but instead of saying "peace be with you," the one to first offer her hand in a gesture of greeting proclaims *"l'humanité"* (humanity), to which the person receiving the greeting, upon shaking the greeter's hand, responds *"la foi"* (faith). This unique form of call-and-response is also enacted whenever anyone takes the microphone to address the congregation, with the speaker saying *"l'humanité"* (or sometimes repeating the greeting in the expanded form, now in Creole, of *"limanite na legliz la"* [humanity in this church]), with the congregation responding collectively *"la foi."* The recently mounted MEC website offers the following explanation for this ritualized greeting:

HUMANITY NEEDS FAITH IN JESUS CHRIST:

Out of all the virtues that relate to the Christian religion, the one that is most difficult to keep is Faith. It is vital for Christians. It gives us the assurance of the existence of God. Even when we walk with God and we benefit from great privileges reserved for the redeemed, we sometimes doubt and face uncertainty. The acts of charity, prayers, thanksgivings, preaching and praises are all important parts of Christian worship. However, none equals a steadfast faith. Jesus Christ, once said, "But when the Son of Man returns, how many will he find on the earth who have faith?" Luke 18 v 8. Thus, the main concern of the Lord is to find faith on earth. . . .

When two Christians from EMC meet, they greet each other in this manner: One says L'Humanite (Humanity) while the other respond La Foi (Faith). It is a mutual engagement to keep the faith in Christ in the entire human race. Other greetings are used as well: Christ reigns, God is Great! All is well in Christ, etc. (missionevangeliqueduchristianisme. org/humanity-faith.html; emphasis in original)

The Miami MEC church edifice is located on one of the neighborhood's main commercial corridors, NW Fifty-fourth Street. The Miami branch serves as the headquarters for Florida, which is home to four MEC churches in all; the others are located in Tampa Bay, Orlando, and Delray. Counting about three hundred members, many of whom are immigrants from the Aquin area in southern Haiti, the Miami MEC church is housed in a cavernous, white, square concrete building, with an unpaved parking lot surrounded by a chain-link fence. Evidently, the building was originally a warehouse or workshop, a space that the congregation has occupied since 1993. The northwest corner lot is the parking area, which fills up regularly by at least fifteen minutes before the 11:00 Sunday worship service begins. An interesting variety of cars can be found here on any given Sunday, ranging from shiny new SUVs to much humbler beat-up jalopies. That there are many cars in general and a few flashy ones in particular clearly indicates that most MEC congregants do not reside in Little Haiti, meaning that this is an example of what Helen Rose Ebaugh and her collaborators (Ebaugh, O'Brien, and Chafetz 2002: 107) refer to as a "niche church," one that attracts "members from a broader geographical area who share identities, interests and/or similar tastes in worship style." By contrast, EDHS is more an example of the "parish model" of church in which "people worship in the same geographical area in which they live." Especially conspicuous in the MEC parking lot are the several taxis often in the lot, each of which had posted on their roofs colorful, racy advertisements for local strip clubs. This incongruity rather strikingly reflects Mircea Eliade's (1959: 25) notion that sacred and profane space are divided by a threshold, namely, in this case, the church door: "The threshold is the limit, the boundary the frontier that distinguishes and opposes two worlds—and at the same time the paradoxical place where the worlds communicate, where passage from the profane to the sacred world becomes possible."

The interior space of the church is also painted white and the floor is smooth concrete. Wooden pews cover about half of the floor space. The ceiling is very high, there are no windows, and along the sidewalls are four air conditioners. Large garage-style doors flank the stage on either side of the rear wall and another makes up the final portion of the northeast wall. The stage in the front is covered in a red carpet on which stands a pulpit, front and center, and four large chairs off to the rear. On the rear wall high above the pulpit is painted the name of the church in large red letters, just like on the outer façade. Beneath this is a painting of a dove in a small circle, carrying a branch in its beak, soaring beneath puffy clouds and pouring blessings over the lush tree where Sévè received his calling to ministry. To the side of this there is a long quotation from the church's founder, Salomon Severe Joseph: *"Si la mission vient de l'homme; le monde avant sa fin verra la fin de la mission. Mais si la mission vient de Dieu; la mission avant sa fin verra la fin du monde"* (If the mission comes from man, then the world will see this mission end before the end of the world. But if the mission comes from God, before its end, the mission will see the end of the world). Below these words is written *Mission Evangelique du Christianisme M.E.C. Fondée en 1934 par Salomon Severe Joseph* (Evangelical Mission of Christianity M.E.C, Founded in 1934 by Salomon Severe Joseph). With the exception of the dove, there are no other religious symbols; most interestingly, not even a single cross is displayed or evident. A number of people have Bibles with them, and a lesser number also carry hymnals, while a few others hold recent editions of the bimonthly MEC newsletter.

Generally women sit on the left side and men on the right side of the church, each in about twenty rows of pews separated by an aisle leading to the stage and pulpit, toward the rear wall. Women rarely, if ever, mount the stage, though they do lead hymns and prayers at its foot by taking the microphone. Women, in fact, lead most of the prayers, although only men preach at MEC, and only men can be pastors.[16] Most sermons are delivered in English, largely for the sake of the children, most of whom understand little Creole and even less French. Children are quite numerous at most services, even if they are absent during the first few minutes because they attend Bible study in an upstairs classroom, which is also conducted in English. MEC members dress very well for services, and most of the women in attendance (though few of the girls) have their heads covered by veils. All of the men wear jackets and ties.

Prayers at MEC services are often spontaneous and moving though seldom, if ever, do people receive the gift of tongues or other charisms; such forms of ecstasy are actually discouraged by MEC pastors, who are clear that their church is not Pentecostal in any way, its rich tradition of faith healing notwithstanding. Still, communal prayers are sweepingly worshipful, and many people sway joyfully with their hands in the air. The content is usually simple and almost like a mantra: *"Jezi sove . . . Jezi sove . . . Jezi sove . . . Se li mem ki mèt mwen . . . "* (Jesus saves . . . Jesus saves . . . Jesus saves . . . It is he who is my master); *"Anba Satan! Anba Satan! Anba Satan . . . Anba Pye'm Satan!"* (Down with Satan! Down with Satan! Down beneath my foot with Satan!). This second prayer is accompanied by the entire congregation heartily stomping their right feet on the ground in cadence with the word "foot," as if stomping on the devil. Throughout the communal prayers one hears spontaneous cries of *"Amen!"* or *"Hallelujah!"*

MEC takes music very seriously, and one member of its Paris congregation, Missoule Guirand, released a CD of original MEC hymns in 2003.[17] The Miami church equips its musicians especially well: electric guitars, bass guitar, a modern drum set, trombone, electronic organ, and large Peavey amplifies. They are very loud, such that it is impossible to hear one's neighbor speak in the pews during hymns, which are often followed by thunderous rounds of applause (see fig. 5.2). MEC features a wider variety of musical styles than most Haitian Protestant churches, as some hymns are even played to the driving rhythms of *konpa*, contemporary dance music that is wildly popular in nightclubs and on the radio in Haiti and its diaspora. This is particularly appealing to young MEC members. Music is robustly featured, furthermore, during the annual MEC convention, which takes place each April at a different church and draws followers from all MEC branches, some of which send their entire choirs and musical groups. The annual convention expands upon a tradition instituted by Sévè long ago: on the first Sunday of each month his followers from throughout Haiti would gather in Aquin at the original MEC church.

Figure 5.2. One of Little Haiti's most thriving Protestant storefront churches, Mission Evangelique du Christianisme (MEC) is part of an international network of churches inspired by the ministry of its Haitian founder, Salomon Severe Joseph. Worship services in this congregation include vibrant choral arrangements, like the one depicted here.

An innovative Protestant adaptation of Haiti's effusive Catholic pilgrimage tradition, this still takes place in Haiti, when thousands of Christianists from throughout the country and even some from the diaspora descend upon Aquin. Replicating this in the Haitian diaspora, members from the three Florida branches also gather at a single church one Sunday each month.[18]

From April 23 to 25, 2004, the annual international MEC convention took place in Miami, with well over one thousand visiting Christianists joining the Miami congregation for three days of worship and fellowship at *"la Grande Convention Annuelle."* They came from Paris, French Guyana, Montreal, Boston, Connecticut, New York, New Jersey, and Florida's four other MEC branches. Music is one of the convention's highlights, as MEC branches from New York, Connecticut, and Tampa showcase their respective choirs, with extra space and time set aside for youth choirs and women's choirs, all quite polished and impeccably and uniformly dressed. Not to be outdone, the Miami MEC youth group performed a hymn of praise to crisp and vivacious *konpa* rhythms; their lead guitarist was as impressive as any professional musician we have ever seen perform this style of music in Haiti, and he could not have been more than sixteen years old. It is an altogether festive and impressive display of faith and musicianship, with prayers and applause interspersed between the musical performances.

Preaching also is featured at the convention, of course, including sermons by local pastors and MEC's international president Rev. Jude Valéry. Members of the MEC governing council also provide updates on church activities, sometimes in a polished French diction rarely heard in local Haitian churches. There is also occasion for witnessing: on April 24, for example, one middle-aged man recounted that as a boy he was unable to walk until cured by Salomon Severe Joseph; and one of the highlights of the convention was when Rev. Saint-Felix, of the Miami MEC church, brought the microphone to his grandmother—a 105-year-old woman who is believed to have been the first person ever healed by Sévè. After recounting the remarkable story of the event, she declared "I only have one regret, and this is that I cannot stand up out of this wheelchair to dance with you all!" She sang, nonetheless, for the entire day, often with arms outstretched in praise.

For the most part, the gender geography of typical Sunday services is kept intact at the annual convention, although somewhat relaxed so that entire families could sit together. Especially striking is the strong family base to MEC membership. Children are in abundance, and they are very well behaved.

Besides being an occasion of renewal and the strengthening of the bonds that makes MEC such a remarkably successful independent and international Haitian church—the only one of its kind, as far as we know—the convention also allows for the MEC central committee to meet and discuss everything from church finances and authority to its future trajectory. Jude Valéry, Sévè's great-grandson, has done as much as anyone to assure growth of the mission, and he heads the eight-member central committee. Each country is represented. The committee also takes time to discuss the states of MEC's two seminaries, one in Port-au-Prince and one in Brooklyn, whose very existences speak to the wealth of foresight of the church's leadership and assure the theological uniformity which is so vital to the success of any church.[19]

The success of any church of course requires sociological forces in addition to theological ones: social capital in addition to religious capital. Clearly the Missionary possessed charisma, in both the theological and sociological sense, and his ministry and message struck a chord with thousands of Haitians who joined his church over the years. That charisma, along with his congregation's claim to be a uniquely indigenous form of Haitian Christianity, infused MEC with the rich store of religious capital that has enabled Sévè's ministry to thrive not only in Haiti but internationally. In Miami, where Haitian immigrants have all too often been confronted with racism and an immigration policy that is stacked against them, to remember that the Holy Spirit found a Haitian prophet *worthy* of bequeathing the charism of healing and the mission to found what is in a real sense the most genuine of all Haitian churches, MEC offers its followers the salvation good of *worthiness* that is beyond compare in Little Haiti's religious marketplace.

Building Transnational Churches

Dozens of founders and/or pastors of Haitian churches in Miami participate in an organization called the Conference of Haitian Pastors United in Christ, Inc. (CHPUCI), which was founded in 1997 in response to "a leadership crisis" facing the Haitian community.[20] CHPUCI usually meets at Eglise Baptiste Haitienne Emmanuel, pastored by Wilner Maxi, which is the largest Haitian Protestant church in Little Haiti, with thirteen hundred members, and also one of the oldest, founded in 1973.[21] Among CHPUCI's founding members are Pastor Harold Vieux, who is also an administrator at the North Miami Health Center, and Pastor Enoch Milien, who is an undertaker. Vieux's clinic offers free HIV testing, which motivated him to found CHPUCI; in the early 1990s Vieux quickly became alarmed by the high seropositivity rate among Haitians then being tested in his clinic, and he decided to take action to mobilize local Haitian churches to concertedly respond to the epidemic. For his part, Milien observed that, around the same time, in one day he had directed funerals for seven Haitians who had died of AIDS. It was in response to this initial crisis that the conference was born, and today periodic health fairs, seven of which were held in 2001, rank among its most notable and successful local initiatives. An earlier fair, in September 2000, drew "647 people in five hours" (Diaz 2001). It is likely that many of the beneficiaries at these events would have turned to Vodou for health concerns in Haiti, and that the fairs might thus serve to contribute to conversions to Protestantism among Haitians in Miami, even if this is nowhere evident among the conference's objectives in orchestrating them. Brodwin (1996) observes that Haitian religious culture is characterized by a "contest for healing power," in which 75 percent of conversions to Protestant Pentecostal sects in Haiti occur "on the occasion of an illness, either their [the convert's] own or that of a parent or child" (Conway 1980: 14). The quest for healing, to recall, is a central feature of the Haitian religious collusio.

Besides the periodic health fairs, CHPUCI also organizes ESL classes and offers counseling for newly arrived Haitians with concerns about deportation. Since the tragic earthquake of January 2010, though, the conference has turned its attention almost entirely to relief efforts in Port-au-Prince and Leogane. Vieux encapsulates some of the challenges as follows:

> The people are overloaded not only with their own personal lives but overloaded with helping the people back home. We're talking about construction, other things that require money. The Conference of Haitian Pastors encounters the same problem the individual churches face. Everyone feels like their hands are tied. The budget I am trying to take care of in Haiti, we still need $200,000 to $250,000 to get it done. I have a pastor in the Conference who is licensed to do pre-construction for homes and churches. His problem is being able to prefabricate what he needs to do. He could do it in 3–4 weeks, but to get the materials is a factor. No matter how you look at it there is some sort of financial obstacle. In that sense the Conference of Pastors cannot do that much. I have already started as you can see from the website, laying the foundation, but I am stuck. A lot of Haitian pastors here have a church over there that they are taking care of. There were so many destroyed and they have to help reconstruct. In Haiti we do not have insurance policies so when it goes down we have to start again. Anyway you look at it, it's not easy.[22]

One result of this urgent shift in the conference's attention is that several other projects in Haiti, namely in Port-au-Prince, Les Cayes,

and in several small towns and villages between Cape Haitian and
Ouanaminthe, like Terrier Rouge and Dolval, have largely been put on
hold. In 2000, Vieux, who holds a Doctor of Divinity, drafted a concept
paper for a $3 million husbandry project and submitted it to USAID in
Port-au-Prince. The proposal was greeted positively by a USAID officer, who informed Vieux that such funding could only go to a Haitian
non-governmental organization (NGO), and so the conference reached
out to several pastors in Port-au-Prince toward establishing a relationship with a Haiti-based counterpart. Once funded, this project would
go toward the purchase and care of livestock for villagers in and around
Terrier Rouge, and toward training in appropriate husbandry technolo-
gies. This, too, has been put on hold because of the earthquake.

Prior to the terrible tragedy of January 2010, the conference had been
making slow and intermittent progress on two projects in Dolval, a
village of two thousand inhabitants located roughly six miles north of
Grand Bassin, in the Department of the North. Besides providing sala-
ries to two school teachers in the village's Baptist school, the conference
had been funding the construction of a relatively large church edifice for
village Baptists. The construction, which began in 1998, remained unfinished during our visit in 2001, as there were no roof, floors, or doors. In
the meantime, the congregation was meeting beneath a makeshift lean-
to covered by a large tent from the 1994–97 U.S. military occupation of
Haiti (the symbolism of which, we think, speaks for itself).

Upon entering Dolval one is immediately struck by the bright yellow Carmel Baptist Church. Naturally when we first visited the village
we assumed this to be the church built with funds from Pastor Vieux's
conference. It was not. Our initial questions to the Carmel elders concerned support from the conference, and they repeatedly indicated that
since Carmel's founding in 1950 they had never received any support
from anyone in the United States, let alone from Miami Haitians. The
yellow church edifice was constructed with the congregants' own funds
and efforts and completed in 1980. And, while over the years a few Haitian pastors had come from abroad to preach at Carmel, their names
have been forgotten. After further discussion, Carmel elders revealed
that two pastors had recently come from Miami, not to visit Carmel
but the church up the road. One of them was a native Dolvalian who
was sometimes based in Port-au-Prince and Cape Haitian, Honoré

Dorceus. Dorceus, incidentally, had spent several years preaching at the Philadelphia Church of God, a Haitian storefront in Little Haiti. The other Miami pastor turned out to be Vieux.

The leading Carmel elder, an energetic man in his eighties named Ameleon, chipped in that Carmel was the first church in Dolval and the village's only church that claimed membership in the Baptist Convention of Haiti (BCH), Haiti's second largest centralized religious institution, after the Roman Catholic Church. The Carmel elders encouraged us to speak with Pastor Zunga Madupinga, a Congolese national who is regional president for the NBC and a professor at the Baptist Seminary in Limbe. It would seem that their stressing Carmel's affiliation with the convention was intended to paste a glaze of legitimacy on their church while casting a pale of illegitimacy on their competition. Apparently a schism in the Carmel Baptist Church occurred some twenty years ago. Ameleon attributed the schism, and the resultant construction project of the village's second Baptist church, to greed: "*chak moun bezwen bagay li*" (Everyone needs his own gig).[23]

Eventually, and somewhat reluctantly, Ameleon led us to that second Baptist church in the village. Since this one, Eglise de Dieu (Church of God), was under construction we thought it an even safer assumption that this was the one being funded by the Miami Conference. Wrong again! Eglise de Dieu, which some locals call Legliz Lafwa Apostolik (Church of Apostolic Faith), counts 165 members; construction of its church edifice began in 1997. Unanimously members of Eglise de Dieu denied either knowing Vieux or benefiting from any foreign aid. When asked to discuss what they would like to derive from such assistance, most members responded: "A floor for our church" (the entire structure in cement block was complete, although the dirt floor often became muddy due to leaks in the tin roof). Eglise de Dieu is considerably larger than Carmel, roughly 175 x 75 feet, and its roof is higher. There are a few benches and chairs but no doors. Colorful strands of paper hang from the rafters, and a table stands in the far end to serve as an altar. A blackboard with biblical lessons hangs in the front end of the church, as at times there is Bible study. There is no pastor in residence, so on most Sundays a pastor drives up from Cape Haitian to preach.

Just two hundred yards down a dry hill from Eglise de Dieu stands still another Baptist church under construction: Eglise Nouvelle

Jerusalem (Church of New Jerusalem). We had finally found what we had come to Dolval looking for! This is bound to be the largest church in the village, measuring roughly 200 x 80 feet, with a mud floor and no roof. There are four principal walls, and an additional three walls that will make a hallway of some kind to one side of the sanctuary. In one corner there is a very large U.S. Army tent set haphazardly as a lean-to, which in lieu of a roof serves to shelter services over about 25 percent of the overall floor space. One church member recalled that it was Pastor Vieux who had brought the tent from Port-au-Prince, a relic of the U.S./ UN occupation of the mid 1990s. The floor is dirt. Beneath the lean-to are some twenty benches and a crude lectern for a pulpit, on which hang some plastic flowers. A doily sits on top of the lectern, before which sits an interesting Haitian musical instrument, a wooden box with some kind of large reed over an opening (they call this a *"bas"*). Two drums are also there, and an accordion.

The dozen Nouvelle Jerusalem members with whom we spoke were very enthusiastic about the construction of the church and expressed much gratitude for the support from Pastors Vieux and Honoré. On occasion, Honoré returns to Dolval to preach at Nouvelle Jerusalem; otherwise the church has no resident pastor, and preaching is taken up by one or another of the elders. At the time of our visit, one of them was enrolled at Ecole Biblique Supérieure in Port-au-Prince. We found it curious that three Baptist churches are found in the same impoverished village. When asked about this, Nouvelle Jerusalem members seemed to find nothing amiss, perhaps having already invested too much of their energy and resources in their church-under-construction to question the economic and social soundness of such a situation.

Notwithstanding the caution of some anthropologists that questions about Vodou in Haiti are rarely frankly answered, after raising relevant questions and getting "a feel" for the place, we became convinced that people in the village and surrounding hills are not very heavily devoted to the Vodou lwa, there being, according to several of our local research consultants, only one *oungan* in the village but no *ounfo* (temple) or shrine anywhere nearby. Protestants take pride in having successfully kept Vodou's influence in Dolval to a minimum. This case is not really unique in contemporary Haitian religion, as we have been to other parts of Haiti where Vodou is not as popular as the geographically limited and largely ahistorical anthropological literature would suggest, even though the largest recent surveys of rural households in Haiti do indicate as much (Woodson and Baros 2001; Woodson and Baros 2002). These surveys demonstrate that one-third of Haitian households today are Protestant, although they are the clear majority in Dolval. Specifically, this means that the struggle over souls in Dolval and environs pits three Baptist churches against one another, as well as a Catholic community that recently constructed a small church in the village. The Baptists, furthermore, were once united but have suffered two schisms over the last ten years. Their differences are certainly deepened by the transnational support Eglise Nouvelle Jerusalem receives while the other Baptist churches receive none. One can sense a strong undercurrent of jealousy and mistrust between the Baptist communities here, which is seemingly exacerbated by Nouvelle Jerusalem's Miami ties.

Why should such a poor, relatively small, abjectly impoverished village, one with no running water, no electricity, and no dispensary or health-care clinic, have three Baptist churches of such size? Why should most villagers seemingly consider their churches to be the most important things in the material world? If religion, as some rational choice theorists would have us believe, is driven by rational calculation and cost-benefit analyses, then wouldn't the villagers in Dolval chose not to build any more churches and instead invest their time and energy and pool their resources to dig a well and install a pump? A Marxist analysis might be tempting here, but it would ultimately be somewhat reductionist. Instead, certain key concepts from Bourdieu's theory of practice—his theory of the religious field in particular—may be saliently applied to an analysis of the Dolvalian religious field. For Bourdieu, the religious field is one of many distinct yet interrelated fields that together constitute human society. Fields are characterized and structured principally by the struggle or competition that takes place within them. In the religious field the struggle is between opposite poles in a regimen of confrontational juxtapositions, principal among which ranks "priest" versus "prophet" and "magician" (Weber), or "church" versus "heresiarch" (Bourdieu), over the production, administration, and control of religious capital and the adherence of the laity. In discussing this competition inherent to the religious field, Bourdieu (1971: 305) stresses that which is ultimately at stake for orthodoxy and its religious specialists or clergy, which constitutes their primary interest: "the monopoly over the legitimate production of religious capital," and the "institutionalization of their dominance in the religious field." To this supreme end, the church and its specialists employ "weapons of symbolic violence" in order to secure the misrecognition, and hence the recognition, of the legitimacy of both their dominant position in the religious field and the resultant gains in the social, cultural, economic, and political fields.

In the case of Dolval, NBC-affiliated Baptists have long dominated the religious field. Now, as their monopoly has been lost (in part due to this field's transnationalization), elders of the Carmel Baptist Church attempt to use their affiliation with the National Baptist Convention as a weapon of symbolic violence against the other Baptist churches in the village. All three Baptist churches, moreover, take pride in the relatively weak presence of Vodou in the village, which evidently has not been much of a competitor in recent decades, although the new Catholic church down the road represents a significant entrant into the fray. What these examples illustrate, most importantly, is that Dolval's religious field is indeed structured by the struggle over the control and legitimate production of religious capital. Bourdieu (1987: 133) reflects the far-reaching significance—*even on the village level*—of this: "Competition for religious power owes its specificity . . . to the fact that what is at stake is the monopoly of the legitimate exercise of the power to modify, in a deep and lasting fashion, the practice and worldview of lay people, by imposing on and inculcating in them a particular religious habitus." The extent to which Dolvalien Baptists, especially Eglise Baptiste Carmel, succeeds in inculcating a pliant religious habitus in the village laity determines the margin of advantage and leverage gained in its struggle against the Protestant heresiarch(s) and, in this case, the Catholic Church. In the first case, if the laity's religious habitus dispose them to recognize as legitimate and effective Carmel membership, they remain consumers of Carmel's salvation goods and thus this church thrives. In the second instance, the other Baptist churches', the Catholic church's, and the Vodou priest's appeal to the villagers will rise in proportion to the degree of failure in the Carmel's attempt to inculcate in the laity a religious habitus in accord with the dominant worldview, for renegade religious interests, ones uncontrolled by Carmel and the NBC, would develop in the laity and lead them to "take their business elsewhere."[24]

Conclusion

Whether in Dolval or in Little Haiti, Haitian Protestant churches must distinguish themselves in order to succeed in attracting new members and retaining old ones. In Dolval, one Baptist church seeks to do this in part by appealing to its formal affiliation with the largest Protestant body in Haiti, while in Little Haiti another seeks to do so by asserting its uniqueness as "the only truly indigenous form of Haitian Christianity," and still another as the first Haitian church in Miami. Without entering too deeply into recent debates in the sociology of religion about the utility of rational choice theory for understanding why some churches grow while others die, we have oriented our analysis with reference to the originator of the notion that, for everything else that they are, religious institutions exist in social arenas that are shaped by economic logic.

One notion that is most fundamental to Weber's theory of religion, and most relevant to the interpretation of immigrant religion in United States, is that the "disprivileged" of any given society are pushed to religious practice by a "hunger for a worthiness that has not fallen their lot, the world being what it is" (Weber 1964: 106), as has already been noted. Weber's needs model of religion posits that the material conditions of one's existence create the needs that determine the kind of religion that s/he inherits or adopts. Bourdieu compellingly refines this line of theorization with his notion of religious habitus, "the principal generator of all thoughts, perceptions and actions consistent with the norms of a religious representation of the natural and supernatural worlds" (Bourdieu 1971: 319). Bourdieu's suggestion that one's religious habitus (as *both* the "matrix of perception" through which one makes sense of religious things *and* the locus of dispositions that manifest as religious belief and practice) is thoroughly conditioned by agents' socioeconomic and cultural background is indeed helpful for understanding why many recent Haitian immigrants join MEC instead of any or other longer-standing churches in Little Haiti, or why Ronald Pierre-Louis gravitated out of a Baptist storefront in Little Haiti and into a Pentecostal one. Immigrants arrive in a country whose Center for Disease Control in 1984 formally listed Haitians, evidently by virtue of something so scientifically verifiable as their ethnicity, as being "at risk" for carrying AIDS, along with homosexual males, hemophiliacs, and heroin addicts.

Worthiness thus ranks paramount among all forms of spiritual capital that are marketed in Little Haiti. This suggests a reiteration of the formula that we proposed in our introduction to this book: *the deeper the discrimination that any given immigrant group experiences upon arrival, the greater value that salvation goods in the form of worthiness will have.*

As applied to the study of religion, rational choice theory has been criticized—rightly so, in our view—for overemphasizing agentival calculation in people's religious behavior. Bourdieu's notion of habitus can go far in correcting this by shedding light on the embeddedness of human behavior in the body. Like anyone else, Haitian immigrants like Ronald Pierre-Louis are thus "embedded" in their language, class, ethnicity, and race, just as they are "situated" by their religious habitus and situated in their religious collusio in ways that in fact greatly limit their religious possibilities. This is a case in point of what Steve Bruce (2002: 182) means in saying that "religious behavior is shaped by social norms that prevent maximizing opportunities: class, race, ethnicity, nationality, and language all limit choice. But religion itself limits choice. To the extent that people are successfully socialized into a particular religion they are not able to see other religions as utility-maximizing opportunities." That species of salvation good called worthiness, in the end, is what truly draws Haitian immigrants to the dozens of storefront Protestant churches in Little Haiti.

Lest we give sociology the final word, we conclude this chapter by suggesting that the image of Little Haiti as a religious marketplace should be transformed into a diptych with the image's other panel being that of a forest whose trees crisscross a sea (markets, trees, and seas, incidentally, are among the most common subjects in Haitian visual art, along with saints, *lwa,* and heroes of the Haitian Revolution). Its trees' trunks and roots are in Haiti, and their branches are clustered in Little Haiti and other inner-city neighborhoods of the Haitian diaspora, branches that themselves sometimes transform into roots for other trunks in Haiti. The branches bear the fruits of the salvation goods that spiritually and materially nourish Haitian immigrants in their struggle for acceptance in a racist society, an instantiation of precisely what Weber (1963: 106) deems to be the ultimate driving force of human religious practice the world over: "the hunger for worthiness." That is a sociological explanation, of course. To a person, Haitian Christians would offer a theological one instead.

Beasts, Gods, and Transnational Transubstantiation

It is the summer of 1994, somewhere at sea between Haiti and Cuba, in the Windward Passage. A young officer of the U.S. Coast Guard stands atop the bridge of his vessel, the USCGC *Hamilton*, and reflects aloud on the scene unfolding on the deck below. There, more than one thousand Haitian *botpipel*, migrants that his crew had detained over the course of the previous three days, are patiently awaiting their arrival at the U.S. naval base in Guantanamo Bay, Cuba: "Just think of all of the man power, ingenuity, and future that Haiti is losing on this boat alone." It is an interesting statement that certainly holds some truth, but all of that "man power" and "ingenuity" is only helpful to Haiti when it is deployable and employable, when it is not driven into hiding out of fear of political oppression, when it is nourished, educated, and healthy. As for the "future" being lost, there is also "future" being gained for Haiti by those migrants on the *Hamilton* who would be granted political asylum and gain residency in the United States, some of them surely benefitting from the assistance from Notre Dame d'Haiti or other Haitian churches in Miami, and most of them faithfully sending remittances to loved ones back home, on the other side of the water.

Nearly half of the *botpipel* on the *Hamilton* that day had been taken from a single wooden sailboat, the *Merci Jésus* (*Thank You, Jesus*), on July 1, and the rest were removed from a few other boats that had also been christened in Haiti with religious names: *Bondye Bon* (*God is Good*), *Mama Mari Avek Nou* (*Mother Mary is with Us*), and *Benissez le Seigneur* (*Bless the Lord*). During their last few minutes aboard the *Merci Jésus*, as they neared the *Hamilton* and the hope of eventually reaching Miami, via Cuba, and gaining political asylum and a new lease on life, the migrants sang a hymn of gratitude to Our Lady of Perpetual Help, their patron saint:

> [T]he skies were bright and Merci Jésus was vibrant with glorious hymns of thanks and praise to the Virgin Mary (Notre Dame du Perpétuel Secours, Priez pour vos enfants toujours: "Our Lady of Perpetual Help, Pray for Your Children Always), and "Queen of the Seas, Mother of God, Mother of Haiti." The united chanting voices of hundreds of sun burnt and exhausted but prayerfully hopeful black people in blazing orange life-jackets rose toward the scorching Caribbean sun, as the boats slowly approached one another. Next to me stood a tall U.S. Marine in tears. (Rey 2006: 206–207)

Just as the African gods had accompanied their ancestors and helped them to endure the brutality of the Middle Passage and create new lives and Creole cultures in the Americas, so too have the saints and gods and the God of Haitian migrants aided and abetted their descendants in this more recent crossing of water to new lands and new lives, hence the abundance of religion, religious imagery, and visual piety in Little Haiti (Rey and Stepick 2010). To paint a mural of, or erect a shrine to, a Catholic saint in Miami is a way for Haitian immigrants to express their gratitude for the saint's or the lwa's assistance in crossing the water and building new lives in America and improving lives in Haiti. The mural inside Notre Dame d'Haiti Catholic Church of Our Lady of Perpetual Help, the patron saint of Haiti who maternally watches over her *botpipel*, her children, does precisely this.

The trauma, drama, and injustices of the experience of Haitian *botpipel* have thus captured the imagination of the muralists of Little Haiti, whose work reflects the deep religious faith of those who have crossed the water from Haiti to Miami. So, too, have they inspired two luminaries of Haiti's extraordinary national arts culture: the late, great poet Félix Morisseau-Leroy, for whom one of Little Haiti's main corridors is named, and Edouard Duval-Carrié, a Haitian immigrant whose art studio is located in Little Haiti. Morisseau-Leroy (1991: 57) links the Middle Passage to the modern *botpipel* experience in his poem by that name, "Botpipel," tragic crossings of water that created, respectively, both Haiti and the Haitian diaspora:

In Africa they chase us with dogs
>Chained our feet, embark us
>Who then called us boat people?
>Half the cargo perished
>The rest sold at Bossal Market
>It's them who call us boat people

>. . .

We looked for jobs and freedom
>And they piled us on again: Cargo—Direct to Miami
>They start to call us boat people
>We run from the rain at Fort Dimanche
>But land in the river at Krome
>It's them who call us boat people
>…
>Except for the Indians—
>All Americans are immigrants

But it's us they call boat people
>We don't bring drugs in our bags
>But courage and strength to work
>Boat people—Yes, that's all right, boat people[1]

Duval-Carrié offers similar reflections in his 2005 painting *Migration of the Beasts*, which depicts Haitian *botpipel* as Vodou spirits, in an affirmation that, despite their being perceived of as "beasts" by certain Americans, these people have gods—in Vodou every human has a spirit, a lwa, living within them as part of her soul—and throughout the crossing their spirits, saints, and gods stood by them and sustained those who survived. One young migrant named Yolande Jean reflects this view with the following observations of her own crossing experience: "My experience on Guantanamo allowed me to see that it was true. These things are their doing. I have no idea what we are to them, maybe their 'bêtes noires' or perhaps their devils. We are not human to them. But I don't know what we are" (in Farmer 1994: 4). Another Duval-Carrié painting depicts the great Vodou goddess of the sea Lasyrenn as watching over *botpipel* sailing across her domain, and another still depicts the recent arrival of *botpipel* as lwa. In the latter painting, the immigrants' spirits are depicted as readying themselves for new lives in America, debarking toward the bright lights of glitzy Miami, with the coquette Ezili Freda trailing behind the group in order to straighten her dress and fix her hair. The Rickenbacker Causeway is in the background, and they are soon to settle, labor, and send money home to Haiti, demonstrating the *botpipel*'s "courage and strength to work" that is lauded by Morisseau-Leroy.

In Miami and wherever else they have settled in the United States, the vast majority of Haitian immigrants have become productive members of American society, having surmounted tremendous obstacles in their quest to not only survive but to thrive (Mooney 2009). As Carolle Charles (2006: 206) correctly observes:

> [O]ne of the most striking characteristics of those experiences is the resilience of these black immigrants "to beat the odds" and to redefine the terms of their incorporation into U.S. society. While resisting or opposing negative representation of otherness, they are also looking for ways that they can become part of the U.S. social mosaic. At the same time, they continue to claim and maintain their rights to be a transnational and diasporic citizenry of Haiti, their country of origin.

These observations recall Pope John Paul II's exhortation to the Miami faithful during his historic visit in 1987. Speaking on the campus of Florida International University beneath a massive cross symbolically adorned with sails like those that powered the odysseys of so many Haitian refugees and Cuban exiles, the pontiff encouraged belief in one's homeland culture as being gifts to the United States:

> As I gaze at this great city with its many peoples and cultures, I pray that you will all help one another with your gifts. Stay in touch with your own roots, your cultures, your traditions; pass on your heritage to your children; and at the same time, place all of these gifts at the service of the whole community. Above all, make every effort to preserve the unity which has the Spirit as its origin and Peace as its binding force. The work of building up the body of Christ rests upon all of us in the church. Certainly! (May 1987: 11)

As if to punctuate the power of this point and make it the pope's final word, lightning began to strike, and the papal Mass had to be cancelled, the first time that this had ever happened in the history of the papacy.

In becoming part of the American social mosaic and securing their rights to a transnational and a Haitian identity at the same time, Haitian immigrants have drawn strength and solidarity from religion, from Haiti's "religious triangle of forces": Catholicism, Protestantism, and Vodou (Woodson 1993: 157). As such, some of the most decisive "terms of their incorporation into U.S. society" have been religious, terms that get redefined in uniquely Haitian American religious ways: the thousands of Charismatic Catholics gathered in ecstatic revival at the Knight Center in downtown Miami; the dozens of Haitian Protestant storefront churches and Vodouist botanicas that animate the Little Haiti cityscape; or dressing in kelly green and draping shamrocks in a Vodou temple for the serpent spirit Danbala. The saints, spirits, gods, and God of these religions have indeed sailed beneath the Rickenbacker Causeway, arrived, survived, and thrived in Miami, just as they have languished in jail cells at the Krome Detention Center, which, somewhat ironically, is actually much closer to West Kendall than to Little Haiti (even though West Kendall Haitians rarely, if ever, find themselves in either). Through it all, they have proven that they are indeed not beasts but dignified human beings with a profound belief that they are children of God, protégés of saints, servants of spirits.

Through their remittances, Haitian immigrants in Miami and throughout their diaspora have also become vital contributors to the largest single segment of the national Haitian economy, subscribing to "a form of morality that links individuals not only to their families but also to the nation," a morality and a reality so pervasive in Haiti that people there feel "that improvements in their lives depend upon assistance from family members abroad," as Nina Schiller and Georges Fouron (2001: 77) explain, and "that they are unable to change conditions on their own." People in Haiti have good reason to feel that way. From the mid-1990s to 2004, the amount of money sent to the homeland by Haitian immigrants increased tenfold to comprise roughly one-quarter of Haiti's total GDP. By 2006, the sum total of their remittances had reached $1.65 billion (Buss and Gardner 2008: 55; Inter-American Development Bank 2007). The 2001 Haitian Census, furthermore, found that one in every five households in Haiti receives some measure of financial support from relatives and friends living in "the tenth department," as the Haitian diaspora is called (there are nine departments [states or provinces] in the Republic of Haiti). By far the largest number of Haitian immigrants live in the Dominican Republic, estimated to number 1.5 million (Ferguson 2003: 8), and in the United States, where Haitian immigrants and people with Haitian ancestry are estimated to number 830,000 (Buchanan, Albert, and Beaulieu 2010), with between a quarter and a third of the latter total residing in South Florida, the most of any state (Orozco 2006). By other estimates, Haitian and Haitian Americans in South Florida number 500,000 (Marcelin and Marcelin 2001). Given the extraordinary obstacles that most of these immigrants have surmounted during the migration and settlement experiences, that they have managed to become a cornerstone to Haiti's national economy through remittances is really quite astounding.

Much of this extraordinary achievement can be attributed to resilience, creativity, entrepreneurship, and hard work. But, from the perspective of those who have made it happen in Miami and elsewhere in the Haitian diaspora, the achievement should also be attributed—first and foremost—to God. This is reflected in the hundreds of churches that they have founded in the United States, more than one hundred in Miami alone, the dozens of Catholic parishes where Mass is said in Haitian Creole, their botanicas, and the names of some of their business enterprises (e.g., Blessing Auto Repair; Thank God Grocery Story; Champions for Christ International Day Care; The Good Shepherd Day Care, and the like). They have crossed the water and kept the faith, a faith that sustains not only their lives abroad but also the lives of so many to whom they are connected in Haiti. Crossing the water has thus never meant leaving Haiti. Instead, it has meant becoming Haitian in a transnational way, a way that is vital to Haiti's other nine departments on the other side of the water.

The Haitian diaspora has already proven to be fascinating and fruitful terrain for the anthropology of religion, and we hope that our effort in this book will contribute to this important literature. Most major studies of religion in Haiti focus on a single faith tradition, whether Catholicism, Protestantism, or Vodou (e.g., Romain 1986, 2004; Greene 1992; Métraux 1972), and this is true of anthropological studies of the religious culture of the Haitian diaspora (Brown 1992; McAlister 2002; Mooney 2009; Richman 2007). With this rich body of literature as a platform, we now realize that studying the three major strands of Haitian religion together can also help inform broader and important sociological questions facing not only Haitian immigrants in Miami but other ethnic or national immigrant groups in the United States. At the same time, we would suggest that the two main theoretical arguments made in our study—(1) that religion provides Haitian immigrants with a "salvation good" in the form of *worthiness* in a society where this might otherwise be elusive, and (2) that there exists across and beneath denominational and theological differences among Haitians a transcendent and unifying Haitian religious collusio—may help shed light on the faith of most immigrants in the history of the United States, if not on religion in general.

The few scholars who have taken a holistic approach to religion in Haiti have reached conclusions that point toward underlying foundations to the Haitian religious triangle of forces, or to key components of a Haitian religious collusio, that there are important features that span and pervade the sometimes nebulous and often contentious boundaries between distinct faith traditions in Haiti. We likewise take a holistic approach to Haitian religion, only this time in an important center of the Haitian diaspora, namely Miami. We have reached a similar conclusion:, one that we further theorize by applying Pierre Bourdieu's theory of practice to suggest that there exists a Haitian religious collusio, which operates in similar ways across Haiti's three major religious traditions. Many Haitian immigrants, as products of and participants in this collusio, believe that a successful quest for legal settlement in the United States requires religious belief and actions, or magic (*maji*) to ensure a safe journey, luck (*chans*) to obtain worthiness in the eyes of U.S. immigration authorities, or *benediksyon* (blessings) to remain healthy through it all. On one side of the triangle, Vodouists believe to have the capacity to augment one's *chans*—that of gaining asylum or a green card—of being deemed *worthy* to stay. As important, Vodou is a wellspring of salvation goods for immigrants in their assertion of worthiness to belong and to thrive in the Magic City (see chap. 5).

Equally critical, the salvation good of worthiness that Haitian religion provides is not merely a substitute for material goods. Rather, it is an experience valued in and of itself that yields material capital both in the diaspora and in Haiti. When, for example, Haitian immigrants are invigorated by Sunday worship services in Protestant storefronts to work hard not only to sustain themselves and any dependents they might have in Miami but also to save enough money to send to relatives in Haiti, and if it is through contacts at church that they secured employment or accessed affordable day care for their children in order to do so, religious capital is indeed transubstantiated into material capital. Many, probably most, Haitians devoutly practice their religion(s) because they believe firmly not only in the promise of eternal salvation but because they derive from their religious faith and practice a profound sense of meaning and an immediate sense of worth, spiritually and materially—worth for and meaning to life in the here and now. As such, Haitian religion is far more than being merely a habituated cultural practice that is rooted in "misrecognition," and it is here that we part company with Bourdieu's ultimately dismissive and adversarial view of religion in general (Rey 2007: 7).

Indeed, Haitian and Haitian American participants of whatever faith commitment(s) share and participate in a transnational Haitian religious collusio, however much their respective theologies, worship styles, and beliefs, their religious habitus and practice may differ, which they sometimes do quite radically. Such a collusio consists of the following features: (1) a deep respect for religious leaders and a conviction that they serve as mediums to and from the unseen, supernatural world(s); (2) a central concern with healing and/or with protection from supernatural forces that are "sent" toward others to inflict harm (Farmer 1992); (3) a profound belief that religious action or ritual, whether in the form of prayer, sacrifice, or possession, elicits supernatural response or intervention by unseen supernatural agents, be they gods, angels, ancestors, lwa, the Holy Spirit, saints, or God; (4) a deeply embodied sense of religious participation and a "pneumacentric" understanding of one's relationship to the divine—spirits are central, integral for humans' accessing the divine (Chesnut 2003); (5) a belief in prophecy and various methods to see into the future; (6) a belief that dreams can and do relay knowledge or prescience; (7) "a persecutory conception of evil" and the need to take religious action to protect oneself from evil (Corten 2001); (8) an incorporation of music not just as an expression of praise but as a means of communion with the sacred; (9) an intuitive sense that healing is a central purpose of religion (Brodwin 1996; Brown 1989; Conway 1978); and (10) a profound faith that religion enhances one's luck (*chans*) and furnishes forms of magic (*maji*) that assist in the negotiation of life.

A related integral feature of the Haitian religious collusio, one that touches all of the other features just listed, is the incorporation or conception as "real" what might be called nonmaterial forces or spirits that have an assumed, often unquestioned, role in one's day-to-day life; and, what we call religion is an institutional means for utilizing, protecting, and addressing those forces in a practical way. All forms of Haitian religion tend strongly to incorporate or embody this characteristic, even as they claim to combat some of these very forces or spirits. Protestants and many Catholics, for instance, disavow Vodou and generally label it as devil worship. Yet, their approach does not deny the power of spirits. Instead, they re-label the spirits as evil or satanic; they enjoin people to pray and be devout to combat such demonic nemeses, which are conceived of as being altogether real, however nonmaterial that they might seem.

Similarly, many Haitian Protestants denounce the Roman Catholic veneration of saints as idolatry, and there is a long history in Haiti of Protestant zealots destroying statues of saints and other religious paraphernalia, although it is a history overshadowed by Christian—both Catholic and Protestant—destruction of the sites and symbols of Vodou worship in Haiti (Métraux 1972; Ramsey 2011). Formal Catholic campaigns to eradicate Vodou from Haitian society, meanwhile, have sometimes targeted Protestant pastors for arrest, like Rev. Salomon Severe Joseph, whose remarkable story we recounted in chapter 4. And, in some ways Vodou has been the most tolerant of Haiti's three major religious traditions, and it has suffered the most persecution among them, a sad historical reality that is making a resurgence in the wake of the tragic earthquake of 2010. Vodou is blamed by many Christians in Haiti, mostly Protestants, as having caused the disaster (McAlister 2012), an etiology of the earthquake that was also prophesied as a pending punishment for the "sins" of Vodou and homosexuality, as many believe, by Fr. Jules Campion at a Catholic Charismatic revival near Port-au-Prince in April of 2009, just nine months before the tragedy (see chap. 2). In any case, laypersons and sacerdotal leaders on each side of this religious triangle of forces frequently reference the others, often confrontationally, with some Catholics and nearly all Protestants demonizing Vodou, while practitioners of Vodou generally also practice Catholicism without any concern with theological contradictions. In fact, a Haitian proverb has it that "you have to be Catholic to serve the lwa," and the Vodou spirits themselves, the lwa, are baptized Catholics who sometimes ask to receive other Catholic sacraments (Métraux 1972).

Differences between and syncretism among them aside, Haiti's religious traditions all respond, although often in different ways, to the existential needs rooted in enslavement and poverty, and this as much as anything has shaped the Haitian religious collusio. Praying to *Bondyè* (God) or the Catholic saints or serving the Vodou lwas (spirits), whether for protection, forgiveness, fullness of life, deliverance, or salvation, arises from an unshakable faith that these spiritual beings can and do respond to humans' needs, and that religious practice elicits such response. Most Haitians expect that God, the saints, the Holy Spirit, or the lwas will intercede in their lives, and they petition them to do so through prayer and ritual. In this sense, Haitians are no different from any Christians who believe that prayer makes a difference in their day-to-day, immediate worlds. Thus, not surprisingly, Catholicism's greatest strengths in Haiti and in the Haitian diaspora are its numerous saint cults, especially that of the Virgin Mary (Rey 1999, 2002). Saints watch over people on demand, and they can pluck you from harm's way, as the Virgin Mary did for the *botpipel* aboard the *Merci Jésus* in the summer of 1994, or at least help you to survive adversity and recover from misfortune. Vodou, likewise, "is a religion of survival, and it counsels what it must to ensure survival" (Brown 1991: 254). The impressive growth of Haitian Protestantism, furthermore, has also been attributed to such factors: "Protestantism [in Haiti] . . . exploits to the hilt a certain psychosis of fear, presenting itself as a refuge that offers a kind of security," as Charles-Poisset Romain (1986: 125), the leading scholar of Haitian Protestantism, concludes. Protection, security, and survival are all things that people need, obviously, and that in Haitian religion, whether in Haiti or the diaspora, are ultimately provided by supernatural forces.

Furthermore, because religion is of such fundamental importance in Haitian history, society, and culture, we are convinced that the Haitian religious collusio is also integral to Haitian national identity. Haitian national identity, especially once "othered" in racist in immigrant contexts as being *unworthy*, is deeply infused with religion in ways that enable and reify expressions of solidarity, despite theological difference and "the contest for healing power" in which all of these strands engage (Brodwin 1996), and despite these strands' not infrequently colliding in their negotiations of a "persecutory conception of evil" (Corten 2001: 30). When evil takes the form of the denial of worthiness, be it worthiness to receive and asylum hearing, justice, or a green card, religion must in turn respond by combating evil and restoring or preserving precisely what evil would deny or take away.

In light of the formidable challenges that most Haitians have experienced in immigrating to and settling in the United States, it is not surprising to find that there is a general increase in religious practice among them, which parallels such an increase in religious participation among immigrant communities in the United States more generally. This in itself is perhaps good enough reason to agree with Timothy Smith's (1978: 1181) assertion that the migration experience is itself "theologizing":

> [T]he acts of uprooting, migration, resettlement, and community-building became for the participants a theologizing experience. . . . The folk theology and religious piety that flourished in immigrant churches from the beginnings of American settlement were not merely traditional but progressive. Belief and devotion were powerful impulses to accommodation and innovation; and both helped legitimate the behavior, the perceptions, and the structures of association that sustained the processes of change.

Although not all immigrants become more religious through the migration and settlement experience, Smith's assertion is consistent with something that Will Herberg (1960) found over fifty years in his landmark study of earlier waves of immigrants and their religious life in the United States: that the process of uprooting and transplanting oneself can be traumatic, and religion often provides familiar reassurances and meaning. Similarly and more recently, Wendy Cadge and Elaine Howard Ecklund (2006) argue specifically that migrants who are less integrated into American society are more likely than others to regularly attend religious services. It matters, of course, that

Haitians, Koreans, and other immigrant groups are migrating to and settling in a deeply "theologized" country, the United States, whose native-born population believe in and practice religion at a much higher rate than those in European nations. America also receive large numbers of immigrants from developing nations. As such, there are ampler opportunities here for native-immigrant religious collaborations, and immigrants have taken full advantage of this, as evinced in the countless immigrant congregations that are today nested in longstanding native churches.

In titling this book *Crossing the Water and Keeping the Faith* we obviously intend to reflect the migratory and settlement experiences of Haitians in Miami who have crossed the water, whether as *botpipel* or members of the American Airlines Frequent Flyers Club, and kept the faith, whether as Catholics, Protestants, or Vodouists, their faith in God, the saints, the lwa, as well as their faith in Haiti. Less obviously, our choice of title conscientiously reflects a recent theory of religion developed by Thomas Tweed, one whose germinating ideas came to Tweed in Miami while he was researching the religious lives of Catholic Cuban exiles. In *Crossing and Dwelling* Tweed (2006: 54) arrives at the following compelling definition of religion: "Religions are confluences of organic-cultural flows that intensify joy and confront suffering by drawing on human and superhuman forces to make homes and cross boundaries." Much wordier surely than E. B. Tylor's (1920: 424) classic definition of religion as "belief in Spiritual Beings," but then again, religion is a much more complicated phenomenon than that.

We have observed that religion's function to "confront suffering" takes the form of a *"bourad"*:

> Besides the universal longings for a sense of meaning and communion with the Sacred, it is to the existential needs born of enslavement and poverty that Haitian religion most forthrightly responds. Paramount among these is the need for a bourad (Creole: "a boost" or "a push"): to the next meal; to making the next rent or tuition payment; to obtaining a visa or green card; to traversing a sea; or to placating a lover. It would be no exaggeration to call bourad one the most important forms of religious capital possessed—if not by all believers—by Haitians, be they Catholic, Vodouist, or Protestant. For most poor Haitians, whether

in Haiti or abroad, religion is essentially not about high-flung cosmology but about supernatural assistance in tackling life's problems as best one can. (Rey and Stepick 2010: 232)

To recall the words that Fr. Reginald Jean-Mary, the present pastor of Notre Dame d'Haiti, used to describe the Jericho Revival at his church in 2010, the year of the earthquake: "After ten months, you can tell people are feeling dispirited. Jericho is about *boosting* their sense of hope" (Miller 2010, emphasis added). For Haitian immigrants, religion provides a critical *bourad* in the migration experience "to cross boundaries," the crossing of water, and in the settlement experience, "to make homes," aiding them materially and spiritually in their negotiations of a new world, in their search for life (*chache lavi*).

Through the course of the research for this book, we have come to see that to the inventory of things toward which religion boosts Haitian immigrants in Miami one could and should add worthiness. We have argued that for many Haitian immigrants in Miami religious practice is a source of worthiness, a form of salvation good that such practice accrues for believers. For Bourdieu, symbolic capital is a power resource because it can be "transubstantiated" into material capital. For Haitians in Miami and elsewhere in the diaspora, the religious capital possessed by churches, temples, priests, pastors, botanicas, *oungan*, and *manbo* generates a wide array of salvation goods that believers pursue, the most obvious being sacraments, luck, magic, and healing. Less obvious, though equally important, especially for poor immigrants, is worthiness: a sense of being worthy of a place in American society; a sense that one's gifts from Haiti are making an important contribution to both the American social fabric and the Haitian; a sense of dignity and respect that transforms boat people into people, beasts into gods, as reflected in the last lines of the Morisseau-Leroy poem:

> One day we'll stand up, put down our feet
> > As we did at St. Domingue
> > They'll know who are boat people
> > That day, be it Christopher Columbus
> > Or Henry Kissinger—They will know
> > Whom we ourselves call people.

These are people whose ancestors derived a *bourad* from their spirits, saints, and gods to overthrow the French colonial slaving regime of Saint-Domingue, the same spirits, saints, and gods who have boosted them in their crossing to the other side of the water and to their dwelling here. Haitian religion in Miami, its salvation good of worthiness, thus enables labor, savings, and remittances to the homeland, illustrating beautifully how religious capital is transubstantiated into material capital, and in this case that transubstantiation is itself transnational. Crossing the water and keeping the faith thus keeps people alive, faithful, and fed on both sides of the water, a faith that, when *All* of this is over and done, one will cross to the truest of all homes, the Kingdom of God, or to *Ginen*—the ancestral home of Africa to which part of one's soul is said to return in Haitian Vodou. In the meantime, hope for Haiti lives in the faith of its living people in Miami.

APPENDIX 1

Churches in the Roman Catholic Archdiocese of Miami that Celebrate
Mass and/or Hear Confessions in Haitian Creole or French

This listing is roughly organized in geographic order, ranging from
north to south in the Archdiocese of Miami. The numbers corre-
sponded to the churches' respective numbered locators on map 2 in the
introduction.

1. St. Elizabeth of Hungary
   3331 NE 10 Terrace
   Pompano Beach, FL 33064

2. Our Lady Queen of Heaven
   1400 South State Road 7
   North Lauderdale, FL 33068

3. St. Clement
   2975 North Andrews Avenue
   Wilton Manors, FL 33311

4. St. Maurice
   2851 Stirling Road
   Dania Beach, FL 33312

5. St. Boniface
   8330 Johnson Street
   Pembroke Pines, FL 33024

6. St. Bartholomew
   8005 Miramar Parkway
   Miramar, FL 33025

7. St. Stephen
   2000 South State Road 7
   Miramar, FL 33023

8. St. Mary Magdalene
   17775 North Bay Road
   North Miami Beach, FL 33160

9. St. Philip Neri
   15700 NW 20th Avenue Road
   Miami Gardens, FL 33054

10. St. James and Our Lady of Perpetual Help
    540 NW 132nd Street
    North Miami, FL 33168

11. Holy Family
    14500 NE 11th Avenue
    North Miami, FL 33161

12. The Cathedral of St. Mary
    7525 NW 2nd Avenue
    Miami, FL 33150

13. Notre Dame d'Haiti
    110 NE 62nd Street
    Miami, FL 33138

14. St. Thomas the Apostle
    7377 SW 64th Street
    Miami, FL 33143

15. Our Lady of Lourdes
    11291 SW 142nd Avenue
    Miami, FL 33186

16. Christ the King
    16000 SW 112th Avenue
    Perrine, FL 33157

17. St. Joachim
    19150 SW 117th Avenue
    Miami, FL 33177

18. Sacred Heart
    106 SE 1st Drive
    Homestead, FL 33030

List of Botanicas in Little Haiti

Botanica Brave Guede
    5857 NE 2nd Avenue
    Miami, FL 33137

Botanica Halouba
    101 NE 54th Street
    Miami, FL 33137

Chez France Botanica*
    5921 NW 2nd Avenue
    Miami, FL 33137

Isidor & Carmel Botanica
    164 NE 54th Street
    Miami, FL 33137

Jn-Simon Brutus Botanica
    8238 NE 2nd Avenue
    Miami, FL 33138

La Belle Déesse Dereale Botanica*
    7728 NE 2nd Avenue
    Miami, FL 33137

Les Trois Mystères Botanica*
    281 NW 79th Street
    Miami, FL 33150

Martha Marombé Botanica Shop
6445 NE 2nd Avenue
Miami, FL

Saint Gerard Botanica Variety Store
5901 NW 2nd Avenue
Miami, FL 33127

Saint-Michel Variety Store: Vodooizan Kilti pa Nou
5919 NW 2nd Avenue
Miami, FL 33137

Santa Barbara 3 x 3 Botanica
5853 NE 2nd Avenue
Miami, FL 33137

St. Lazard Variety Store
5903 NW 2nd Avenue
Miami, FL 33127

Tipa Tipa & Danger La Croix Botanica
7736 NE 2nd Avenue
Miami, FL 33138

Toute Division Botanica
135 NE 54th Street
Miami, FL 33137

Varieté Shop and Botanica*
5742 NW 2nd Avenue
Miami, FL 33127

Vierge Miracle et St. Philippe Botanica
5912 NE 2nd Avenue
Miami, FL 33138

*connotes botanicas that we believe to be defunct since we conducted our fieldwork in Little Haiti.

Protestant Churches in Little Haiti

Ambassadors for God*
  8370 NE 2nd Avenue
  Miami, FL 33138

Assembly Kingdom of Elohim, Inc.
  House of Elohim (God)
  8267 NE 2nd Avenue
  Miami, FL 33150

Bethel Pentecostal Holiness Church of the Apostolic Faith
  4772 NW 7th Avenue
  Miami, FL 33127

Bethlehem Baptist Church
  6534 NW 7th Avenue
  Miami, FL 33150

Calvary Holiness Church of God #2
  7614 NW 7th Avenue
  Miami, FL 33150

Church of Christ Redeemer Haitian Assembly of God
  4314 NW 2nd Avenue
  Miami, FL 33127

Church of God
  267 NE 79th Street
  Miami, FL 33138

Church of God of Prophecy
    4528 NW 1st Avenue
    Miami, FL 33127

Church of Jesus Christ of Latter Day Saints*
    Morningside (Haitian Creole) Branch
    8515 Biscayne Boulevard
    Miami, FL 33161

Church of Perfection
    585 NW 7th Street
    Miami, FL 33150

Community Christian Church
    311 NE 7th Street
    Miami, FL 33138

Cornerstone Haitian Baptist Church
    7194 NW 6th Court.
    Miami, FL 33150

Crusade for Christ Church
    7798 NW 7th Avenue
    Miami, FL 33150

Discipleship Baptist Church
    8272 NE 2nd Avenue
    Miami, FL 33138

Divinity Baptist Church
    6400 NE 2nd Avenue
    Miami, FL 33138

Drake Memorial Baptist Church
    5800 NW 2nd Avenue
    Miami, FL 33150

Eben Ezer Haitian Baptist Church
   6985 NW 2nd Avenue
   Miami, FL 33150

EDEN Eglise Adventiste du Septieme Jour
   777 N. Miami Avenue
   Miami, FL 33150

Eglise Alliance Evangelique
   8323 NE 2nd Avenue
   Miami, FL 33150

Eglise Ambassadeurs pour Christ du Dernier Temps
   Church of the Ambassadors for Christ for the Last Time
   233 NE 76th Street
   Miami, FL 33138

Eglise Baptiste Bethel
   3600 NW 7th Avenue
   Miami, FL 33125

Eglise Baptiste d'Expression Française, Inc.
   375 NE 54th Street
   Miami, FL 33150

Eglise Baptiste de la Régénération
   6319 NW 2nd Avenue
   Miami, FL 33150

Eglise Baptiste de la Renaissance
   8255 NW 2nd Court
   Miami, FL 33150

Eglise Baptiste Phare Lumineux
   8397 NE 2nd Avenue
   Miami, FL 33150

Eglise Baptiste Terre Promise, Inc.
200 NW 77th Street
Miami, FL 33150

Eglise Baptiste Haitienne Emmanuel
New Vision Emmanuel Baptist Mission
7321 NE 2nd Avenue
Miami, FL 33150

Eglise Baptiste Un Seul Dieu
4312 NW 7th Avenue
Miami, FL 33150

Eglise Bethesda Baptiste
132 NW 54th Street
Miami, FL 33150

Eglise Chretienne Baptiste de Canaan, Inc.
274 NE 59th Street
Miami, FL 33150

Eglise Chretienne par la Foi de Dieu
63 NW 54th Street
Miami, FL 33150

Eglise de Dieu
7140 N Miami Avenue
Miami, FL 33150

Eglise de Dieu Apostolique
88 NW 54th Street
Miami, FL 33150

Eglise de Dieu du Dernier Temps*
8380 NE 2nd Avenue
Miami, FL 33138

Eglise de Dieu l'Arche de Délivrance
   147 NW 71st Street
   Miami, FL 33150

Eglise de Dieu l'Arch de Noe
   141 NW 71st Street
   Miami, FL 33150

Eglise de Dieu de la Prophétie
   48 NW 54th Street
   Miami, FL 33127

Eglise de Dieu Sanctifiée Haitienne
   5121 NW 2nd Avenue
   Miami, FL 33127

Eglise de Dieu Missionaire de Miami
   180 NE 65th Street
   Miami, FL 33150

Eglise de Dieu Mont des Oliviers
   Church of God Source of Victory
   45 NE 54th Street
   Miami, FL 33150

Eglise de Dieu de Siloe
   Pentecostal Church off Miami, Inc.
   90 NW 54th Street
   Miami, FL 33127

Eglise de Dieu du Temps de la Fin
   End Time Church of God
   4852 NW 2nd Avenue
   Miami, FL 33127

Eglise de Dieu Indépandante
    275 NW 54th Street
    Miami, FL 33127

Eglise de Dieu pour Jesus Christ
    6007 NW 7th Avenue
    Miami, FL 33127

Eglise de la Nouvelle Alliance, Inc.*
    8411 Biscayne Boulevard
    Miami, FL 33138

Eglise de St. Paul et les Martyrs d'Haiti
    6744 N. Miami Avenue
    Miami, FL 33150

Eglise des Freres Unis en Jesus-Christ
    4900 NW 2nd Avenue
    Miami, FL 33127

Eglise des Rachetés
    8320 NE 2nd Avenue
    Miami, FL 33150

Eglise Devoué pour Christ
    6234 NE 2nd Avenue
    Miami, FL 33150

Eglise du Christ de North Miami
    8343 NE 3rd Court
    Miami, FL 33150

Eglise du Nazaréen*
    8288 Biscayne Boulevard
    Miami, FL 33138

Eglise du Nazareen Libre
  Free Church of the Nazareen by Faith
  7640 NE 2nd Avenue
  Miami, FL 33150

Eglise du Nouveau Testament
  281 NW 79th Street
  Miami, FL 33150

Eglise Ephatha Church
  5800 NW 2nd Avenue
  Miami, FL 33150

Eglise Evangelique Baptiste de Bethesda
  7037 NW 2nd Avenue
  Miami, FL 33150

Eglise Evangelique Baptiste Mt. Sion (2001)
  Mount Zion Evangelical Baptist Church of Morningside (2012)
  6720 NE 5th Avenue
  Miami, FL 33147

Eglise Evangelique Baptiste Salem (2001)
  First Salem Evangelical Church and Community Center (2012)
  140 NW 79th Street
  Miami, FL 33150

Eglise Evangelique Chrétienne*
  292 NE 71st Street
  Miami, FL 33138

Eglise Evangelique de la Bible*
  500 NW 54th Street
  Miami, FL 33127

Eglise Evangelique du Grand Berger, Inc.
260 NE 59th Street
Miami, FL 33150

Eglise Evangelique Maranatha
7297 NW 2nd Avenue
Miami, FL 33150

Eglise Horeb Adventiste du 7eme Jour
7403 NE 4th Court
Miami, FL 33138

Eglise Methodiste Libre
101 NW 71st Street
Miami, FL 33150

Eglise Missionaire Trompette de Sion, Inc.
7642 NW 7th Avenue
Miami, FL 33150

Eglise par la Foi en Christ
759 NW 54th Street
Miami, FL 33127

Filadelfia Seventh Day Adventist Church
8017 NE 2nd Avenue
Miami, FL 33138

First Haitian Church of God
7140 North Miami Ave.
Miami, FL 33150

First Haitian Church of the Living God, Inc.
132 NW 54th Street
Miami, FL 33127

First Interdenominational Haitian Church
5832 NE 2nd Avenue
Miami, FL 33150

First International Pentecostal Church of God, Inc.
5706 NW 7th Avenue
Miami, FL 33127

Free Methodist Christian Community Church
101 NW 71st Street
Miami, FL 33150

French Speaking Baptist Church
6985 NW 2nd Avenue
Miami FL, 33150

Friendship Missionary Baptist Church
740 NW 58th Street
Miami, FL 33127

Full Gospel Assembly
3901 NW 2nd Avenue
Miami, FL 33127

Gospel Arena International Ministries Incorporated of Miami, Florida
7511 NW 7th Avenue
Miami, FL 33150

Grace Memorial House of Prayer for All People
6511 NW 7th Avenue
Miami FL 33150

Grace United Methodist Church
(First Haitian Free Methodist Church)
6501 N. Miami Avenue
Miami, FL 33150

Haitian Baptist Church of the Living God (2001)
  Eglise Baptise de Dieu Vivant (2001)
  Outreach Mission Church of God in Christ (2012)
  7751 NE 4th Court
  Miami, FL 33150

Haitian Baptist Refugee Center
  6985 NW 2nd Avenue
  Miami, FL 33150

Heart of God Ministries Church, Inc.
  980 NW 7th Street
  Miami, FL 33150

Holy Church of the Nazarene
  130 NW 79th Street
  Miami, FL 33150

House of the Living God
  6620 N. Miami Avenue
  Miami, FL 33150

House of Prayer Holiness and Fire Baptized Church, Inc
  118 NW 79th Street
  Miami, FL 33150

Iglesia Cristiana Refugio de Amor
  2810 NW 2nd Avenue
  Miami, FL 33127

Iglesia Cristiana Unidos en Cristo
  4386 NW 2nd Avenue
  Miami, FL 33127

Iglesia de Dios Rios Pentecostal
  2610 NW 36th Street
  Miami, FL 33142

Iglesia Pentecoste Hermanos Unidos en Cristo
    4810 NE 2nd Avenue
    Miami, FL 33137

Independent Eglise de Dieu
    1290 NW 36th Street
    Miami, FL 33142

Jehovah's Witness Kingdom Hall
    7790 NW 4th Avenue
    Miami, FL 33150

Jerusalem Eglise Adventiste du Septième Jour
    4201 NE 2nd Avenue
    Miami, FL 33150

La Nueva Jerusalem Church
    4528 NW 1st Avenue
    Miami, FL 33127

Lighthouse Christian Center, Inc.*
    300 NE 62nd Street
    Miami, FL 33132

Lively Stone Church of Miami
    8025 NW Miami Court
    Miami, FL 33150

Miami Bethany Church of the Nazarene, Inc.
    2490 NW 35th Street
    Miami, FL 33142

Miami Hosanna Church of the Nazarene
    195 NW 39th Street
    Miami, FL 33127

Miami Peniel Church of the Nazarene
5801 NW 2nd Avenue
Miami, FL 33127

Miami Victory Church*
215 NW 36th Street
Miami, FL 33127

Ministerio Evangelico en Espiritu
2010 NW 36th Street
Miami, FL 33142

Mission Evangelique du Christianisme
535 NW 54th Street
Miami, FL 33127

Mount Clair Holiness Church
4421 NW 7th Avenue
Miami, FL 33127

Mount Sinai Missionary Baptist Church
698 NW 47th Terrace.
Miami, FL 33127

Nazareth Haitian Mission
47 NW 67th Street
Miami, FL 33150

New Beginnings Baptist Church
6311 NW 2nd Avenue
Miami, FL 33150

New Beginnings Community Church
7140 NW Miami Court
Miami, FL 33150

New Bethany Baptist Church
   777 NW 54th Street
   Miami, FL 33127

New Birth Enterprise
   8400 NE 2nd Avenue
   Miami, FL 33138

New Canaan Baptiste Church*
   301 NE 59th Street
   Miami, FL 33150

New Canaan Missionary Baptist Church
   703 NW 56th Street
   Miami, FL 33127

New Hope Baptist Church
   4606 NW 7th Avenue
   Miami, FL 33127

New Mount Pleasant Institutional Baptist Church, Inc.
   7610 Biscayne Boulevard
   Miami, FL 33138

New St. Mark MB Church
   744 NW 54th Street
   Miami, FL 33127

New St. Paul Missionary Baptist Church
   4755 NW 2nd Avenue
   Miami, FL 33127

Nouvelle Eglise Baptiste Bethanie (2001)
   Bethany Baptist Church (2012)
   787 NW 54th Street
   Miami, FL 33150

Oasis Chritian Ministries
   4801 NW 7th Avenue
   Miami, FL 33127

Pentecostal Church of Miami, Inc.
   81 NW 54th Street
   Miami, FL 33150

Philadelphia Church of God, Inc.
   125 NE 54th Street
   Miami, FL 33137

Philadelphie Seventh Day Adventist Church
   74 NE 75th Street
   Miami, FL 33138

Potential Release Ministries
   54 NE 54th Street
   Miami, FL 33137

Premiere Eglise des Elus, Inc.
   8344 NE 2nd Avenue
   Miami, FL 33150

Première Eglise Universelle du Seigneur
   521 NW 54th Street
   Miami, FL 33127

Salle de Royaume des Temoins de Jehovah
   241 NW 54th Street
   Miami, FL 33150

Second Corinth M.B. Church
   6200 NW Miami Court
   Miami, FL 33150

Shalom Seventh Day Adventist Church
    7430 NE 4th Court
    Miami, FL 33138

South Florida Haitian Christian Center, Inc.
    111 NW 54th Street
    Miami, FL 33127

Spring Hill Revival Center
    4740 NW 7th Avenue
    Miami, FL 33127

St. Luke Free Will Baptist Church
    749 NW 62nd Street
    Miami, FL 33150

St. Mary's House of Prayer—Apostolic Faith
    6313 NW 2nd Avenue
    Miami, FL 33150

St. Matthew's Free Will Baptist Church
    6700 NW 2nd Avenue
    Miami, FL 33150

St. Peter's African Orthodox Cathedral
    4841 NW 2nd Avenue
    Miami, FL 33127

Tabernacle de Dieu en Christ (2001)
    Tabernacle of God in Christ (2012)
    3825 NW 2nd Avenue
    Miami, FL 33127

Tabernacle Seventh Day Adventist Church
    8017 NE 2nd Avenue
    Miami, FL 33138

Temple de l'Eternel
    2225 NW 7th Avenue
    Miami, FL 33127

The Bible Way Prayer Mission
    5757 NW 7th Avenue
    Miami, FL 33127

The First Tabernacle of Jesus Christ
    7426 NE 2nd Avenue
    Miami, FL 33138

The Tabernacle Ark of Jesus Christ, Inc.
    6391 NW 2nd Avenue
    Miami, FL 33150

Trinity Evangelical Baptist Church
    6777 NW 7th Avenue
    Miami, FL 33150

True Gospel Unity Tabernacle
    5000 NW 7th Avenue
    Miami, FL 33127

Un Seul Dieu, Inc.
    761 NW 62nd Street
    Miami, FL 33150

Union Chretienne
    6701 NW 7th Avenue
    Miami, FL 33150

United Christian Fellowship
    Gospel Truth Ministry, Inc.
    769 NW 54th Street
    Miami, FL 33127

United Christian Praise and Worship Center, Inc.
  7626 NW 77th Street
  Miami, FL 33150

United House of Prayer for All People
  4600 NW 2nd Avenue
  Miami, FL 33127

Westminster Presbyterian Church
  4201 NE 2nd Avenue
  Miami, FL 33137

Youth Crusade Deliverance Church
  7600 NW 7th Avenue
  Miami, FL 33150

NOTES

INTRODUCTION

1. Manbo Margaret Armand, interview with Terry Rey, Plantation, Florida, June 4, 2004.

2. This data dates from the late 1990s, and it should be admitted that it may no longer be the case that Haitians practice religion communally with greater frequency than any other immigrant group in the United States. That said, religious life in Little Haiti seems to be every bit as vibrant today as it was in the 1990s, if not more so. For comparison's sake, consider recent survey data about foreign-born ethnic minorities in North Philadelphia, Pennsylvania, mostly Latinos, which indicate that a relatively paltry 11 percent regularly participate in communal religious services (Stern, Steifert, and Vitiello 2010: 38).

3. Though Philadelphia is not usually counted among cities with a large Haitian diasporic community, Terry Rey has begun preliminary research on a book project about Haitian churches in the "city of brotherly love" and estimates there to be over thirty thousand Haitians now residing in or near the city, where there are now about sixty Haitian churches in all.

4. That Calvinism transformed work into a virtue and thus provided the theological impetus for the Protestant work ethic is of course Weber's (1958) most famous argument concerning religion.

5. Rev. Fritz Bazin, interview with Terry Rey, Miami, February 6, 2004.

6. This and all other translations in this book are by the authors.

7. Lest one argue that worthiness described here by Weber is precisely the kind of "compensator" that rational choice theorists perceivably identify as the virtual essence of religion, remember that Weber (1963: 107) also identified worthiness, or at least the legitimation of their right thereto, as the motivating force (actually, the *sole* motivating force) behind the religious practice of those who hardly require of religion compensation for material want, namely "the privileged classes."

8. Religious capital is one of a several forms of "symbolic capital" conceptualized by Bourdieu, and others, the best known and most widely used form in scholarship being "social capital." As summarized by Portes and some of his collaborators (e.g., Portes 1998, 2000b; Portes and Landolt 2000; Portes and

Mooney 2002), the concept of social capital was developed independently by Bourdieu (1983) and the American sociologist James Coleman (1988a; 1988b). "Capital, defined implicitly as attributes, possessions, or qualities of a person or a position exchangeable for goods, services, or esteem, exists in many forms— symbolic, cultural, social, linguistic, as well as economic," as Paul DiMaggio explains (1979: 1463). The key is that something symbolic can be transformed into something material, like an academic degree (symbolic capital) landing someone a job and an income (material capital), and a process that Bourdieu (1986: 242) refers to as "transubstantiation." Similarly, social capital—one's network of social relations and resultant knowledge of how to "play the system"— can result in material advantages. As such, social capital theorizes the cliché that "It's not what you know, but who you know." In religious contexts, religious capital functions in a similar vein.

9. Religion is more than economics, however. Richman (2005) indicates how Haitian Protestants use the church as their primary social group. Moreover, she explains how Haitians can use Protestantism to escape transnational social obligations, which are tied to the traditional religion of Vodou. Protestantism's impact on an individual's direct relationship to God relieves one of Vodou's imperatives to share, give to one's capacity, and engage in reciprocal relationships. Haitian converts to Protestantism are relieved of the burden of sponsoring religious events in the home country and of Vodou's explicit moral imperative to share one's material resources. Richman's arguments are similar to earlier research that addressed why Latin American peasants were converting to Protestantism (Annis 1987; Falla 2001; Garrard-Burnett and Stoll 1993; Junker-Kenny and Tomka 1999; Stewart-Gambino 2001).

10. Schrauf (1999) argues that religious practice is one of the few factors that preserves native language among immigrants and their offspring.

11. In a rare exception, one boatload of Haitian migrants that arrived in Pompano Beach on December 12, 1965, did receive political asylum, as its passengers had "shot up Haiti's presidential palace" before fleeing Haiti (Dunne 1997: 322).

12. Saint-Domingue and its people were widely understood to be the source of the yellow fever epidemics that ravaged Philadelphia in 1793 and 1797; thus Haitians have been considered diseased in American popular consciousness since then. In the 1970s, meanwhile, "a hysterical scare swept through south Florida that tuberculosis was endemic among Haitians and was likely to spread through the general population" (Stepick 1992: 58). That said, the association with AIDS proved to be the most devastating of the disease rumors in Haitian and Haitian American history.

13. The Roman Catholic Diocese of Miami was founded in 1958. In 1968 it became an archdiocese.

14. Thomas Wenski, interview with Terry Rey and Alex Stepick, Miami, September 26, 2002.

CHAPTER 1

1. The Venerable Pierre Toussaint (1766–1853), was born a slave in Saint-Domingue and came to New York with the wife of his owner in 1787, where he became a successful hairdresser, eventually supporting her after her husband had died in Saint-Domingue. After she died, Toussaint was freed and invested much of his fortune in charitable works, including the construction of an orphanage and Old Saint Patrick's Cathedral in Manhattan. Pope John Paul II pronounced Toussaint as Venerable in 1996 (the first degree of sanctity in Roman Catholic theology). His remains lie in a crypt at St. Patrick's Cathedral in New York, the first layperson to receive this honor. On Toussaint, see Jones 2003 and Tarry 1998.

2. Msgr. Thomas Wenski, interview with authors, September 26, 2000, Miami.

3. Ibid.

4. Known popularly as "Papa Doc," Dr. François Duvalier ruled Haiti from 1957 until his death in 1971. He was succeeded by his son, Jean-Claude Duvalier ("Baby Doc"), who was ousted by rising popular discontent in 1984. The human rights record of the Duvaliers is one of the worst in Latin American history, with much of the persecution orchestrated by the notorious paramilitary organization known as the Tonton Macoutes. On Duvalier, see Diedrich and Burt 1986. The Namphy regime ruled and terrorized Haiti from 1986 to 1988, and that of Cédras from 1991 to 1994.

5. *Lavwa Katolik* (The Catholic Voice) was founded in 1981. See also Martinez 1983.

6. See also Thompson 1987 and Lee 1988.

7. For a moving account of the St. Jean Bosco massacre, see Aristide 1993.

8. See, for example, Kollin 1993.

9. Wenski's commitment to Catholic sexual morality led to clashes with local Haitian community leaders who were promoting the use of condoms as part of a safe-sex campaign as the AIDS epidemic surged in the Haitian immigrant community in the 1980s and 1990s. Larry Pierre, then the director of the Center for Haitian Studies in Little Haiti, dispatched a volunteer to Notre Dame to lead an AIDS prevention discussion, only to be angrily confronted by Wenski with over the phone: "I received a call from him and said, 'Hi, Tom. How you doing?' . . . . But he shouted, 'I'm not calling you to bullshit around. I'm calling you to tell you don't you dare distribute information about condoms at my church.' . . . He even called the director of our foundation, saying I was encouraging people to have sex. . . . Without a doubt, he was trying to get our funding cut" (Miller 2010b).

10. Although Vatican II, Puebla, and Medellín inspired some measure of enculturation of the Catholic Mass in Haiti, homiletic denunciations of "superstitions" and "the ancestors" remain common in the Haitian Church.

11. The *poto mitan* is the center pole that runs from the floor and to the roof of a Vodou temple. Vodouists believe that this is the point at which the spirits enter their midst in ceremonial ritual. Colloquially in Haitian Creole the term *poto mitan* is equivalent to the English term "pillar of strength."

12. Reginald Jean-Mary, interview with Alex Stepick, Miami, June 15, 2010.

13. Notre Dame is also a key congregation in Miami's largest interfaith community-based organization, PACT (People Acting for Community), which, as Mooney (2009: 85) explains "is unique . . . because it goes beyond charitable actions and aims at mobilizing people to participate in politics."
14. Nonciature Apostolique en Haïti. 2010. Letter of Tarcisio Cardinal Bertone to Msgr. Bernadito Auzo, September 20, Port-au-Prince. http://www.newmiamiarch. org/Atimo_s/news/0083_001.pdf.

CHAPTER 2

1. The median household income in Miramar is $64,547 (http://quickfacts.census.gov/qfd/states/12/1236121.html; last accessed December 30, 2011), while the median household income in Little Haiti is slightly less than $19,000 (http://www. miamigov.com/Planning/pages/services/Census.asp; last accessed December 30, 2011).
2. Mirlène Jeanty is a pseudonym. Jeanty was interviewed on several occasions by Terry Rey between 1998 and 2005. Some of her biographical details have been altered on her request to further conceal her identity.
3. In this regard Kendall differs radically from North Miami, where violent gang-related crime is generally as fearsome as, and often directly related to, that found in Little Haiti (Clary 2002).
4. Anonymous, interview with Terry Rey, Miami, January 4, 2005.
5. This sermon was captured on film and may be seen on youtube: http://www. youtube.com/watch?v=rqKNui3xCEc; last accessed March 20, 2012.
6. We adopt the term "pneumacentric" from Chesnut 2003.

CHAPTER 3

1. Bel-Air is the Port-au-Prince neighborhood that is home to the Church of Our Lady of Perpetual Help and hence the site of an important pilgrimage tradition there, while Limonade is a coastal village in the north of Haiti that is home to both the Church of St. Ann and the Shrine of St. Philomena, hence the home to two other important Haitian pilgrimages (Rey 1999; O'Neil and Rey 2012).
2. Campion has subsequently warned Haiti of even worst disasters if people do not repent and convert to Catholicism (Jean 2011).
3. Paul Brodwin (2003: 87–88) echoes Hurbon's and our own observations about Haitian Pentecostalism: "Pentecostal doctrine demands that Christians separate totally from the fallen world and seek direct encounters with God." For Brodwin, becoming Pentecostal clearly entails rejecting Vodou spirits *as objects of worship*. Critical of anthropological accounts of Pentecostalism in Brazil for having ignored "believers' explicit commitments," which are inspired by a theology that "demonizes other religious paths," he stresses that like among Haitian Pentecostals vis-à-vis Vodou, Brazilian Pentecostals "would surely deny they share anything in common with Umbanda devotees and their practice of spirit possession."

4. With the exception of carnival, which takes place just before Lent, the annual National Charismatic Congress has become the biggest public gathering in Haiti and is arguably the largest religious gathering in all of the Caribbean. Begun in 1995, the congress today draws upwards of ninety thousand Catholics daily over its three-day duration (Cleary 2011; Norton 2003; Rey 2010).

5. Anonymous, interview with Terry Rey, Miami, June 28, 2002.

6. The Magnificat is Mary's most extensive statement in the Bible (Luke 1:46–55).

7. The escapist tendency of the Renewal is emphasized by Brodwin (2003: 85) in his analysis of Haitian Pentecostalism in general, which he classifies as a "world-rejecting religion."

8. Msgr. Guire Poulard, interview with Terry Rey, Jacmel, Haiti, February 17, 2002; Msgr. Joseph Serge Miot, interview with Terry Rey, Port-au-Prince, Haiti, March 1, 2002.

9. A health and education fair was held in the churchyard from 9:00 to 3:00 on Saturday, June 29, 2002. Unfortunately, heavy rains caused most of the fair's booths to close early. That evening there was also an inter-parish concert (*Concert Marial*), which we were unable to attend.

10. Although the feasts of Mount Carmel in New York may have been the largest gathering of Haitian immigrants for religious purposes in the United States when McAlister did her research there in the 1990s, we suspect that today the largest such gathering is the annual meeting of the Catholic Charismatic Congress of Overseas Haitians, whose location rotates annually. In 2002, the congress was held in Miami and drew more than seven thousand participants, most of them present for all three days of the gathering (see chap. 1).

11. In a 2006 letter to Terry Rey, Msgr. Thomas Wenski encouraged Rey, who had just moved from Miami to Philadelphia, to make the effort to write an ethnographic study of Haitian pilgrims to the Feast of Czestochowa in Doylestown. In addition to making pilgrimage to the Doylestown shrine, many Haitians in the diaspora, according to Karen McCarthy Brown (1999: 90), also visit for the Feast of Our Lady of Mount Carmel, incorporating this shrine into their re-creation of the Saut-d'Eau pilgrimage in Haiti.

CHAPTER 4

1. See also Dubocq 1993.

2. For press accounts of this incident, see Rhoten 1993 and Yanez et al. 1993.

3. See also Charles 2003. On Vodou in Broward County, see Monnay 1998, and in Palm Beach County, see Richman 2008a and 2008b.

4. On the use of audio-cassette tapes in Haitian religion, see also Richman and Rey 2009.

5. Although beyond the scope of our present study, it is important to note the presence of thousands of Central Africans in Saint-Domingue, especially enslaved people from the Kingdom of Kongo, who were Catholic long before being brought in chains to the French Caribbean colony (Rey 2002).

6. Margaret Armand, personal electronic communication, June 10, 2004.

7. Benjamin Hebblethwaite, guest lecture in Terry Rey's African Religions graduate seminar, Temple University, February 23, 2012. We are most grateful to Professor Hebblethwaite for having brought Societe Linto Roi to our attention. On Vodou songs, see Hebblethwaite 2011.

8. St. Ann Mission is the spiritual home of thousands of Mexican immigrant farm workers in the fields of rural south Miami-Dade County and home to South Florida's swelling devotion to Our Lady of Guadalupe, Mexico's national patron saint, whose feast day celebrations span several days and attract thousands (Báez, Rey, and Rey, 2009: 206, n3).

9. *Asogwe* is the highest rank for a Vodou priestess or priest. We have the impression that Vodou Fest in Miami did not endure annually beyond 2005.

10. Margaret Armand, interview with Terry Rey, June 4, 2004.

11. For further discussion on the efforts of Armand, de Lynch, Llera, and other leading *manbo* in South Florida, see Mapou 2002.

12. See also Sandoval 1979.

13. Wagner St. Pierre, interview with Terry Rey, November 22, 2001, Miami. On his request, Wagner St. Pierre is a pseudonym, and the name of the botanica that helped him regain his health is not included in our discussion.

14. Guerda Joseph (pseudonym), interview with Terry Rey, Miami, June 15, 2002.

15. See chap. 2 for further discussion about the Feast of Caridad in Miami.

16. On Sunday, February 29, 2004, for example, on the day that President Aristide was forced from power by an armed rebellion, Roman led a pilgrimage of two hundred Cubans from the shrine to Notre Dame d'Haiti in Little Haiti to deliver a homily of solidarity with the Haitian people.

17. Fr. Timothy Hopkins. Interview with Terry Rey, Miami, September 15, 2001.

18. On popular American misrepresentations of Vodou, see also McGee 2012.

19. A leading Miami Santería (Lukumi) priest, Oba Ernesto Pichardo, took the City of Hialeah to the U.S. Supreme Court for the City's ban of the ritual sacrifice of animals. Pichardo and his Church of the Lukumi Babalu Aye won a victory for all practitioners of African-derived religions in the United States in 1997. See O'Brien 2004.

20. Face Of The Gods: Art and Altars Of Africa And The African Americas, an exhibit curated by Robert Farris Thomspon. Florida International University, Miami, 2001. For examples of some of the altars on display, see Thompson 1993.

21. Leslie Desmangles, personal electronic communications, September 29, 2011; October 10, 2011. Desmangles was judicious in accepting the invitation to testify in this case: "I studied the case very carefully before I accepted to testify on behalf of the nursing home's management and as I read the transcripts of all the meeting that preceded the court procedure, I became convinced that the evidence was quite clear." Terry Rey did likewise before testifying in the 2002 SEIU case.

22. Anonymous, interview with Terry Rey, Miami, March 13, 2002. In addition to being subpoenaed by SEIU to appear as an expert witness on Haitian Vodou at

this trial, Rey was paid by the nursing home to do so, only after carefully reviewing the circumstances and, like Desmangles, being convinced that the union was using religion as a scare tactic.

23. Jean-Baptiste's daughter was a co-defendant in the trial. Terry Rey served as an expert witness on Haitian Vodou at the trial. The defense initially asked for Rey's assistance with the case, though he found their arguments about Vodou to be spurious. He was later hired by the prosecution instead. Both Marie Jean-Baptiste and her daughter appealed their convictions, in part by asserting that Rey's testimony at the trial should have entirely been stricken from the record. *United States of America v. Sophia Jean-Baptiste, Marie Jean-Baptiste.*

24. Luckner Thomas is a pseudonym.

25. We have also frequently encountered a belief in the spiritual power of Haiti among Haitian Catholics and Protestants, both in Miami and in Haiti. Rey (1999: 311) documents a case of revelations made by the Virgin Mary to a Haitian nun that the Blessed Mother had chosen Haiti as "my hot land . . . the center of the universal conversion."

26. Marie-Carmel Fontus is a pseudonym, as is the name of her botanica, and, on her request, we have likewise concealed the location of her Vodou temple in Haiti. Otherwise, the description of the botanica, temple, and related events are all accurate.

27. On the significance of trees in Haitian Vodou, see Hurbon 1987 and Rey 2005b.

28. Marie-Carmel Fontus, interview with Terry Rey, Miragoane, Haiti, October 15, 2002.

29. In saying "Miami," Richman's research consultants, like many Haitians, mean anywhere in South Florida and not just the City of Miami or Miami-Dade County.

CHAPTER 5

1. By the term "religioscape" we mean a more specific version of Arjun Appadurai's (1996: 33) term "ethnoscape": "the landscape of persons who constitute the shifting world in which we live: tourists, immigrants, refugees, exiles, guest workers, and other moving groups and individuals constitute an essential feature of the world and appear to affect the politics of (and between) nations to a hitherto unprecedented degree." We thought that we had coined the term "religioscape" in the early stages of our research for this book, only to realize that Elizabeth McAlister (1998: 156) had done so at around the same time, also drawing on Appadurai to suggest the same term in her work on immigrant Haitian religion, meaning specifically "the suggestive religious maps (and attendant theologies, of diasporic communities who are also in global flow and flux." Part of this section of this chapter and the following section are adapted from Rey 2007b.

2. In Haiti, meanwhile, Protestants have been renting and purchasing buildings designed for other purposes, like warehouses and theaters, as sanctuaries independent of any African American or other foreign influences.

3. For a glimpse of this, see the interview with "Madame Clobert" by Raoul Peck in his film *Desounnen: Dialogue with Death*.

4. Rev. Fritz Bazin, interview with Terry Rey, February 6, 2004, Miami.

5. There are certainly churches that we were unable to find; many congregations meet in private unmarked spaces, while others change location frequently. Thus, while we have located ninety-five churches in the neighborhood, there are easily more than one hundred.

6. The Islamic temples are not Haitian and the Mormon branch, whose opening ceremony Rey attended in 2003, has closed. On the establishment of the Mormon branch for Haitians in Miami, see Yardley 2003.

7. Rev. Devil Legrand, interview with Emmanuel Eugène, October 5, 2001. Eugène conducted several interviews on behalf of the Pew-funded project that supported much of our research in Haiti and Miami. Evidently Legrand's efforts to found a church in Miami, which today has a more recent sister congregation in Dania Beach, Palm Beach County, were supported by World Mission Ministries, a Miami-based organization that has its most extensive missionary programs in Belize (http://www.worldmissionministries.com/index.htm; last accessed April 28, 2012).

8. The oldest Haitian church the United States is the First Haitian Baptist Church, which was founded in 1965 in New York City by Rev. Pierre Ludovic Saint-Phard. http://www.fsbconline.org/index-1.html; last accessed April 25, 2012. Charles-Poisset Romain (2004: 73) lists the following pastors as Haitian Protestant "pioneers" in Miami, assessing that because of their work and that of their cohorts in other cities of their diaspora, "The Haitian churches of the diaspora are bubbling with activity. The future looks very promising: Elie Dumeny, Amos Eugène, Mariot Valcin, Renaud Balzora, Renaud Pierre-Louis, Clorin Calixte, Jonas Georges, Jean Fritz Bazin . . . Emmanuel César, Gonel Joseph, Jacques Dumornay, Félix Saint-Louis, Brésil Saint-Germain, Amos Myrthil, Mathieu Jean-Baptiste."

9. Rev. Jacques Clotaire, interview with Terry Rey, March 21, 2004.

10. This hymnal is used widely in most Haitian congregations both in Haiti and the Haitian diaspora. *Chants D'esperance et les melodies joyeuses*, 42nd ed. (Port-au-Prince: La Librerie de la Presse Evalngelique, 1995).

11. Rev. Fandor Saint-Felix, interview with Terry Rey, March 21, 2004, Miami.

12. According to Paul Brodwin (2003: 86), indeed "most Pentecostal churches in Haiti" were "founded by visiting missionaries from North America."

13. Details about the life of Joseph here summarized are entirely derived from Valéry 2000.

14. We have done the math: this equals 10,197 mystical kisses; add to this the three first kisses and you get 10,200.

15. The youth of the Montreal MEC branch have recently mounted a Facebook page on the Internet: http://www.facebook.com/group.php?gid=24980570480. Last accessed on March 26, 2010.

16. There is one exception to this rule: Dr. Kathleen Burton, a white American professor who joined the MEC in Connecticut and serves a number of important

leadership functions in the church. She has been ordained as a pastor by the MEC, the only woman in the church's clerical ranks. "In her case, we made an exception," explained the pastors in Miami.

17. For a glimpse of Guirand singing in an MEC congregation, see http://www.you-tube.com/watch?v=VtH75PmGNQ8; last accessed October 14, 2011.

18. In October 2005 the MEC Florida convention was scheduled to take place in Fort Meyers on the very same weekend that Hurricane Wilma, the strongest Atlantic hurricane ever recorded, was predicted to slam into the west coast of Florida. Gravely concerned, the Florida MEC pastors gathered in Fort Meyers a few days early to pray to God to delay the hurricane so that the convention could take place and all attendees would have enough time to return home safely. Much to the surprise of meteorologists covering the storm, Wilma slowed dramatically over the Yucatan Peninsula and arrived in Florida more than two days later than expected. Miracles, it would seem, continue in the MEC church. Pastor Kersaint Joseph, telephone interview with Terry Rey, November 1, 2005.

19. On the role of religious leadership in immigrant churches in Miami, see Stepick, Rey, and Mahler 2009.

20. Pastor Harold Vieux, interview with Alex Stepick and Terry Rey, September 21, 2002, Miami.

21. Eglise Baptiste Haitienne Emmanuel sponsors eight churches in Haiti. Juan Perez, "Pastor Wilner Maxion Emmanuel Baptist Church and the Crisis in Haiti." *Miami Evangelical Protestant Examiner*, October 28, 2010, http://www.examiner.com/ evangelical-protestant-in-miami/pastor-wilner-maxy-on-emmanuel-haitian-baptist-church-and-the-crisis-haiti; last accessed September 24, 2011. For a video clip of this church's thirty-seventh anniversary celebration in 2010, see http:// www.youtube.com/watch?v=Tnrg3P78Cps; last accessed September 24, 2011. In 2010, the State of Florida named several blocks of NE 73rd St. "Pastor Wilner Maxi Street." Florida Senate, 2010 Committee Bill no. 1033, http://laws.flrules. org/2010/233; last accessed September 24, 2010.

22. Harold Vieiux, interview with Alex Stepick, June 17, 2010, Miami.

23. Ameleon Juste, interview with Terry Rey, September 23, 2001, Dolval, Haiti.

24. Over the last few years, a Baptist pastor from Dolval named Oris Guillaume immi-grated to Georgia where he became involved with a missionary organization (Haiti Cheri Ministries), which has built and finances the operations of, a school in the village. From their website, it is unclear which Baptist church in Dolval enjoys the support of Haiti Cheri Ministries, but we suspect that this association will deepen the competition in the village's religious field. See www.haiticheri.org; last accessed October 30, 2011.

CONCLUSION

1. Fort Dimanche was a prison in Port-au-Prince, notorious for the persecution of political prisoners in Haiti during the Duvalier regime. Bossal Market is a refer-ence to slave markets in Saint-Domingue, the word "Bossal" (*bosal* in Haitian Creole) meaning African-born.

Abdullah, Zain. *Black Mecca: The African Muslims of Harlem*. New York: Oxford University Press, 2010.

Adhar, Rex. "The Idea of 'Religious Markets.'" *International Journal of Law in Context* 2, 1 (2006): 49–65.

Al-Ahmary, Abdullah Arib. "Ethnic Self-Identity and the Role of Islam: A Study of the Yemeni Community in the South End of Dearborn and Detroit, Michigan." PhD diss., University of Tennessee, Knoxville, 2000.

Annis, Sheldon. *God and Production in a Guatemalan Town*. Austin: University of Texas Press, 1987.

Aristide, Jean-Bertrand. *Aristide: An Autobiography*. New York: Orbis, 1993.

Appadurai, Arjun. *Modernity at Large: Cultural Dimensions of Globalization*. Minneapolis: University of Minnesota Press, 1996.

Báez, Noemí, María de los Ángeles Rey, and Terry Rey. "Faith in the Fields: Mexican Marianism in Miami-Dade County." In Stepick et al., eds., *Churches and Charity in the Immigrant City*, 190–207.

Balmaseda, Liz. "Prayer Vigil is a Protest for Haitians." *Miami Herald*, February 10, 1983.

Barm-S. Diaz, Madeline. "Health Fairs Serve as Haitian Lifeline." *Sun Sentinel*, April 27, 2001.

Bankston, Carl. L., III. "Bayou Lotus: Theravada Buddhism in Southwestern Louisiana." *Sociological Spectrum* 17, 4 (1997): 453–472.

Bankston, Carl L., III, and Min Zhou, M. "De Facto Congregationalism and Socioeconomic Mobility in Laotian and Vietnamese Immigrant Communities: A Study of Religious Institutions and Economic Change." *Review of Religious Research* 41, 4 (2000): 453–470.

Barnard, Anne. "Quake a Defining Crisis for Two Priests in Queens." *New York Times*, February 7, 2010(a).

———. "Suffering, Haitians turn to Charismatic Prayer." *New York Times*, November 24, 2010(b).

Bastian, Jean-Pierre. "La nouvelle économie religieuse de l'Amérique latine." *Social Compass* 53, 1 (2006): 65–80.

BBC News. "Haitian Migrants Found Dead off Cuba's Coast." December 24, 2011. http://www.bbc.co.uk/news/world-latin-america-16328342; last accessed March 11, 2012.

BBC World News. "Voodoo in Florida's Little Haiti." May 16, 2010. http://news.bbc.
co.uk/2/hi/8682605.stm; last accessed September 30, 2011.

Bébel-Gisler, Dany, and Laënnec Hurbon. *Cultures et pouvoir dans la Caraïbe: Langue créole, vaudou, sectes religieuses en Guadeloupe et en Haïti.* Paris: L'Harmattan, 1975.

Béchacq, Dimitri. "Pratiques migratoires entre Haïti et la France: Des élites d'hier aux *diasporas* d'aujourd'hui." PhD diss., École des Hautes Études en Sciences Sociales, 2010.

Bohning, Don, "Duvalier Keeps Grip on Haiti." *Miami Herald,* February 1, 1986.

Bourdieu, Pierre. "Genèse et structure du champ religieux." *Revue française de sociologie* 12, 2 (1971): 295–334.

———. *Outline of a Theory of Practice.* Translated by Richard Nice. Cambridge: Cambridge University Press, 1977.

———. *Le sens pratique.* Paris: Editions de Minuit, 1980.

———. "The Forms of Capital." In John G. Richardson, ed., *Handbook of Theory and Research for the Sociology of Education.* Translated by Richard Nice. New York: Greenwood Press, 1986, 241–258.

———. "Legitimation and Structured Interest in Weber's Sociology of Religion." In Scott Lash and Sam Whimster, eds., *Max Weber, Rationality and Modernity.* Translated by Chris Turner. London: Allen and Unwin, 1987.

———. *In Other Words.* Translated by Richard Nice. London: Polity Press, 1990.

———. "Genesis and Structure of the Religious Field." Translated by Jenny B. Burnside, Craig Calhoun, and Leah Florence. *Comparative Social Research* 13, 1 (1991): 1–44.

———. *The Logic of Practice.* Translated by Richard Nice. Stanford: Stanford University Press, 1992(a).

———. "Tout est social: Propos recueillis par Pierre-Marc de Biasi." *Magazine littéraire* 303, October 1992(b), 104–111.

———. *Pascalian Meditations.* Translated by Richard Nice. Stanford: Stanford University Press, 2000.

Brodwin, Paul. *Medicine and Morality in Haiti: The Contest for Healing Power.* New York: Cambridge University Press, 1996.

———. "Pentecostalism in Translation: Religion and the Production of Community in the Haitian Diaspora," *American Ethnologist* 30, 1 (2003): 85–101.

Brown, Karen McCarthy. "Olina and Erzulie: A Woman and a Goddess in Haitian Vodou." *Anima* 5, 2 (1979): 110–116.

———. "Afro-Caribbean Spirituality: A Haitian Case Study." In Lawrence Sullivan, ed., *Healing and Restoring: Medicine and Health in the World's Religious Traditions.* New York: Macmillan, 1989, 255–285.

———. *Mama Lola: A Vodou Priestess in Brooklyn.* Berkeley: University of California Press, 1991.

———. *Tracing the Spirit: Ethnographic Essays on Haitian Art.* Seattle: University of Washington Press, 1995.

———. "Staying Grounded in a High-Rise Building: Ecological Dissonance and Ritual Accommodation in Haitian Vodou." In Robert A. Orsi, ed., *Gods of the City:*

Religion and the American Urban Landscape. Bloomington: Indiana University Press, 1999, 79–102.

Bruce, Steve. *Religion and Choice: A Critique of Rational Choice Theory.* Oxford: Oxford University Press, 1999.

———. "The Poverty of Economism or the Social Limits on Maximizing." In Ted G. Jelen, ed., *Sacred Markets, Sacred Canopies: Essays on Religious Markets and Religious Pluralism.* Lanham, MD: Rowman and Littlefield, 2002, 167–185.

Buchanan, Angela B., Nora G. Albert, and Daniel Beaulieu. "The Population with Haitian Ancestry in the United States: 2009." Washington, DC: U.S. Census Bureau, October 2010.

Buss, Terry F., and Adam Gardner. *Haiti in the Balance: Why Foreign Aid Has Failed and What We Can Do About It.* Washington, DC: The Brookings Institute, 2008.

Caistor, Nick. "Obituary: Félix Morisseau-Leroy." *Independent*, September 11, 1998.

Candido, Sergio N. "Little Haiti Church Tree Removal Permit Appealed." *Miami Herald*, October 4, 2011.

Casimir, Leslie. "Support Urged for Honoring Slain Haitians," *Miami Herald*, September 18, 1994.

———. "Little Haiti Church Wants Homeless Out: They've Taken over Carnival Site." *Miami Herald*, January 11, 1996.

Chai, Karen Jung Won. "Protestant-Catholic-Buddhist: Korean Americans and Religious Adaptation in Greater Boston." PhD diss., Harvard University, 2000.

Charles, Carolle. "Political Refugees or Economic Migrants? A New 'Old Debate' within the Haitian Immigrant Communities but with Contestations and Division." *Journal of American Ethnic History* 25, 2/3 (2006): 190–209.

Charles, Jacqueline. "Vodou's Veil." *Miami Herald*, May 3, 2003.

Chaves, Mark. "On the Rational Choice Approach to Religion." *Journal for the Scientific Study of Religion* 34, 1 (1995): 98–104.

Chesnut, R. Andrew. *Competitive Spirits: Latin America's New Religious Economy.* New York: Oxford University Press, 2003.

Chomsky, Noam. "World Order and Its Rules: Variations on Some Themes." *Journal of Law and Society* 20, 2 (1993): 145–165.

———. *Year 501: The Conquest Continues.* Cambridge: South End Press, 1993.

Chou, Shie-Deh Chang. "Religion and Chinese Life in the United States." *Studi Emigrazione* 28, 103 (1991): 455–464.

City of Miami, Planning Department. "Census Information." 2011. http://www.miamigov.com/Planning/pages/services/Census.asp; last accessed July 7, 2012.

Clark, Kamari Maxine. "Normalizing Practices and Ritualizing Acts: The Mapping of Yoruba Transnational Identities." Paper presented to the *From Local to Global: Rethinking Yoruba Religious Traditions for the New Millennium* conference, Florida International University, Miami, December 10, 1999.

Clary, Mike. "M. O. B. (Money Over Bitches): Thug Life Ain't No Good Life, But It's My Life." *Miami New Times*, November 14, 2002.

Cleary, Edward L. *The Rise of Charismatic Catholicism in Latin America*. Gainesville: University Press of Florida. 2011.

Coleman, James S. "Social Capital in the Creation of Human Capital." *American Sociological Review* 94 (1988): S95–S120.

Commission Justice et Paix du Diocèse de Gonaïves. *La répression au quotidien en Haïti*. Paris: Karthala, 1995.

Conway, Frederick J. "Pentecostalism in Haiti: Healing and Hierarchy." In Stephen D. Glazier, ed., *Perspectives on Pentecostalism: Case Studies from Latin America and the Caribbean*. Washington, DC: University Press of America, 1980, 7–25.

Corten, André. *Misère, religion et politique en Haïti: Diabolisation et mal politique*. Paris: Karthala, 2001.

Cosentino, Donald J. "It's All for You, Sen Jak!" In Donald J. Cosentino, ed., *Sacred Arts of Haitian Vodou*. Hong Kong: South Sea International, 1995, 243–263.

Cottman, Michael J. "Miami Mass Celebrates New Haiti." *Miami Herald*, February 10, 1986.

Csordas, Thomas J. *Language, Charisma, and Creativity: Ritual Life in the Catholic Charismatic Renewal*. New York: Palgrave, 2001, 1997.

David, James D. "Catholics Assist Haitians, Volunteers Sought to Help Refugees." *Sun Sentinel*, December 11, 1991.

———. "Call of Two Shepherds." *Sun Sentinel*, September 3, 1997.

Del Pino-Allen, Isabel. "*La Catedral Del Exilio*: A Nicaraguan Congregation in a Cuban Church." In Stepick et al., eds., *Churches and Charity in the Immigrant City*, 132–150.

Delva, Joseph Guyler. "Haiti's Voodoo Priests Object to Mass Burials." Reuters, January 17. http://www.reuters.com/article/2010/01/17/us-quake-haiti-voodoo-idUS-TRE60G2DF20100117. Last accessed October 28, 2010.

de Lynch, Carole. "Lakou Hounto Press Release." Miami, 2003.

DeMarinis, Valerie, and Halina Grzymala-Moszczynska. "The Nature and Role of Religion and Religious Experience in Psychological Cross-Cultural Adjustment: Ongoing Research in the Clinical Psychology of Religion." *Social Compass* 42, 1 (1995): 121–135.

Denis, Lorimer, and François Duvalier, *Le problème des classes à travers l'histoire d'Haïti*. Port-au-Prince: Au Service de la Jeunesse, 1948.

Desmangles, Leslie G. *The Faces of the Gods: Vodou and Roman Catholicism in Haiti*. Chapel Hill: University of North Carolina Press, 1992.

Dibble, Sandra. "Archbishop asked to Oppose Transfer." *Miami Herald*, October 17, 1988.

DiMaggio, Paul. "On Pierre Bourdieu." *American Journal of Sociology* 84, 6 (1979): 1460–1474.

DiMaggio, Paul, and Patricia Fernández-Kelly, eds. *Art in the Lives of Immigrant Communities in the United States*. New Brunswick, NJ: Rutgers University Press, 2010..

Dolan, Jay. *The American Catholic Experience: A History from Colonial Times to the Present*. Notre Dame: University of Notre Dame Press, 1992.

Doup, Liz. "Santería and Voodoo Skulls and Saints." *Miami Herald*, November 10, 1987.

Dunne, Marvin. *Black Miami in the Twentieth Century*. Gainesville: University Press of Florida, 1997.

Dubocq, Tom. "Pilot Won't Face Piracy Charges; Cuban Airliner's Diversion to Miami Not Hijacking, US Says." *Miami Herald*, September 30, 1993.

Dupuy-McCalla, Regine. "Haitian Boat People." Special Report, Forced Migrations Project, Open Society Foundations, 1997. http://www.osi.hu/fmp/html/haitian_full.html; last accessed October 28, 2011.

Durkheim, Émile. *The Elementary Forms of Religious Life*. Translated by Karen E. Fields. New York: Free Press, 1995.

Ebaugh, Helen Rose, and Janet Saltzman Chafetz, eds. *Religion and the New Immigrants: Continuities and Adaptations in Immigrant Congregations*. Walnut Creek, CA: AltaMira Press, 2000.

Ebaugh, Helen Rose, Jennifer O'Brien, and Janet Saltzman Chafetz. 2002. "The Social Ecology of Residential Patterns and Membership in Immigrant Churches." *Journal for the Scientific Study of Religion* 39, 1(2002): 107–116.

Evans, Christine. "6,000 Protest Haiti Election Turmoil." *Miami Herald*, December 6, 1987.

Falla, Ricardo. *Quiché Rebelde: Religious Conversion, Politics, and Ethnic Identity in Guatemala*. Translated by Phillip Berryman. Austin: University of Texas Press, 2001.

Farmer, Paul. *AIDS and Accusation: Haiti and the Geography of Blame*. Berkeley: University of California Press, 1992.

———. *The Uses of Haiti*. Monroe, ME: Common Courage, 1994.

Fass, Simon. *Political Economy in Haiti: The Drama of Survival*. New Brunswick, NJ: Transaction Publishers, 1988.

Ferguson, James. "Migration in the Caribbean: Haiti, the Dominican Republic and Beyond." London: Minority Rights Group International, 2003.

Fernandez, Guillermo. 1991. "Haiti: Laying to Rest the Ghost of Duvalier?" *Barricada Internacional*, March 4, 1991. http://www.greenleft.org.au/back/1991/03/03p14.htm; last accessed January 4, 2012.

Françisque, Edouard. *La structure économique et sociale d'Haïti*. Port-au-Prince: Deschamps, 1986.

French-Speaking Baptist Church of New York. www.fsbconline.org; last accessed April 25, 2012.

Gaither, Dorothy. ". . . to see a Born-Again Haiti." *Miami Herald*, November 27, 1987.

Gans, Herbert J. "Symbolic Ethnicity and Symbolic Religiosity: Towards a Comparison of Ethnic and Religious Acculturation." *Ethnic and Racial Studies* 17, 4 (1994): 577–592.

Garrard-Burnett, Virginia, and David Stoll, eds. *Rethinking Protestantism in Latin America*. Philadelphia: Temple University Press, 1993.

Gibb, Camilla. "Religious Identification in Transnational Contexts: Being and Becoming Muslim in Ethiopia and Canada." *Diaspora* 7, 2 (1998): 247–269.

Gersuk, John. "Surviving Haitians Quiet After Ordeal." *Palm Beach Post*, October 27, 1981.

Green, Nadege. "Notre Dame Will Get New $3.2 Million Church." *Miami Herald*, July 1, 2011(a).

———. "Little Haiti Church Ticks Off Tree Lovers." *Miami Herald*, July 11, 2011(b).

Hansing, Katrin, and Sarah J. Mahler. "Toward a Transnationalism of the Middle: How Transnational Religious Practices Help Bridge the Divides Between Cuba and Miami. *Latin American Perspectives*, 32, 1 (2005): 121–146.

Hebblethwaite, Benjamin. *Vodou Songs in Haitian Creole and English*. Philadelphia: Temple University Press, 2011.

Harrison, Ian E. "The Storefront Church as a Revitalization Movement." *Review of Religious Research* 7, 3 (1966): 160–163.

Herberg, Will. *Protestant, Catholic, Jew: An Essay in American Religious Sociology*. Garden City, NY: Doubleday, 1960.

Herskovits, Melville J. *Life in a Haitian Valley*. New York: Doubleday, 1938.

Hervieu-Léger, Danièle. *Religion as a Chain of Memory*. Translated by Simon Lee. New Brunswick: Rutgers University Press, 2000.

Hoffmann, Leon-François. *Haïti: couleurs, croyances, créole*. Montreal: CIDIHCA, 1990.

Houtart, François, and Anselme Rémy. *Les référents culturel à Port-au-Prince*. Port-au-Prince: CRESFED, 1997.

Hurbon, Laënnec. *Dieu dans le vaudou haïtien*. Port-au-Prince: Deschamps, 1987.

———. *Voodoo: Search for the Spirit*. Translated by Lory Frankel. New York: Abrams, 1995 (1993).

———. "Pentecostalism and Transnationalism in the Caribbean." In André Corten and Ruth Marshall Fratani, eds., *Between Babel and Pentecost: Transnational Pentecostalism in Africa and Latin America*. Bloomington: Indiana University Press, 2001(a), 124–141.

———. "Current Evolution of Relations between Religion and Politics in Haiti." In Patrick Taylor, ed., *Nation Dance: Religion, Identity, and Cultural Difference in the Caribbean*. Bloomington: Indiana University Press. 2001(b), 118–125.

———. "Haitian Vodou in the Context of Globalization." Translated by Terry Rey. In Jacob K. Olupona and Terry Rey, eds., *Òrìsà Devotion as World: The Globalization of Yorùbá Religious Culture*. Madison: University of Wisconsin Press, 2008, 263–277.

Hurh, Wan Moo, and Kwang Chung Kim. *Korean Immigrants in America: A Structural Analysis of Ethnic Confinement and Adhesive Adaptation*. Madison, NJ: Fairleigh Dickinson University Press, 1984.

———. "Religious Participation of Korean Immigrants in the United States." *Journal for the Scientific Study of Religion* 29 (1990): 9–34.

Iannaccone, Laurence R. "Religious Practice: A Human Capital Approach." *Journal for the Scientific Study of Religion* 29, 3 (1990): 297–314.

———. "Religious Markets and the Economics of Religion." *Social Compass* 39, 1 (1992): 123-131.

———. "Rational Choice: Framework for the Scientific Study of Religion." In Lawrence A. Young, ed., *Rational Choice Theory and Religion*. London: Routledge, 1997, 25–44.

James-Johnson, Alva. "Vodou Priest Wants Haiti Religion Recognized." *Sun Sentinel*, April 22, 2004.

Jean, Marc-Henry. "Le Père Jules Campion appelle à la conversions des cœurs." *Le Nouvelliste*, May 3, 2011.

Jean-Mary, Reginald. "Voodoo and Catholicism: An Analysis of the Religious Syncretism among Voodoo Practitioners." Master's thesis, St. Vincent de Paul Regional Seminary, 2000.

Juliani, Richard N. *Priest, Parish, and People: Saving the Faith in Philadelphia's Little Italy*. Notre Dame: Notre Dame University Press, 2006.

Juan Pablo II. *Mensajes sociales de Juan Pablo II en América Latina*. Bogotá: CELAM, 1986.

Kasinitz, Philip. *Caribbean New York: Black Immigrants and the Politics of Race*. New York: Cornell University Press, 1992.

Kay, Jennifer. "Rite Gives Respite from Deadly Year." *Sarasota Herald Tribune*, November 28, 2008.

Kim, Kwang Chug, and Shin Kim. "Ethnic Role of Korean Immigrant Churches in the United States." In Ho Yu Kwan, Kwang Chung Kim, and R. Stephen Warner, eds., *Korean Americans and Their Religions: Pilgrims and Missionaries from a Different Shore*. University Park: Pennsylvania State University Press, 2001, 71–95.

Kollin, Joe. "Mass Mourns Ferry Casualties, Priest Rips Haitian Government." *Miami Herald*, February 22, 1993.

Kostarelos, Frances. *Feeling the Spirit: Faith and Hope in an Evangelical Black Storefront Church*. Columbia: University of South Carolina Press, 1995.

Kurien, Prema. "Becoming American by Becoming Hindu: Indian Americans Take Their Place at the Multicultural Table." In R. Stephen Warner and Judith G. Wittner, eds., *Gatherings in Diaspora: Religious Communities and the New Immigration*. Philadelphia: Temple University Press, 1998, 37–70

———. "Religion, Ethnicity and Politics: Hindu and Muslim Indian Immigrants in the United States." *Ethnic and Racial Studies* 24, 2 (2001): 263–293.

———. "'We Are Better Hindus Here': Religion and Ethnicity among Indian Americans." In Pyung Gap Min and Jung Ha Kim, eds., *Religions in Asian America: Building Faith Communities*. Walnut Creek, CA: AltaMira Press, 2002, 99–120.

Kwon, Victoria Hyonchu, Helen Rose Ebaugh, and Jacqueline Hagan, "The Structure and Functions of Cell Group Ministry in a Korean Christian Church." *Journal for the Scientific Study of Religion* 36, 2 (1997): 247–256.

Laguerre, Michel S. "The Voodooization of Politics in Haiti." In Arlene Torres and Norman R. Whitten, Jr., eds., *Blackness in Latin America and the Caribbean: Social Dynamics and Cultural Transformations,* vol. 2. Bloomington: Indiana University Press, 1998, 495–439.

Lammoglia, José A. "Botanicas: Absence in Cuba, Proliferation in the United States." Master's thesis, Florida International University, 2001.

Lee, Felicia R. "Haitians Urge End of Regime." *Miami Herald*, January 2, 1988.

Legged, Jerome S., Jr. "The Religious Erosion-Assimilation Hypothesis: The Case of U.S. Jewish Immigrants." *Social Science Quarterly* 78, 2 (1997): 472–486.

LeMaire, Sandra. "As World Attention Wanes, Miami Church Increases Effort to Help Haiti." *Voice of America*, March 4, 2010.

Leonard, Karen I. "State, Culture and Religion: Political Action and Representation among South Asians in North America." *Diaspora* 9, 1 (2000): 21–38.

Leonard, Karen I., Alex Stepick, Manuel A. Vasquez, and Jennifer Holdaway, eds., *Immigrant Faiths: Transforming Religious Life in America*. Lanham, MD: Rowman Altamira, 2005.

Levine, Daniel H. *Popular Voices in Latin-American Catholicism*. Princeton: Princeton University Press, 1992.

Levitt, Steven D., and Stephen J. Dubner. *Freakonomics: A Rogue Economist Explores the Hidden Side of Everything*. New York: Harper Perennial, 2009.

Libowitz, Larry. "Santería Powder Making Mess at Money-Laundering Trial Site." *Miami Herald*, December 16, 2003.

Lin, Ann Chih, and Amaney Jamal. "Muslim, Arab, and American: The Adaptation of Arab Immigrants to American Society." Paper presented at the Social Science Research Council Working Group on Religion and Immigration, Seattle, December 20, 2001.

Little, Cheryl, and Charu Newhouse al-Sahli. "Haitian Refugees: A People in Search of Hope." Miami: Florida Immigrant Advocacy Center, 2004.

Louissaint, Nadine. "Compilation of Herbs and Home Remedies Commonly Used in the Haitian Community." Community Voices, Little Haiti Collaborative, Sant La, Miami, unpublished manuscript, 2002.

Lowenthal, Ira P. "Ritual Performance and Religious Experience: A Service for the Gods in Southern Haiti." *Journal of Anthropological Research* 34, 3 (1978): 392–414.

———. "Marriage Is 20, Children Are 21: The Cultural Construction of Conjugality and the Family in Rural Haiti." PhD diss., Johns Hopkins University, 1987.

Lundahl, Mats. *Peasants and Poverty: A Study of Haiti*. London: Croom-Helm, 1979.

———. "Government and Inefficiency in the Haitian Economy: The Nineteenth Century Legacy." *The Economics of the Caribbean Basin*. Santa Barbara: Praeger, 1985, 175–218.

———. *Politics or Markets? Essays on Haitian Underdevelopment*. New York: Routledge 1992.

Maass, Harold. "Haitian Priests in Dade Stay Involved with Struggle." *Miami Herald*, January 19, 1992.

———. "Creole 'Voice of Calm' is Heard above Political Din." *Miami Herald,* January 21, 1993.

Maduro, Otto. *Religion and Social Conflicts*. Translated by Robert R. Barr. Maryknoll: Orbis 1982.

Manigat, Sabine. "The Popular Sectors and the Crisis in Port-au-Prince." In Alejandro Portes, Carlos Dore y Cabra, and Patricia Landholt, eds., *The Urban Caribbean*. Baltimore: Johns Hopkins University Press, 1997, 87–123.

Mapou, Jan. "Vodou nan miyami: Sèt manbo, 7 fanm total-kapital." *Haïti en Marche*, February 27, 2002.

Marcelin, Louis, and Louise Marcelin. "Ethnographic Social Network Tracing Among Haitian Migrant Workers in South Florida." Washington: Decennial Management Division, U.S. Bureau of the Census, 2001.

Mardy, Hans. "Festival Has a New Purpose: Raising Cash to Fix Up Church." *Miami Herald*, January 14, 1999.

Markowitz, Arnold. "Priest Back with Haitians' Notes," *Miami Herald,* December 31, 1991.

Marotte, Cécille, and Hervé Rotoko Razafimbahiny. *Mémoire oubliée: Haïti 1991–1994.* Montréal: CIDIHCA, 1997.

Marquardt, Marie Friedmann. "Structural and Cultural Hybrids: Religious Congregational Life and Public Participation among Mexicans in the New South." In Leonard et al., *Immigrant Faiths*, 189–219.

Martikainen, Tuomas. "Religion, Immigrants and Integration." Academy for Migration Studies in Denmark Working Series Paper 43. 2005. http://www.amid.dk/pub/papers/AMID_43-2005_Martikainen.pdf; last accessed July 7, 2012.

Maternowska, M. Catherine. *Reproducing Inequities: Poverty and the Politics of Population in Haiti.* Chicago: University of Chicago Press, 2006.

Martinez, Guillermo. "A Catholic Lay Worker is Beaten in Haiti Jail." *Miami Herald,* March 24, 1983.

Maxwell, John. "Racist Antecedents of US Haiti Policy: Imagine! Niggers Speaking French!!!" *The Black Commentator*, n.d., http://www.blackcommentator.com/74/74_reprint_french_pf.html, last accessed April 14, 2012

May, Patrick. "Pope Comes to Miami as a Pilgrim of Peace." In Allison Owen, ed., *The Papal Visit: Pope John Paul II in Miami*. Bay Harbor Islands: Miami Herald Publishing and Surfside Publishing, 1987.

McAlister, Elizabeth. "The Madonna of 115th Street Revisited: Vodou and Catholicism in the Age of Transnationalism." In Steven R. Warner and Judith G. Wittner, eds., *Gatherings in Diaspora: Religious Communities and the New Immigration*. Philadelphia: Temple University Press, 1998, 123–160.

———. *Rara! Vodou, Power, and Performance in Haiti and its Diaspora.* Berkeley: University of California Press, 2002.

———. "From Slave Revolt to a Blood Pact with Satan: The Evangelical Rewriting of Haitian History." *Studies in Religion/Sciences religieuses* 42, 2 (2012): 187–215.

McCarthy, Kathy. "A Newspaper for the People." *Miami Herald*, July 4, 1985 (a).

———. "Expelled Catholic Priests to lead Little Haiti Mass." *Miami Herald*, August 4, 1985 (b).

———. "Haitians Send Pope a Message of Thanks." *Miami Herald*, October 17, 1985(c).

———. "Bishop Urges Local Haitians to Return to Help Rebuild Country." *Miami Herald,* March 16, 1986.

McGee, Adam M. "Haitian Vodou and Voodoo: Imagined Religion and Popular Culture." *Studies in Religion/Sciences religieuses* 42, 2 (2012): 231–256.

Miami Herald Staff. "Local Fund-Raisers Scheduled Today for Haiti's New Government." *Miami Herald*, April 7, 1991.

———."Church Raises Funds to Help Haitians." *Miami Herald*, August 20, 1992.

Michel, Claudine. "Le vodou haïtien est-il un Humanisme?" *Journal of Haitian Studies* 12, 2 (2006): 116–136.

Miller, Michael. "Jericho Revival Draws Thousands to Notre Dame d'Haiti 10 Months After Earthquake." *Miami New Times*, October 18, 2010 (2010a).

———. "Archbishop Thomas Wenski: Tea Party Conservative and Church Radical." *Miami New Times*, November 18, 2010 (2010b).

Min, Pyong Gap. "The Structure and Social Functions of Korean Immigrant Churches in the United States." *International Migration Review* 26 (1992):1370–1394.

———. "Immigrants' Religion and Ethnicity: A Comparison of Korean Christian and Indian Hindu Immigrants." *Bulletin of the Royal Institute for Inter-Faith Studies* 2, 1 (2000): 121–140.

———. "Religion and the Maintenance of Ethnicity among Immigrants: A Comparison of Indian Hindus and Korean Protestants." In Leonard, *Immigrant Faiths*, 99–122.

Monnay, Thomas. "Voodoo Emerges from the Shadows." *Sun-Sentinel*, April 6, 1998.

Mooney, Margarita A. *Faith Makes Us Live: Surviving and Thriving in the Haitian Diaspora*. Berkeley: University of California Press, 2009.

Morisseau-Leroy, Felix. *Haitiad and Oddities*. Translated by Jeffrey Knapp. Miami: Pantaléon Guilbaud, 1991.

Murphy, Joseph M. *Santería: An African Religion in America*. Boston: Beacon, 1993.

Nonciature Apostolique en Haïti. Letter of Tarcisio Cardinal Bertone to Msgr. Bernadito Auzo. Port-au-Prince. September 20, 2010. http://www.newmiamiarch.org/Atimo_s/news/0083_001.pdf.

Norton, Michael. "Thousands Turn out at Haitian Conference to Ward off Forces of Evil." *Miami Herald*, April 28, 2003.

O'Brien, David. *Animal Sacrifice and Religious Freedom: Church of the Lukumi Babalu Aye v. City of Hialeah*. Lawrence: University Press of Kansas, 1994.

O'Neil, Deborah, and Terry Rey. "The Saint and Siren: Liberation Hagiography in a Haitian Village." *Studies in Religion/Sciences Religieuses* 42, 2 (2012): 166–186.

Olupona, Jacob K., and Terry Rey. "Introduction." In Jacob K. Olupona and Terry Rey, eds., *Òrìsà Devotion as World Religion: The Globalization of Yorùbá Religious Culture*. Madison: University of Wisconsin Press, 2008, 3–28.

Orozco, Manuel. "Understanding the Remittance Economy in Haiti." The World Bank, 2006.

Orsi, Robert A.. *The Madonna of 115th Street: Faith and Community in Italian Harlem, 1880–1950*. New Haven: Yale University Press, 1988.

———. "The Religious Boundaries of an Inbetween People: Street Feste and the Problem of the Dark-Skinned Other in Italian Harlem, 1920–1990." *American Quarterly* 44, 3 (1992): 313–347

———. "Is the Study of Lived Religion Irrelevant to the World We Live In? Special Presidential Plenary Address, Society for the Scientific Study of Religion, Salt Lake City, November 2, 2002." *Journal for the Scientific Study of Religion* 42, 2 (2003): 169–174.

Paquin, Lionel. *The Haitians: Class and Color Politics*. Brooklyn: Multitype, 1983.

Portes, Alejandro. "Social Capital: Its Origins and Applications in Modern Sociology." *Annual Review of Sociology* 24 (1998):1–24.

———. "The Two Meanings of Social Capital." *Sociological Forum* 15, 1 (2000): 1–12.

Portes, Alejandro, and Patricia Landolt. "Social Capital: Promise and Pitfalls of Its Role in Development." *Journal of Latin American Studies* 32, 2 (2000): 529–547.

Portes, Alejandro, and Margarita A. Mooney. "Social Capital and Community Development." In Mario F. Guillén, Randall Collins, Paula England, and Marshall Meyer, eds., *The New Economic Sociology: Developments in an Emerging Field*. New York: Russell Sage Foundation, 2002, 3003–3329.

Portes, Alejandro, and Rubén Rumbault. *Immigrant America: A Portrait*. 3rd ed. Berkeley: University of California Press, 2006.

Portes, Alejandro, and Alex Stepick, *City on the Edge: The Transformation of Miami*. Berkeley: University of California Press, 1994.

Price-Mars, Jean. *Ainsi parla l'oncle*. Port-au-Prince: Fardin, 1998 (1928).

———. *La vocation de l'élite*. Port-au-Prince: Patrimoine, 2001 (1919).

Proudfoot, Wayne. *Religious Experience*. Berkeley: University of California Press, 1985.

Proust, Mary De Turris. "Bishop Wenski Q & A." *Our Sunday Visitor*. 2010. http://www.osvcurriculum.com/haiti/qa.html, last accessed December 24, 2011.

Ramsey, Kate. *The Spirits and the Law: Vodou and Power in Haiti*. Chicago: University of Chicago Press, 2011.

Remennick, Larissa I. "Identity Quest among Russian Jews of the 1990s: Before and After Emigration." *Sociological Papers* 6 (1998):241–258.

Rey, Terry. *"Lavyèj Kafoufey ki rive Miyami*: Haitian Devotion at a Cuban Catholic Shrine in Miami." Paper presented to the Haitian Studies Association, Port-au-Prince, Haiti, October 28, 1998.

———. *Our Lady of Class Struggle: The Cult of the Virgin Mary in Haiti*. Trenton: Africa World Press, 1999(a).

———. "Junta, Rape, and Religion in Haiti: 1991–1994," *Journal of Feminist Studies in Religion*, 15, 2 (1999b): 73–100.

———. "'The Virgin's Slip is Full of Fireflies': The Multidimensional Struggle over the Virgin Mary's *legitimierende Macht* in Latin America and its U.S. Diasporic Communities." *University of California-Davis Law Review* 33, 3 (2000): 955–972.

———. "Kongolese Catholic Influences on Haitian Popular Catholicism: A Sociohistorical Exploration." In Linda M. Heywood, ed., *Central Africans and Cultural Transformations in the American Diaspora*. New York: Cambridge University Press, 2002, 265–285.

———. "Marketing the Goods of Salvation: Bourdieu on Religion." *Religion* 34, 4 (2004a): 331–343.

———. "Marian Devotion at a Haitian Catholic Parish in Miami: The Feast Day of Our Lady of Perpetual Help." *Journal of Contemporary Religion* 19, 3 (2004b): 353–374.

———. "Toward an Ethnohistory of Haitian Pilgrimage." *Journal de la Société des Américanistes* 91, 1 (2005a): 161–183.

———. "Trees in Haitian Vodou." In Bron Taylor, eds., *The Encyclopedia of Religion and Nature*. London: Continuum, 2005(b), 1658–1659.

———. "Vodou, Water, and Exile: Symbolizing Spirit, Passage, and Pain in Port-au-Prince." In Oren Baruch Stier and J. Shawn Landres, eds., *Religion, Violence, Memory, and Place*. Bloomington: Indiana University Press, 2006, 198–213.

———. *Bourdieu on Religion: Imposing Faith and Legitimacy*. London: Equinox, 2007(a).

———. "Worthiness as Spiritual Capital: Theorizing Little Haiti's Religious Market." In Jörg Stoltz, ed., *Salvation Goods and Religious Markets: Theory and Applications*. Bern: Peter Lang, 2007(b), 189–206.

———. "Catholic Pentecostalism in Haiti: Spirit, Politics, and Gender." *Pneuma: Journal of the Society of Pentecostal Studies* 32, 1 (2010): 80–106.

———. "The Spirit(s) of African Religion in Miami." In Robin Poynor and Amanda Carlson, eds., *Africa in Florida*. Gainesville: University Press of Florida, forthcoming.

Rey, Terry, and Karen E. Richman. "The Somatics of Syncretism: Tying Body and Soul in Haitian Religion." *Studies in Religion/Sciences Religieuses* 39, 3 (2010): 379–403.

Rey, Terry, and Alex Stepick. "Visual Culture and Visual Piety in Little Haiti: The Sea, the Tree, and the Refugee." In DiMaggio, *Art in the Lives of Immigrant Communitie*, 229–248.

Richman, Karen E. "Anchored in Haiti and Docked in Florida." Paper delivered to the Social Science Research Council Group on Religion, Immigration and Civic Life, December 20, 2001.

———. "Miami Money and the Home Gal." *Anthropology and Humanism* 27, 2 (2003): 119–132.

———. "The Protestant Ethic and the Dis-Spirit of Vodou." In Leonard, *Immigrant Faiths*, 165–188.

———. *Migration and Vodou*. Gainesville: University Press of Florida, 2005(b).

———. "Peasants, Migrants, and the Discovery of African Traditions." *Journal of Religion in Africa* 37, 3 (2007): 371–397.

———. "A More Powerful Sorcerer: Conversion, Capital, and Haitian Transnational Migration." *New West Indian Guide/Nieuwe West-Indishe Gids* 82, 1/2 (2008): 3–45.

Richman, Karen E., and Terry Rey. "Congregating by Cassette: Vodouist and Catholic Recordings in Haitian Transnational Spaces." *International Journal for Cultural Studies* 12, 2 (2009): 149–165.

Robertson, Roland. "The Economization of Religion? Reflections on the Promise and limitations of the Economic Approach." *Social Compass* 39, 1 (1992): 147–157.

Robinson, Catherine. "Being *Somewhere*: Young Homeless People in Inner-city Sydney." PhD diss., University of New South Wales, 2002.

Rodriguez-Soto, Ana. "'After Death . . . New Life': Members of Divine Providence Haitian Mission Turn Their Merger with St. Clement into a 'Procession of Faith' Through Streets of Wilton Manors." *Florida Catholic*, October 9, 2009.

———. "Plans Made to Rebuild Haiti's Church: Haitian Bishops Approve Program to Ensure 'Efficient, Transparent' Use of Donors Money." *Florida Catholic*, September 27, 2010.

Rohter, Larry. Untitled article. *New York Times*, December 30, 1992.

———. "Haitian Man Hijacks a Missionary Plane to Miami." *New York Times*, February 19, 1993.

———. "Mission to Haiti; Haiti's Priest-President Faces a Hostile Catholic Hierarchy." *New York Times*, September 26, 1994.

Romain, Charles-Poisset. *Le protestantisme dans la société haïtienne: Contribution à l'étude sociologique d'une religion.* Port-au-Prince: Deschamps, 1986.

———. *Le protestantisme dans la société haïtienne: Contribution à l'étude historique, sociographique et descriptive d'une religion, Tome II.* Coconut Creek: Educa Vision, 2004.

Romero, Simon, and Marc Lacey. "Fierce Quake Devastates Haitian Capital." *New York Times*, January 12, 2010.

Roumain, Jacques. *Masters of the Dew.* Translated by Langston Hughes and Mercer Cook. New York: Reynal and Hitchcock, 1947.

San Martin, Nancy. "Miami's Haitians Rejoice." *Miami Herald*, February 8, 1991.

Sandoval, Mercedes Cros. "Santería as a Mental Health Care System: An Historical Overview." *Social Science and Medicine* 13, B (1979): 137–151.

———. *Worldview, the Orichas, and Santería: From Africa to Cuba and Beyond.* Gainesville: University Press of Florida, 2006.

Shaffer, Gina. "Priest Uses Ethnicity to Reach Out the Flock." *Miami Herald*, February 16, 1989.

Schiller, Nina Glick, and Georges Eugene Fouron. *Georges Woke Up Laughing: Long-Distance Nationalism and the Search for Home.* Durham, NC: Duke University Press, 2001.

Schmich, Mary T. "Haitian Refugees Find a Champion in Miami." *Chicago Tribune*, November 29, 1991.

Schrauf, Robert W. "Mother Tongue Maintenance among North American Ethnic Groups." *Cross-Cultural* Research 33, 2 (1999): 175–192.

Shogan, Robert. "Bush Ends His Waiting Game, Attacks Reagan." *Los Angeles Times*, April 14, 1980.

Sharot, Stephen. "Beyond Christianity: A Critique of the Rational Choice Theory of Religion from a Weberian and Comparative Religions Perspective." *Sociology of Religion* 63, 4 (2002): 427–454.

Sick, Jessica. "Ingrid Llera, Vodou Expert." *Street*, April 30–May 6, 2004.

Smith, Timothy L. "Religion and Ethnicity in America." *American Historical Review* 83, 5 (1978): 1155–1185.

Stark, Rodney, and Roger Finke. *Acts of Faith: Explaining the Human Side of Religion.* Berkeley: University of California Press, 2000.

Stepick, Alex. "The Refugees Nobody Wants: Haitians in Miami." In Gilberto Grenier and Alex Stepick III, eds., *Miami Now! Immigration, Ethnicity, and Social Change.* Gainesville: University Press of Florida, 1992, 57–82.

———. *Pride against Prejudice: Haitians in the United States.* Boston: Allyn and Bacon, 1998.

———. "God Is Apparently Not Dead. The Obvious, the Emergent, and the Unknown in Immigration and Religion." In Karen J. Leonard, Alex Stepick, Manuel A. Vasquez, and Jennifer Holdaway, eds., *Immigrant Faiths: Transforming Religious Life in America.* Lanham, MD: Alta Mira Press, 2005, 11–37.

Stepick, Alex, and Alejandro Portes. "Flight into Despair: A Profile of Recent Haitian Refugees in South Florida." *International Migration Review* 20, 2 (1986): 329–350.

Stepick, Alex, Terry Rey, and Sarah Mahler, eds. *Churches and Charity in the Immigrant City: Religion, Immigration, and Civic Engagement in Miami.* New Brunswick, NJ: Rutgers University Press, 2009.

Stern, Mark J., Susan C. Seifert, and Dominic Vitiello. "Migrants and the Transformation of Philadelphia's Cultural Economy." In DiMaggio, *Art in the Lives of Immigrant Communities,* 23–51.

Stewart-Gambino, Hannah W. "'Religious Consumers' in a Changing 'Religious Marketplace.'" *Latin American Research Review* 36, 1 (2001): 193–206.

Stoltz, Jörg. "Salvation Goods and Religious Markets: Integrating Rational Choice and Weberian Perspectives." *Social Compass* 53, 1 (2006): 13–32.

Suh, Sharon A. "Buddhism, Rhetoric, and the Korean American Community: The Adjustment of Korean Buddhist Immigrants to the U.S." Paper presented at the Social Science Research Council Working Group on Religion and Immigration, Seattle, WA, September 2001.

Suro, Roberto. "The Papal Visit; Pontiff Embraces Welcome in Miami; Deflects Queries." *New York Times,* September 11, 1987.

Taft, Adon. "Black Catholics: Their Numbers Are Small; Their Devotion Is Steady." *Miami Herald,* January 31, 1986.

———. "How Widespread is Voodoo Locally? Experts Disagree." *Miami Herald,* January 12, 1990.

Tempels, Placide. *Bantu Philosophy.* Translated by Colin King. Paris: Présence Africaine, 1959 (1944).

Terrazas, Aaron. "Haitian Immigrants in the United States." Migration Policy Institute, 2010. http://www.migrationinformation.org/usfocus/display.cfm?id=770; last accessed June 25, 2012.

Thompson, M. Dion. "Haitians Pray for Peace in Homeland." *Miami Herald,* November 26, 1987.

Thompson, Robert Farris. *Faces of the Gods: Art and Altars of Africa and the African Americas.* New York: Museum for African Art, 1993.

Tiryakian, Edward. "L'Exceptionnelle vitalité religieuse aux Etats-Unis: Une relecture de Protestant-Catholic-Jew." *Social Compass,* 38, 3 (1991): 215–238.

Tomasi, Silvano M. *Piety and Power: The Role of Italian Parishes in the New York Metropolitan Area, 1880–1930.* New York: Center for Migration Studies, 1975.

Tracy, Tom. "Remembering Haiti's Dead: Journalists Create Database to Register Names of Loved Ones Killed in Earthquake." *Florida Catholic,* October 19, 2010(a).

http://www.miamiarch.org/ip.asp?op=Article_101019183123190; last accessed January 8, 2012.

———. "Parish Kicks off Week of Spiritual Renewal: Thousands Celebrate Opening of Jericho in Little Haiti with Songs, Prayers." *Florida Catholic*, October 19, 2010(b). http://www.miamiarch.org/ip.asp?op=Article_101019175035631; last accessed January 8, 2012.

———. "Haiti: A Year after Quake: Archbishop Wenski to Lead Memorial Mass at Cathedral; Other Events Planned." *Florida Catholic*, January 6, 2011. http://www.miamiarch.org/ip.asp?op=Article_1116161035431; last accessed January 11, 2012.

Trouillot, Michel-Rolph. *Haiti, State Against Nation: The Origins and Legacy of Duvalierism*. New York: Monthly Review Press, 1990.

Tweed, Thomas A. *Our Lady of the Exile: Diasporic Religion at a Cuban Catholic Shrine in Miami*. New York: Oxford University Press, 1997.

———. *Crossing and Dwelling: A Theory of Religion*. Cambridge, MA: Harvard University Press, 2006.

Tylor, E. B. *Primitive Culture, Volume I*. London: Murray, 1920.

United States Coast Guard. "Alien Migrant Interdiction." (n.d.). http://www.uscg.mil/hq/cg5/cg531/AMIO/amio.asp#Statistics; last accessed March 18, 2012.

United States Court of Appeals, Eleventh Circuit. *United States of America v. Sophia Jean-Baptiste, Marie Jean-Baptiste*. August 11, 1996. http://www.ca11.uscourts.gov/unpub/ops/200512697.pdf; last accessed September 28, 2011.

United States Department of Justice, Executive Office for Immigration Review, "Withholding of removal and deferral of removal under Article 3 of the Convention Against Torture," March 18, 2003.

Valéry, Jude. *Biographie d'un grand missionare: Salomon Sévère Joseph (1891–1973)*. Port-au-Prince: Fardin, 1983.

———. *Manifestation du Saint Esprit dans le ministère du Rév. Salomon Sévère Joseph (1891–1973)*. Port-au-Prince: Fardin, 2000.

———. "Quand on celèbre les morts en Haïti." (n.d.) http://missionevangeliqueduchristianisme.org/messages.html, last accessed July 7, 2012.

Vaughan, Chris. "Churches Vie for the Soul of Little Haiti." *Miami Herald*, April 16, 1983(a).

———. "Tribute Stirs Memories of Haitians Who Drowned." *Miami Herald*, October 28, 1983(b).

———. "Radio Unites, Divides Haitians." *Miami Herald*, June 9, 1983(c).

Viglucci, Andres. "God's Man in Little Haiti." *Miami Herald*, February 26, 1995.

Vonarx, Nicolas. "Les Églises de l'Armée Céleste comme Églises de guérison en Haïti: Un Développement qui repose sur une double légitimité." *Social Compass* 54, 1 (2007): 113–127.

Washington, Jr., Joseph R. *Black Sects and Cults: The Power Axis in an Ethnic Ethic*. Garden City, NY: Doubleday, 1972.

Weber, Max. *The Protestant Ethic and the Spirit of Capitalism*. Translated by Talcott Parsons. New York: Scribner's, 1958.

———. *The Sociology of Religion*. Translated by Ephraim Fischoff. Boston: Beacon, 1963.

Williams, Raymond Brady. *Religions of Immigrants from India and Pakistan: New Threads in the American Tapestry*. Berkeley: University of California Press, 1988.

Witt, April. "Two Popular Priests Ordained as Bishops," *Miami Herald*, September 4, 1997.

———. "A New Era at Notre Dame d'Haiti," *Miami Herald*, February 27, 1998.

WLRN. "Faith in the Aftermath." 2010. http://wlrnunderthesun.org/wp-content/uploads/2011/01/Faith_MEATC_FINAL.mp3, last accessed December 24, 2011.

Woodson, Drexel G. "Review of Bellegarde-Smith, *Haiti: The Breached Citadel.*" *New West Indian Guide/Nieuwe West-Indische Gids* 67, 1/2 (1993): 156–159.

Woodson, Drexel G., and Mamadou A. Baro. *A Baseline Study of Livelihood Security in the Southern Peninsula of Haiti*. Tucson, AZ: The Bureau of Applied Research in Anthropology, University of Arizona, 1996.

———. *A Baseline Study of Livelihood Security in the Department of the Artibonite, Center, North, Northeast, and West, Republic of Haiti*. Tucson: The Bureau of Applied Research in Anthropology, University of Arizona, 1997.

Yanez, Luiza. "Miami-Dade Leaders See Magic in New Name." *Sun Sentinel*, November 15, 1997.

Yanez, Luiza, et al., "Passengers Persuade Hijacker on Haitian Flight to Surrender." *Sun Sentinel*, February 19, 1993.

Yardley, William. "Mormons Reach Out to Haitians." *Miami Herald*, June 10, 2003.

Yoo, Jin-Kyung. *Korean Immigrant Entrepreneurs. Network and Ethnic Resources*. New York: Garland Publishing, 1988.

Abitasyon, 127

Adhar, Rex, 153

Adrien, Antoine, 42

Africa: influence on Haitian religion, 2, 4, 50, 90, 116–118, 122–123, 131–132; 136, 142, 149, 190; as place of exile, 1; as resting place of the living dead, ancestors, 148; slavery and, 3, 19, 116–117, 122, 190–191, 202

African Americans: churches of, 23, 128, 157, 160, 162, 165, 173; and civil rights, 1; demographics and Miami Neighborhoods, 26, 157; identity among Haitian youth and, 150; religious leadership among, 23, 160, 173; support for Haitian refugees, 23

Agua Florida, 125

AIDS, xi, 22, 36, 180, 187, 228n12, 229n9

Alisma, Michelet Tibosse, 121–125, 128

All Saints Day, 50, 122

All Souls Day, 50, 122

American Airlines Arena, 131

amulets, 7, 115, 117

ancestors (*lemò*): and Africa, 50, 121–123, 190; Catholic demonization of, 91, 229n10; and Haitian history, 31, 202; in the Haitian religious collusio, 191; Vodouist veneration of, 7, 50, 115, 117–118, 121–123, 129, 141, 143–148

Annunciation of the Blessed Virgin Mary, 99–100

antisuperstition campaigns, 85

apparitions (of the Virgin Mary), 13

Aquin, 170–178

Archbishop Curley High School, 39

Aristide, Jean-Bertrand: as critic of conservatism in Haitian Catholic Church, 42, 79; and liberation theology, 23, 25, 37, 42–45; 96; popularity in Haiti, 45, 73, 96; as president of Haiti, 25, 37–38, 45–46, 119

Armand, Margaret, 121, 127, 148

Armée Céleste (Celestial Army churches), 153

art, 115, 121, 127, 136, 188, 190

Artibonite Valley, 46, 86, 162

assimilation, xii, 12, 70, 83, 120

asylum: among Cuban exiles, 113–114; among Haitian immigrants, xi, 21, 25, 28, 37, 41, 140, 189, 195, 199

Atlanta, 23

Auzo, Bernadito, 230n14

Babaluaye (Santería spirit of disease), 142

Bahamas, 74, 114, 139, 152

Bahamians, 70, 162, 173

balseros (Cuban rafters), 21

Balzora, Renaud, 234n8

Bankston, Carl, 12

Baptist: African American churches in Miami, 23; churches in Haiti, 172, 182–187; Haitian churches in Miami, 152–153, 158–164, 180, 187; pre-Haitian presence in Miami, 24

Baptist churches : Eglise Baptiste de la
Régénération, 161, 211; Eglise Baptiste de
la Renaissance, 161, 211; Eglise Baptiste
Emmanuel, 158, 162–164, 169, 180, 212,
235n2; First Haitian Baptist Church,
234n7; Friendship Missionary Baptist
Church, 23, 217; Nouvelle Eglise Bap-
tiste Bethanie, 162, 222
Baptist Convention of Haiti (*Convention
Baptiste d'Haïti*), 183–186
Baptist Missionary Society of London, 172
Barnard, Anne, 74, 77
Baro, Mamadou A., 6, 89
Bastian, Jean-Pierre, 156
Bayfront Park, 127
Bazile, Clotaire, 128
Bazin, Fritz, 160–161
Beauvoir, Max, 122, 126–127
Bel-Air, 86, 101, 110, 230n1
Belize, 234n7
Belle Glade, 39
Benedict XVI, Pope, 56
Bennett, Michèle, 48
Bertone, Tarcisco Cardinal, 230n14
Bible: and American courts of law, 135; as
carried by Christians in Little Haiti, 2,
97, 156, 176; commentaries by Jean-Ber-
trand Aristide, 45; evocations in Vodou
ritual, 124; instruction to Haitians in
Miami, 164; readings/enactments in
Miami Haitian churches, 62, 72, 74, 95,
100, 169; and Salomon Severe Joseph,
172; study in Haiti, 183; study in Little
Haiti Protestant churches, 166, 177; use
as an amulet among Haitian Protes-
tants, 7
Bimini, 152–153
Biscayne Bay, 26, 48, 127, 131
Black Baptist Alliance, 23
bokò (sorcerer), 137
Bondyè (God), 51, 90, 117, 169, 189, 198
Bossal Market, 191, 235n1
Boston, 6, 19, 21, 23, 28, 74, 141, 178

botanicas: Botanica Brave Guede, 115,
207; Botanica Halouba, 121, 127, 207;
Botanica Mawu-Lisa, 142–144; Cuban,
67, 118, 127–129; Haitian, 3–4, 26, 29, 86,
103, 115, 118–122, 127–130, 142–148, 156,
162, 198; list of Little Haiti botanicas,
207–208
bourad (boost), as primary function of
Haitian religion, 200–202
Bourdieu, Pierre, 7–10, 14–15, 30, 154–156,
185–188, 195–196, 201, 227–228n8
Bourjolly, Nancy, 43
Brazil, 142, 230n3
Brodwin, Paul, 5, 10, 14, 59, 80, 173, 181,
230n3, 231n7, 234n12
Broward County, 27–28, 60, 79, 116, 164
Brown, Karen McCarthy, 88, 90, 119, 123,
135, 140–141, 149, 231n11
Bruce, Steve, 154–155, 188
Brutus, Ferry, 95, 97
Bryan, Williams Jennings, 22
Burt, Al, 229n4
Burton, Kathleen, 234n16
Bush, George H. W., 135
Bush, George W., 38

Cadge, Wendy, 199
Calixte, Clorin, 234n8
Calvinism, 227n4
Campion, Jules, 72–75, 87, 89, 197, 230n2
Candomblé, 142
Cape Haitian, 113, 133, 182–183
Capuchins, 117
Caribbean Market (Miami), 2, 26
Carmel Baptist Church, 182–183, 186
carnival, 231n4
Carrefour-Dufort, 145
Carrefour-Feuilles, 132
Carroll, Coleman, 39
Carter, Jimmy, 21
casa de santo (Santería temple), 128
Castro, Fidel, 129
Catholic Charismatic Renewal: attitudes

toward Vodou, 91; clerical concerns with, 98–99; healing in, 106–107; history and scope of, in Haiti, 71, 83, 87, 99–100; in Miami, 71–78; saint cults in, 87; and social class, 80, 64, 107, 231n7

Catholic Charities, 47, 49

Catholic Church: and Cubans in Miami, 24–25; in Haiti, 3, 5, 8–10; and Haitian social class, 60–62, 65–71, 77–80; Notre Dame d'Haiti Catholic Church in Miami, 33–57; social ministry to Haitian immigrants in South Florida, ix-x, 12, 17–18; transnationalism and Haitian politics in, 33–57

Catholic churches: (see also Notre Dame d'Haiti); Cathedral of Our Lady of the Assumption, 56, 91; Cathedral of St. Mary, 39–40, 43, 56–57, 158–159, 204; Our Lady of Mount Carmel, 88; Our Lady of Perpetual Help (Opa Locka), 131; Our Lady of Perpetual Help (Port-au-Prince), 110, 230n3; Sacred Heart Catholic Church (Homestead), 95, 205; Sacred Heart Catholic Church (Port-au-Prince), 87; St. Ann Mission, 126, 232n8; St. Bartholomew Catholic Church, 60, 95, 203; St. James Catholic Church, 55, 60, 126, 204; St. Rose de Lima Catholic Church, 56

Catholic saints: assimilation with Vodou lwa, 83–84, 87–90, 117, 122–124, 126, 131, 133–134, 144; in the Haitian Charismatic Renewal, 86–87, 126n1; Our Lady of the Assumption, 84, 126, 148; Our Lady of Charity of El Cobre, ix, 37, 62, 86, 131–132; Our Lady of Czestochowa, 109, 231n11; Our Lady of Fatima, 73, 83, 87; Our Lady of Guadalupe, 70, 232n8; Our Lady of the Immaculate Conception, 84; Our Lady of Lourdes, 2, 52–53, 93, 149; Our Lady of Mount Carmel, 84, 87–89, 101, 109, 126, 144, 231n10, 231n11; Our Lady of Perpetual Help, 29, 33–36,

55–56, 70, 84–85, 92–111, 131, 190, 230n1; popularity in Haiti, 87, 198; Saint Ann, 70, 126, 230n1; Saint Barbara, 142; Saint Gabriel the Archangel, 99–100; Saint James the Greater, 84, 126; Saint Lazarus, 125, 128, 142–144; Saint Patrick, 122–125; Saint Philomena, 62–65, 126, 133–134, 230n1

Cédras, Raoul, 40, 46–47, 229n4

Center for Haitian Studies, 229n9

Centers for Disease Control and Prevention (CDC), 22

Central High School, 141

Centre Biblique Notre Dame de Fatima (Our Lady of Fatima Biblical Center), 83, 87

César, Emmanuel, 234n8

Charles, Carolle, 192

Charles, Gabriel, 98

Charles, Jacqueline, 128

Charles, Robès, 95–96, 99

Chicago, 6, 19, 21, 28, 55, 74

Chirac, Jacques, 38

Chita Tande, 42

choirs, xi, 3, 52, 54, 60, 70, 95, 170, 177–178

Christ the King Catholic Church, 34, 60, 65, 75, 85, 205

Christian Community Service Agency, 23

church (see also under Catholic, Baptist, and Protestant): niche church, 175; parish model, 175; storefront, 128, 151–188

Church of Our Lady of Perpetual Help: in Florida 131, 204; in Haiti, 110, 230n1

Church of St. Ann, 230n1

Church of St. John Bosco, 45

Church of the Lukumi Babaluaye, 232n19

Cité Soleil, 68

City of Hialeah, 232n10

City of Miami, 53, 66–68

Civil Rights Movement, 1, 20, 23

Clarke, Kamari M., 129

class. See social class

Coleman, James, 237n8

collusio: introduced and defined, 4–5, 7, 9; and Haitian Catholicism, 71, 83, 85, 89, 100–104, 107–110, 116, 129, 149; and Haitian Protestantism 151, 154, 166, 188; Haitian religious collusio, 7–10, 15, 31, 59, 68, 71, 76, 80–81 89, 154, 156, 196–198; Marian collusio, 81; and rational choice theory, 154–156, 181; and social class, 68, 80; and Vodou, 116, 129, 149
colonialism (*see also* Saint-Domingue), 2, 19, 22, 36, 78, 116–117, 202, 231n5
Conference of Haitian Pastors United in Christ, Inc. (CHPUCI), 180–181
Confraternity of Christian Doctrine (CCD), 65
Congrès National du Renouveau Charismatique Catholique d'Haïti (National Convention of the Catholic Charismatic Renewal of Haiti), 71, 83
Connecticut, 234n16
Conseil du Renouveau Charismatique des Haïtiens d'Outre-Mer (Council of the Catholic Charismatic Renewal of Haitians Overseas), 71–76
Constant, Hugh, 92, 107, 108
conversion, 73, 90–91, 120, 169, 181, 233n
Corten, André, 5, 10
courts of justice, 21, 118, 135–140
"Cry of Midnight," 166
Csordas, Thomas J., 87
Cuba, 57, 113, 121, 129, 131, 189
Cubans, 78, 101, 113–114, 118, 128, 130–132, 135, 142, 152–153, 192, 200, 232n16
culture: xi-xii, African, 117, 129; American, 116; Creole, 190; Haitian, 34, 59, 88 104, 116, 121, 140, 181, 195, 198; immigrant religion and maintenance of, 11, 192; of "superstition," 85; visual, 115

Dabady, Gilbert, 72
Dade County, 66
Dania Beach, 234n7
Danroc, Gilles, 42, 46–47

Darbouze, Gérard, 39, 48–52, 79, 108, 161
Delray, 104, 175
de Lynch, Carol, 121, 127, 232n11
demographics (religious), 5–10, 188
Desmangles, Leslie G., 88, 122–123, 136, 232n21
Desquirons, Lilas, 120
Diedrich, Bernard, 229n4
divination, 18, 103, 117, 128, 131, 143–144, 148
Divine Mercy Haitian Catholic Mission, 62
Dolan, Jay, 11
Dominican Republic, 160, 194
Dominicans (religious order), 117
Dominique, Max, 42
Dorceus, Honoré, 182–183
Doylestown, 109, 231n11
drums (and drumming), 2, 43, 54, 70, 85, 95, 117–118, 120, 125, 128, 133, 167, 177, 184
Duclair, F. F., 168
Duclair, François, 168
Duclair, Pascal, 165, 168
Duclerville, Gérard, 41,48
Dumeny, Elie, 234n8
Dumornay, Jacques, 234n8
Dunne, Marvin, 23
Dupuy-McCalla, Regine, 114
Durkheim, Émile, 98
Du Sable, Jean-Baptiste, 19
Duval-Carrié, Edouard, 115, 149, 190–191
Duvalier, François, 20, 40–41, 229n4, 235n1
Duvalier, Jean-Claude, 24, 40–42, 229n4, 235n1

earthquake (of 2010 in Haiti), 6, 36, 38, 52–57, 73–79, 89, 104, 116, 122, 150, 164, 173, 181–182, 197, 201
Ebaugh, Helen Rose, 175
ecclesiology, 16, 41, 49–51, 158
Ecklund, Elaine Howard, 199
Ecole Biblique Supérieure, 184
economics, 15, 154–155, 170, 228n9

Edouard, Woody Marc, 113–115, 130
education, 27–28, 38, 48, 93, 170, 173, 231n9
Eliade, Mircea, 175
Elks lodge, 162
Episcopal, 124, 134, 160, 187–188
ESL, 40, 55, 181
ethnic parish, x, 24, 40
ethnicity, 8, 39, 70
Eugène, Amos, 234n8
Eugène, Emmanuel, 234n7
Evangelicalism, 150, 161–164. *See also* Protestant churches, Mission Evangélique du Christianisme
evil, 7, 10, 59, 78, 83–84, 97, 104, 129, 136, 151, 166, 196, 199
evil spirits (*move zesprit*), 171, 166, 197
exorcism, 73, 91, 134, 166

Facebook, 132, 141–142, 234n15
Fauntroy, Ray, 23
FBI, 113
field theory of religion, 151
Finke, Roger, 154
Florida Everglades, 66, 68, 139
Florida International University, 4, 136, 166, 192, 232n20
Fon, 117
Fontus, Marie-Carmel, 142–148, 26n233
food, 2, 23, 27–28, 38, 64, 84, 124, 135
Ford Foundation, 24
Fort Lauderdale, 39, 60, 62, 104,
Fort Lauderdale Women's Club, 127
Fort Liberté, 92, 107
Fouron, Georges, 193
France, 1, 19, 43, 145, 164, 173
Freemasonry, 162
fund raising, 45, 49, 53, 55, 69, 158, 162, 165
funerary rites, 117–118, 122, 172

Gagné, Claire, 72
gender (*see also* women), 179
George, Jonas, 161, 234n8
Georgia, 235n24

glossolalia, 168
God (*Bondye*): dominion over Haiti, 13, 31, 45, 55; faith in, 30–31, 50, 78, 97, 171, 190, 193–194, 196, 198, 200, 202; and healing, 130, 171, 174–176; and Pentecostal spirituality, 71, 74; and Saint Philomena, 71; and sin, 14; 73; and the Virgin Mary, 96–100; in Vodou, 14, 90, 117, 124, 130; worship of, 104, 168–169, 198
Golgotha, 87
Gouveneurs de la rosée (Roumain), 20
Grand Bahama Island, 74
Grand Bassin, 182
grottoes, 2, 52–53, 91–95, 104, 106–107
Groupe Effusion, 72
Guantanamo Bay, 46, 189, 191
Guillaume, Oris, 235n24
Guirand, Missoule, 177, 235n17

habitus, 8–10, 14, 16, 81, 153–155, 186–188, 196
Haiti: bicentennial celebration, 36; emigration from, 19–21, 165, 189; Gross Domestic Product, 193; human rights, 21, 42, 44, 47–49, 100, 140, 229n4; national origins, 2, 19; political persecution in, 1, 48–59, 113, 140, 160; ; politics, 16, 24–26, 36, 40–47; population of, 19; religious demographics, 2–3, 5–7, 30, 50, 68, 85, 88–92, 184–185; remittances to, 13, 90, 110, 120, 189, 193–194, 196, 202; as spiritually empowered land, 13, 116–117, 141 145, 148; 2001 Census, 193–194; tourism, 23; U.S. military occupations of, 22, 182, 184
Haiti Cheri Ministries, 235n24
Haiti Memorial Database, 56
Haitian Army (*Force Armée d'Haïti*), 44, 85, 172
Haitian Constitution, 44, 119
Haitian Refugee Center 23–25, 45, 161

Haitian refugees (*botpipel*; Haitian boat people): Catholic ministry to, 34, 52; depicted in Haitian art and poetry, 115, 190–192; experience at sea, 152–153, 189–190; history and reception in South Florida, 21–25, 46, 57; and identity, 31; use of religion and magic among, 7, 133, 198, 200
Haitian Revolution, 19, 66, 188
Harlem, 89
Harlem Renaissance, 20
Harrison, Ian, 157–158
Havana, 113, 129
healing: in Haitian Catholicism, 38, 64–65, 71–76, 80–85, 91, 103, 106–107, 116, 118, 120, 196–201; in Haitian Protestantism, 18, 153, 165–166, 169–173, 177, 180–181; in the Haitian religious collusio, 7, 10, 14, 59, 151; in Vodou, 129, 135, 145, 149
health care, 38, 55, 108, 129–130, 180, 185
Hebblethwaite, Benjamin, 232n7
Herberg, Will, 159–160, 199
herbs/herbalism, 2, 128–129, 141, 144–147
heresiarch/heresiarchy, 10, 185–186
Hillsboro Beach, 7, 36
Hispaniola, 19
HIV (*see also* AIDS), 180
Holy Family, 52
Holy Family Catholic Church, 95, 204
Holy Spirit: in the Catholic Charismatic Renewal, 72, 74, 76–77, 92, 97, 107; in Haitian Protestant Pentecostalism, 151, 153, 166, 168–169; in the Haitian religious collusio, 196, 198; and Salomon Severe Joseph, 151, 180
Homestead, 28, 70, 95, 126
homiletics, 169–173
homosexuality, 22, 73, 89, 187, 197
Hopkins, Timothy, 63–65, 134,
Hostens, Jan, 42
Houtart, François, 6
Hughes, Langston, 20
Hurbon, Laënnec, 89, 92, 98, 133, 230n3, 233n27

Hurricane Wilma, 235n18
hymns: in Haitian Catholicism, 2, 46, 54, 62, 72, 95, 98–99, 103–107, 190; in Haitian Protestantism, 2, 3, 167–169, 234n10; 177, 179, in Vodou, 123

Iannaccone, Laurence, 154
icons, 2, 9, 53, 70, 87, 94, 101–104, 141, 144–145, 172, 174
identity: cultural, 11–12, 37, 40, 159; ethnic, xii, 157; formation, 11; among Haitian youth, 23, 150; religion and, 159–160, 193, 198
Ile Orunmila, 162
immigrants: appeal of Protestant churches to, 159, 166, 187–188; and the Catholic church, ix–xii, 2, 12, 24–25, 110; and education, 28; frequency of religious practice among, 4–5, 13, 159–160, 199; function of religion for, 11, 200–201, 228n10; Haitian, number of, 195; Korean, 13; mode of arrival in the United States, 28; Notre Dame d'Haiti and, 33–58; and religious conversion, 120; and social class, 59, 62; 66–68, 78–81; and symbolic capital, 11, 13, 18, 159, 188
immigration: "new immigration," ix, 12, 13, 159; "old immigration," 12, 159; policy and proceedings, 106, 114, 118, 130, 135, 139–142, 155, 180, 195; and social mobility, 60; variety of experience, 67, 80
initiation, 88, 118, 121, 123, 125, 131, 141–142, 148, 156
Institut Biblique Logos, 164
Internet (*see also* Facebook), 142, 234n15
Ireland/Irish, 22, 125
Iron Market, 26, 115, 145
Islam, 148
Israel, 167
Italians/Italian Americans, 11, 70–71, 74, 79

Jadotte, Jean, 60
Jakmel Art Gallery, 115, 121
Jamaican Baptist Missionary Society, 172

Jamaicans, 70, 137, 162
Jamal, Amaney, 12
James L. Knight International Center, 72–75, 193
Jean, Dorcely, 45
Jean-Baptiste, Marie, 137–139, 233n23
Jean-Baptiste, Mathieu, 234n8
Jean-Baptiste, Sophia, 233n23
Jean-Juste, Gérard, 23, 161
Jean-Mary, Reginald, 36, 38, 51–57, 78–79, 100, 105–106, 201
Jean-Philippe, Marie, 136
Jeanty, Mirlène, 64–66, 69–73, 76, 230n2
Jehovah's Witness, 162, 222
Jenkins, James, 23
Jérémie, 39, 43, 48
Jericho Revival, 56–57, 201
Jerusalem, 148
Jesuits, 117
Jesus Christ: faith in, 73, 97, 105, 169, 171, 174; and justice, 106; and miracles, 73, 152; as redeemer, 13, 77, 169; and the Virgin Mary, 64, 99; and Vodou, 124, 128; 152, 169, 171, 174, 177
Jews, 3, 24
Jocelyn, Yves, 95–97, 99
John Paul II, Pope, 41–43, 108, 192, 229n1
Jonc d'Audin d'Aquin, 170
Joseph, Gonel, 234n8
Joseph, Guerda, 131, 232n14
Joseph, Pierre, 165
Joseph, Salomon Severe, 165, 170–180
Josue, Erol, 122
Judaism, 148
Juste, Ameleon, 183

katolik fran (frank Catholics), 6, 88, 103
konpa, 72, 177, 179
Kendall (see also West Kendall), 78–80, 107, 233n3
King, Martin Luther, 1, 23
Kennedy, John F., 20
Kongo, 117, 231n5

Koreans (Korean Americans), 11–13
Kostarelos, Frances, 157
kouche kanzo, 125, 141
kouche yam (manje yam), 121
Krome Detention Center, 37, 39, 139, 191, 193

labor, 27
La Deesse De La Mer, 141–142
La Nativité, 36
Lakou Badio, 123
Lakou Hounto, 127
Lakou Joseph, 171, 173
Lakou Soukri, 123
Lakou Souvenance, 123
Lammoglia, Jose Antonio, 118, 129
language: and Catholic liturgy, x, 2, 34, 39–40, 46, 52, 54, 60–62, 68–69, 80, 124; Creole, x, 1–2, 16, 34, 39, 42, 52, 52, 62, 68, 72, 89; English, 16, 69, 89; French, 2, 16, 34, 39, 54, 62, 68–69, 72, 100; in Haitian Protestant worship in Miami, 16, 168; and immigrants, xii, 1, 159, 228n10; and immigrants, classes for, 17; and social class in Haiti and the Haitian diaspora, 34, 39, 68–69, 80; Italian, 89, as restricting religious choice, 156, 188; Spanish, x, 39, 62, 89, 152
Lavwa Katolik, 41, 229n5
Legion of Mary, 55
Legrand, Devil, 162, 234n7
Lemon City, 26, 39, 158, 165
Leogane, 4, 56, 141, 145, 149
Les Cayes, 19, 39, 108, 165, 170, 181
Levine, Daniel, 86–87
liberation theology, 23, 40, 48–49, 76, 86–87
Liberty City, 23, 26
Libowitz, Larry, 136
Libreri Mapou, 115
Ligondé, François Wolff , 48, 79
Limonade, 70, 86, 133, 230n1
Lin, Ann Chih, 12

Little, Cheryl, 39

Little Haiti: botanicas in, 193, 207–208; crime in, 27, 49, 139, 330n3; and Haitian class distinctions, 68–69, 78; history of, 24–26, 39–40; location and size, 4, 26; median household income in, 27, 67, 230n1; Protestant churches in, 30, 151–188, 209–225; as a religious market, 188; visual culture in, 26–27, 190; Vodou in, 127–130. *See also* Catholic Churches, Cathedral of St. Mary; Notre Dame d'Haiti Catholic Church

Little Havana, 60, 63, 66

lived religion, 16

Llera, Ingrid, 115, 121–122, 127, 232n11

Loray Gronde Bon Houngan, 141

Los Angeles, 12

loup garou (werewolves), 3

Loussaint, Nadine, 129

luck (*chans*), 5, 59, 114, 116, 130, 135, 139, 149, 195, 197

Lukumi, 118, 232n19

lwa (Vodou spirits): Agwe (spirit of the sea), 114, 127; assimilation with Catholic saints, 83–84, 87–90, 117, 122–124, 125, 131, 133–134; Ayizan (spirit of ritual purity), 126; Catholic demonization of, 91, 98; Danbala (serpent spirit of regeneration) 122–123, 193; Ezili (female spirits of sensuality and motherhood), 84, 88, 126, 132–133; Ezili Dantò, 90, 149 ; Ezili Freda, 131, 192 ; Ezili Kawoulo, 144, 148; Gede (chief spirit of death and dying; trickster spirit) 50, 122; Lasyrenn (mermaid spirit), 125, 132–133, 141–142, 191; Linto Roi, 125; Loko, 126; and nature, 83; Ogou (spirit of iron and warfare), 84, 126; and pilgrimage, 83; rituals for, 116–118, 121–125, 133–134; Simbi (spirits of lakes, lagoons, and ponds), 126

magic (*maji*), 5, 7, 59, 114, 140–149, 190, 197

Magnificat, 72, 98, 231n6

Malagreca, Joseph, 74

Mami Wata, 142

manbo (Vodou priestess), 3, 6, 114, 117–118, 127–128, 133, 136–137, 142, 201, 232n11

Mariani, 127

market theory of religion (*see also* rational choice theory), 154

Martikainen, Tuomas, 80

Marxist theory of religion, 18, 185

Massachusetts Institute of Technology (MIT), 22

McAlister, Elizabeth, 90, 109, 120, 231n10, 233n1

McCarthy, Edward, 24, 39–40, 43, 48, 68

Mecca, 148

medsin fey, 130, 171

Métraux, Alfred, 85, 91

Mexicans (Mexican Americans), 70, 78

Miami (*see also* City of Miami; Miami-Dade County): appeal to Haitian immigrants, 21, 26; and the Civil Rights Movement, 20; geography, 26, 39, 66, 68; in popular Haitian imagination 57, 149, 160, 233n9, 234n3

Miami Baptist Association, 164

Miami Dade College, 67

Miami-Dade County (Dade County): distinct from Miami, 233n9, ethnicity in, 67; formally Dade County, 66; geography, 27–28, 64, 79, 131; and Haitian labor, 27; Haitian population of, 118; mean household income, 27; rural, 232n8; topography, 67

Miami Design District, 157

Miami Gardens, 66

Miami Herald, 56

Miami Lakes, 66

Miami Shores, 26, 66

Miami Springs, 27, 66

Michel, Claudine, 88

Migration of the Beasts (Duval-Carrié), 149, 191

Middle Passage, 122, 190

Milien, Enoch, 180
Miot, Joseph Serge, 231n8
miracles (*see also* healing), 44, 84
Miragoane, 142–148
Miramar, 27, 60, 95, 230n2
Mooney, Margarita A., 4, 36, 50, 76, 126, 159, 230n13
Montreal, 6, 74, 126, 142, 178, 234n15
Morisseau-Leroy, Félix, 1, 20, 190, 192, 201
music (*see also* choirs; hymns), 2, 26, 55, 62, 66, 72, 177–179, 196
Myrthil, Amos, 234n8

Namphy, Henri, 40, 44, 229n4
National Labor Relations Hearing Board, 177
National Monument to the Refugees, 87
Nassau, 114
New Orleans, 12, 19, 22
New York City, 11, 19–20, 26–28, 70, 74, 77, 89–90, 109, 120, 124, 128, 140–142, 161, 178, 229n1, 231n10, 234n8
New Zealand, 142
Newark, New Jersey, 6
Noel, Papa Paul, 121
North Miami, 123, 131, 142, 164, 169
North Miami Beach, 27, 60, 66
Notre Dame Academy, 39
Notre Dame d'Haiti Catholic Church: and earthquake relief, 55–56; ecclesiology at, 16, 50–51; as ethnic parish, x, 35; Eucharistic services at, 54–55, 107–109; founding and early history, ix, 39–40, 160; and Haitian politics, 40–47; language at, 16; new church construction, 53–54; New Year's Day celebration at, 36–37; patron saint feast day celebrations at, 92–111; and social service to immigrants, xi–xii, 25, 34, 50, 55, 160; symbolism at, 33, 35, 190; and Vodou, 50, 84–86; youth at, 51
nuns, 72, 74, 95, 100, 233n25
Nyack, 74

O'Brien, David M., 232n19
Ochun, 131–132
Old Saint Patrick's Cathedral, 229n1
one-drop rule, 20
O'Neil, Deborah, 134
Opa Locka, 131
Orange County, 27
Orlando, 27, 53, 175
oricha, 128, 131, 134, 136
Orsi, Robert A. ,89
oungan (Vodou priests), 3, 6, 114, 117–118, 121–128, 130, 133, 136, 138, 141, 184, 201
Ouanaminthe, 182

Palm Beach County, 3–4, 27–28, 231n3
Palo Monte, 118
parish model church, x, 175
pastoral ministry, xii
pastors (Protestant), 3, 13,108, 160, 162, 176, 180, 182, 197, 201, 234n8, 234–235n16, 235n18
Peck, Raoul, 234n3
Pentecostalism (*see also* Catholic Charismatic Renewal), 90–91, 153, 159, 161–170, 234n12
People Acting Together for Community (PACT), 230n13
Perez, Juan, 235n21
Perrine, 27, 59–60, 68, 75–76, 80
Pestel, 152
Philadelphia, 6, 13, 19, 28, 74, 227n2, 227n3, 228n12, 231n11
Pichardo, Ernesto, 232n19
Pierre, Jean, 60
Pierre, Larry, 229n9
Pierre Toussaint Haitian Catholic Center, 25, 33–39, 49, 55, 57, 60, 70, 94, 160
Pierre-Louis, Renaud, 234n8
Pierre-Louis, Ronald, 152–156 ,187–188
pilgrimage, 70, 83–88, 101–102, 109, 122, 133–134, 178, 230n1, 231n11
politics, 35, 40–47, 65, 87, 65, 161, 230n13
Pollefeyt, Ivan, 42

polyglossia, 168

Pompano Beach, 39, 228n11

Porcel, Carlos Cancio, 113

Port-au-Prince, 47, 55–56, 73, 78–79, 83, 87, 91, 101, 110, 113–114, 119, 122, 129, 133–134, 173, 179, 181–182, 230n1, 235n1

Portes, Alejandro, 78, 119, 227n8

poverty: in Haiti, xii, 10, 40, 44, 57, 59, 160, 198, 200; in South Florida, 27–28, 49, 67, 79, 156

preaching. *See* homiletics

Presbyterian, 161

Presumé, Marc, 105

Préval, René, 64, 122

priestesses. See *manbo*

priests (Catholic), 24, 40, 42, 46, 48, 50–51, 62, 65, 72, 74, 79, 84, 95–99, 103–109. *See also specific priests by their last names*

PROCHE (Partnership for the Reconstruction of the Church in Haiti), 55–56

protest, 40–48

Protestant churches (*see also* Baptist churches): Eglise de Dieu, 153; Eglise de Dieu de la Prophétie, 165, 213 ; Eglise de Dieu du Temps de la Fin, 161, 213; Eglise de Dieu l'Arche de Délivrance, 161, 213; Eglise de Dieu Sanctifiée Haïtienne, 158, 164–170; Eglise de Saint Paul et les Martyrs d'Haiti, 157, 160, 214 ; Eglise du Christ de North Miami, 157, 214; Eglise Evangélique Maranatha, 161, 216; Eglise Missionaire Trompette de Sion, Inc, 161, 216 ; Eglise Nouvelle Jerusalem, 183–184; First Haitian Free United Methodist Church (Grace United Methodist Church), 17, 157–158, 217; First Interdenominational Haitian Church, 158, 164, 217; Legliz Lafwa Apostolik, 183; Mission Evangélique du Christianisme, 164, 170–180; Philadelphia Church of God, 13, 183, 222 ; Première Eglise Universelle du Seigneur, 161, 222; Premiere Haitian Baptist

Church, 164; St. Paul's Episcopal Church (St. Paul et les Martyrs d'Haiti), 157, 160, 214; Temple de L'Eternel, 161–162, 224

Protestant work ethic, 227n4

proverbs, xi, 40, 42, 131, 198

Proudfoot, Wayne, 30

Puerto Rico, 23

pwen, 134, 146

Queens Village, 74

race, ix, 8, 20, 188

racism, 20, 22–23, 114, 119–120, 160, 180

radio, 41–42, 46–48, 114, 162, 177

rara, 120–121

rational choice theory, 15–16, 154–156, 187–188

Reagan, Ronald, 43, 135

refugees: and African American churches, 160; Cuban, ix, xi, 192 ; Dominguean, 19, Haitian, ix, xi, 18, 21–28, 39–40, 79, 192; Haitians in 1994 exodus, 47; settlement in Miami, 18, 59, 67, 119, 161; from the 2001 earthquake, 171; Vodou and, 115, 119

religion (see also *collusio*; healing; religious capital; religious field): African, 14, 50, 117, 123; defined, 200; functions for Haitian immigrants, 5, 114; in Haiti, 6, 29, 89; and immigrants in America, 11–13; 158–160; pneumacentric, 107; and salvation, 14; and social class, 59, 80–81; transnational, 148; world religion, 129, 148; as worldview, 115–116

religious capital, 9–10, 13–17, 154, 156, 165, 170, 174, 180, 185–186, 196, 200–202, 227–228n8

religious field, 10, 14–15, 154–155, 185–186, 235n24

remittances, 13, 90, 110, 120, 189, 193–194, 202

Rémy, Anselm, 6

Rey, Terry, 81, 134, 140, 227n3, 231n11, 232n31, 233n33

Richard Gerstein Justice Building, 136

Richman, Karen E., 4, 13, 90, 116, 149, 228n9

Rickenbacker Causeway, 192–193

Ricodel, Fr., 172

ritual paraphernalia, 85, 101, 103, 128, 137, 145, 151, 156, 172

Robertson, Roland, 155–156

Robinson, Catherine, 9

Romain, Charles-Poisset, 198, 234n8

Roman, Augustín, 37, 132

Roman Catholic Archdiocese of Miami, 2, 24–25, 33, 49, 55, 61–63, 85, 134, 160, 203–205, 228n13

Roman Catholic Diocese of Fort Liberté, 107

Roman Catholic Diocese of Jérémie, 39, 43, 48

Roman Catholic Diocese of Orlando, 53

Romélus, Willy, 42–44

Roosevelt, Franklin Delano, 22

Roumain, Jacques, 20

rum, 145–146

Rumbaut, Rubén, 78

Sabel Palm Court, 3

sacraments, 14, 18, 65, 92, 198, 201

Saint-Domingue, 2, 19, 116–117, 119, 122, 202, 228n12, 229n1, 231n4, 235n1

Saint Marc, 19

Saint-Felix, Fandor, 171

Saint-Germain, Brésil, 234n8

Saint-Louis, Felix, 234n8

Saint-Phard, Pierre Ludovic, 234n8

Salvador da Bahia, 129

salvation goods, 5, 10–18, 80, 97, 110, 114–115, 135, 149–150, 154–156, 165, 174, 186, 188, 195, 201

Sandoval, Mercedes Cros, 129

Sant La, 129

Santería, 103, 118, 125, 128, 131–135, 142–143, 232n19

Saut-d'Eau, 84, 90, 101, 231n11

Schiller, Nina Glick, 193

Schrauf, Robert W., 228n10

Scofield, Calvin, 160

Second Vatican Council, 63–64, 229n9

Sermons. See homiletics

Service Employees International Union (SEIU) 136–137, 232n21, 232–233n22

Seventh Day Adventist, 13, 162

Shango, 142

Shrine of Our Lady of Guadalupe, 70, 232n8

Shrine of St. Philomena (Haiti),133, 230n1

Shrine of St. Philomena (Miami), 60–65, 134

Shrine of the Virgin of Charity of El Cobre, ix, 101, 131–133, 232n15

Simbi, 126

slavery, 31, 36, 57, 78, 116, 119–122, 229n1, 235n1

Smith, Timothy, 199

social capital, 60, 180, 227–228n8

social class: and the American Catholic Church, ix-x, and collusio, 8; in Haiti, 20, 34, 44, 46, 59; in Miami, 25–27, 34, 59–62, 65–71, 75–81; at Notre Dame d'Haiti, 95, 107; as restraint on rational choice, 188

Societe Linto Roi Trois Mysteres, 121–128, 143, 232n7

sorcery, 118, 135–139, 166

Sosyete La Deesse De La Mer, 141–142

South Miami, 66

South Miami Heights, 66

Southern Christian Leadership Council, 23

spirit possession, 72, 76, 117–118, 126, 138, 140 153, 166, 171, 230n3

St. Francis Nursing Home, 136–137, 232–233n22

St. Lucie County, 116

St. Michel de l'Attalaye, 162

St. Pierre, Wagner, 130, 232n4

St. Vincent de Paul Society, 55

Stark, Rodney, 15, 154

Stepick, Alex, 119
Stolz, Jörg, 156
storefront churches, 128, 151–188
Sts. Joachim and Anne Catholic Church
    74
students (*see also* education), 4, 166
Swidler, Leonard, 14
symbolic capital (*see also* social capital;
    religious capital), 11, 17, 201, 227–228n8
syncretism, 81, 85, 117, 126, 198

Tabarre, 87
Tanzania, 134
Tap Tap Restaurant, 115
teledjòl (word of mouth), 37
Temple Yehwe, 127
Terrier Rouge, 182
theology (*see also* liberation theology) 7,
    97, 168, 173, 230n3
Thegenus, Jude (Papaloko), 115, 121
Thémistocle, Jean-Robert, 72
Thérèse, Sister, 161, 162
Thomas, Luckner, 139, 233n24
Thomson, Robert Farris, 232n20
Tilegliz. See liberation theology
Tonton Macoutes (*tonton makout*),
    229n4
tourism, 23–24
Toussaint, Pierre, 34, 229n1
Traditionalist Catholicism, 60, 63, 134
transnationalism: and the Catholic Char-
    ismatic Renewal, 60; and collusio,
    194; and Haitian Catholicism, 181; and
    Haitian identity, 192–194; Protestantism
    and, 3, 151, 156, 164; 173–174, 180–188,
    228n9; and social class, 34, 59; and the
    transubstantiation of symbolic capital,
    202; and Vodou, 29, 116–118, 140–148,
    174, 228n9
trees, 36, 53, 93, 108, 127, 144, 188, 233n27
Triduum, 93–100
Triest, Hugo, 42
Trinidadians, 70

Trujillo, Rafael, 160
tuberculosis, 228n12
Tweed, Thomas A., 101, 132–133, 150, 200

Umbanda, 230n3
United Nations, 47, 64, 140, 184
United States Agency for International
    Development (USAID), 182
United States Catholic Bishops Confer-
    ence, 46
United States Coast Guard, 21, 46–47, 189
United States Immigration and Customs
    Enforcement (ICE), 22
United States Immigration and Natural-
    ization Service (INS), 22
United States Supreme Court 232n19
U.S. military occupations of Haiti, 22, 182,
    184
USCG *Hamilton*, 189

Valcin, Mariot, 234n8
Valéry, Jude, 173, 179
Varadero, 113
Vietnamese, 12
Vieux, Harold, 180–184
Ville-Bonheur, 84, 87–88
Vincent, Jean-Marie, 42, 47
Virgin Mary. *See* Catholic saints
Vodou (*see also* lwa): at Catholic feast
    day celebrations, 84–86, 90; and col-
    lusio, 10; in Haiti, and the land, 29; in
    Haiti, as majority religion, 3, 88–89;
    in Haiti, persecution of, 85, 113–150;
    and healing, 129, 135, 145, 149; his-
    tory and structure, 116–118; in Miami,
    demographics of, 6; in Miami, practice
    of, 113–150; in Miami, temples of, 26,
    26; transnational dimensions of, 29,
    116–118, 140–148, 174, 228n9; as world-
    view, 115–116
Vodou-Fest, 126–127
Vonarx, Nicolas ,153
Voodoo Squad, 136

Waller, Littleton, 22

wanga (*see also* sorcery), 136–138

Washington, DC, 6, 127

Weber, Max, 154–156, 159, 187–188, 227n4

Wenski, Thomas: and Catholic sexual morality, 229n9; and the Charismatic Renewal, 78; consecrating the Marian grotto at Notre Dame, 92–95, 107; and Cubans in Miami, 132; and the development of Miami's Haitian Catholic ministry, 16, 39–41; on the earthquake of 2010, 78–79; ecclesiology of, 51, 158; investiture as archbishop of Miami, 47–48, 53; and politics in Haiti, 42–47; and Vodou, 50, 115–116, 119

West Africa, 123, 142

West Central Africa, 117

West Kendall (*see also* Kendall), 59, 64–69, 79–80, 193

West Palm Beach, 13, 28, 194, 113

Wet Foot-Dry Foot policy, 113

WGLY (radio station), 42

Williams, Raymond, 159–160

Wilson, Woodrow, 22

Wilton Manors, 27

Windward Passage, 189

Woodson, Drexel G., 3, 89

women, 2, 52, 54, 64, 74, 86, 94–95, 98, 100–101, 104, 107, 121, 125, 127, 166–169, 176–178

yellow fever, 228n12

Yemaya, 142

Yucatan Peninsula, 235n18

Youth, xi, 2, 23, 51, 72, 93, 150, 178, 234n15

Zhou, Min, 12

zonbi (zombies), 3, 91

Formerly *Professeur de Sociologie des Religions* at *Université d'État d'Haïti* and Associate Professor of Religious Studies at Florida International University, Terry Rey is Associate Professor of Religion at Temple University.

Alex Stepick is Professor of Sociology at Portland State University and Professor of Global and Sociocultural Studies at Florida International University, where he also is director of the Research Institute on Social and Economic Policy.